POWER WITHOUT PERSUASION

POWER WITHOUT PERSUASION

THE POLITICS OF DIRECT
PRESIDENTIAL ACTION

William G. Howell

PRINCETON UNIVERSITY PRESS   PRINCETON AND OXFORD

Library of Congress Cataloging-in-Publication Data

Howell, William G.
Power without persuasion : the politics of direct presidential action / William G.
Howell.
p.   cm.
Includes bibliographical references and index.
ISBN 0-691-10269-4 (acid-free paper) — ISBN 0-691-10270-8 (pbk. : acid-free paper)
1. Executive orders—United States.   2. Executive power—United States.
3. Presidents—United States.   I. Title.
KF5053.H68 2003
352.23'5'0973—dc21   2003048607

British Library Cataloging-in-Publication Data is available

This book has been composed in Palatino

Printed on acid-free paper. ∞

www.pupress.princeton.edu

Printed in the United States of America

10 9 8 7 6 5 4 3 2

ISBN-13: 978-0-691-10270-2 (pbk.)

ISBN-10: 0-691-10270-8 (pbk.)

For Marcy

Contents

List of Figures

List of Tables

Preface

THIS book traces back to a conversation with Paul Peterson during the spring of 1996. For his introductory American politics textbook, Paul wanted a figure that showed the number of executive agreements issued by presidents over time. Having collected the data, we were struck by two things: the precipitous and uninterrupted rise in agreements issued during the modern era, and a literature on presidential bargaining that highlighted the personal differences among individual presidents. What presidents were doing, and what scholars were studying, appeared distinctly out of sync.

Much of the presidency literature focused on the persuasive, and mostly personal, powers of presidents—their reputations, prestige, and leadership styles. The literature's analytic focus centered on the ability of individual presidents to bargain with members of Congress, shape public opinion, solicit compliance from the bureaucracy, and place like-minded judges in the judiciary. While presidents, all presidents, were issuing all kinds of unilateral directives, few within political science appeared to take much notice, and fewer still had much to say about the implications of these directives for the foundations of presidential power.

Scholarly disinterest, I assumed, stemmed from an impression that very little of consequence came of these unilateral powers, that executive agreements, executive orders, proclamations, and other kinds of directives were generally used for mundane administrative matters. If true, then political scientists were right to pay them little mind. But upon investigation, this notion proved mistaken. Many of the most important policy changes in the modern era came at the hands of presidents going it alone: Roosevelt's orders to implement the National Industrial Recovery Act, Truman's order to compel loyalty oaths from federal employees, Kennedy's efforts to control racial violence in Alabama, and Johnson's subsequent establishment of the first affirmative action policy. Further, an impressive number of law review articles call upon judges and congressional representatives to rein in errant presidents who, by all accounts, regularly flout the Constitution's separation-of-powers doctrine (Cash 1965; Chemerinsky 1983, 1987; Hebe 1972; Neighbors 1964). In addition, a slate of recent books— including Kenneth Mayer's historical survey of executive orders, Phillip Cooper's overview of "the tools of presidential direct administration," and Greg Robinson's probing account of FDR's decision to intern the Japanese during World War II—show that the president's capacity for unilateral action is a formidable force in American politics (Cooper 2002; Mayer 2001; Robinson 2001).

The time has come to specify the logic of unilateral action in systems of separated powers. Institutional theories must begin to incorporate the president's ability to write public policy without the expressed consent of either Congress or the courts, and often over their vocal objection. This book initiates the process of theory building. It moves beyond the recognition that presidents have unilaterally issued all kinds of important policy changes that have the force of law in order to scrutinize the politics of direct presidential action.

To begin, clarity is essential. "Direct presidential actions" or "unilateral actions" refers to the wide array of public policies that presidents set without Congress. They include foreign and domestic policies, policies directed at both government personnel and the broader citizenry, policies that are recorded in the *Federal Register* and others that are filed away as confidential, policies that immediately attract widespread political controversy and those that enter the books with little fanfare. "Power" also has a very specific definition, and one that differs from that of other scholars. In this book, "power" refers to the president's capacity to influence the content of public policy. It is silent on the matter of public policy's implementation, which is a critical component of Richard Neustadt's conception of power.[1] As such, this book juxtaposes unilateral directives and laws, contrasting the president's powers of direct action with the persuasive powers that often are central to negotiations with Congress over legislative enactments.

The first chapter of this book examines how the president's ability to unilaterally set public policy fits within and challenges more conventional scholarly assessments of presidential power. It introduces some of the more controversial, and consequential, orders presidents have issued in the modern era, reviews the legal foundations of the president's unilateral powers, and hints at some of the strategic considerations presidents face when thinking about exercising these powers.

The second chapter presents a simple spatial model of unilateral action that specifies when presidents will unilaterally set public policy and when they will try to rally support within Congress for their legislative initiatives. The unilateral politics model critically examines how different institutional contexts affect the opportunities and incentives for the president to act unilaterally. The president, Congress, and the federal courts all play integral roles in the model, each with the opportunity to amend the actions of previous players therein.

The reader is here forewarned that portions of chapter 2 are somewhat technical. While proofs have been relegated to an appendix, some basic algebra is required to figure out precisely when presidents will unilaterally set public policy and to calculate the influence they glean from doing so. Because the model establishes a framework for thinking about the president's unilateral powers and acts as a point of reference for future chapters, I encourage readers not to proceed directly to the empirical findings. Readers need not have any formal training to discern the model's underlying logic. Indeed, its central proposition can be stated quite simply: the president's freedom to act unilaterally is defined by Congress's ability, and the judiciary's willingness, to subsequently overturn him. Rather than being a distraction, the simple math that runs through chapter 2 hopefully adds clarity and care to the presentation of a theory of direct presidential action.

Chapter 3 links theory to real-world politics. It lays out several case studies of unilateral policy making—Truman's desegregation of the military, Reagan's imposition of sanctions on South Africa, and Clinton's ban on the permanent replacement of striking workers—and shows how the unilateral politics model highlights the political dynamics of each. After establishing a preliminary basis for accepting the validity of the unilateral politics model, the chapter then sets a higher standard of proof, drawing out a host of testable hypotheses. The model predicts, for example, that presidents will exercise their unilateral powers most when Congress has an especially difficult time enacting legislation, weakening the institution's capacity to constrain the president. The model further suggests that presidents will act unilaterally more frequently during periods of unified government (when the same parties govern the legislative and executive branches) than periods of divided government (when different parties govern), contrary to much of the existing literature on the subject. Finally, it predicts that when the challenging party wins a presidential election, the president will act unilaterally more often than when the incumbent party is reelected.

All of these propositions are subject to empirical verification, which is the central objective of chapter 4. To examine these issues, I focus on executive orders. Presidents have at their disposal numerous alternative mechanisms to make policy unilaterally: proclamations, directives, memoranda, and executive agreements. For three reasons, however, executive orders present an ideal opportunity for study. First, the record of executive orders is relatively clear. Unlike national security directives (which are confidential) and executive memoranda (which are not systematically catalogued), executive orders are easily referenced. Since the 1935 Federal Register Act, presidents have had to register, and thus make public, all executive orders. More recently, efforts have been made to collect these published orders so that they can be more easily compared and understood as a corpus of law.[2] In addition to their accessibility, executive orders are particularly interesting because, unlike executive agreements, they involve both foreign and domestic policy making. Presidents issue executive orders in all sorts of policy domains, from foreign trade to agriculture subsidies, providing a unique opportunity to compare what presidents accomplish by acting unilaterally to what they gain by introducing legislation to Congress. Finally, executive orders present the clearest alternative presidents have to the traditional legislative process. By focusing on executive orders, then, we may better understand some of the limitations of the existing literature on congressional lawmaking, and the president's perceived role within it.

While previous works have tried to explain trends in executive order issuance, few have differentiated more important orders from less important ones.[3] This distinction is crucial. Without it we cannot distinguish between the management of administrative affairs and the creation of actual public policy. Chapter 4 therefore constructs a timeline of significant executive orders that covers the entire twentieth century and then employs a battery of event count models to test the predictions of the unilateral politics model.

Game theoretic models like the one presented in chapter 2 do some things very well, and other things not so well. Their parsimony is simultaneously their greatest strength (for they distill the most important facets of an empirical phenomenon and explain the underlying logic that ties them together) and their greatest weakness (for they necessarily omit important aspects of politics). We can learn a fair amount from the unilateral politics model and the tests to which we subject it, but the model need not define the bounds of our analysis entirely. The model, for example, assumes that Congress is completely and perfectly informed about what presidents have done unilaterally, that Congress can enact legislation without incurring any kind of cost, and that the judiciary will vigorously enforce a clear set of constitutional and statutory restrictions on unilateral powers. But as soon as we begin to think outside of the model, these assumptions prove troublesome.

In the second half of this book, therefore, I expand the scope of the analysis in order to consider the institutional capacities of Congress and the courts to check the president's powers of unilateral action. Chapter 5 starts with Congress and examines how historically it has responded to presidential policy making, both legislatively and in the appropriations process. There is good reason to believe that Congress, on the whole, will have a difficult time constraining the president.

Congress's internal organization, especially its party leadership, can impose a modicum of order on member behavior, thereby giving the institution a certain capacity to guard its power. Nevertheless, disabling collective action problems run rampant. A body of 535 members in two chambers, scattered among dozens of committees and facing multiple veto points, not the least of which is the president's, will likely have a very difficult time constraining a president who can unilaterally shift policy without ever having to assemble an enacting coalition or face a legislative veto.

To investigate what Congress has been able to actually accomplish, I have assembled a database of congressional bills that sought to amend, extend, overturn, or codify in law an executive order between 1945 and 1998. These data allow us to see whether the story of unilateral politics is one of presidents acting strictly according to the will of Congress, or whether presidents occasionally set policy in ways that a majority of congressional members dislike, but which institutional problems prevent them from effectively undoing.

When presidents unilaterally set policies that do not require any positive congressional action, they enjoy tremendous discretion; nonaction on the part of Congress and the courts is functionally equivalent to support. But frequently presidents create programs and agencies that require appropriations, and here Congress enjoys unique opportunities of influence. If members object to the president's project they can simply refuse to allocate funding, leaving it with a mandate but no staff or facilities of which to speak. And even if members decide to fund the project, they can attach any number of stipulations on how the president can spend the money.

Consequently, the second half of chapter 5 delves into the budgetary politics of unilateral action. It examines how Congress has used the budget to constrain unilateral powers, and how presidents have found ways around the formal appropriations process. Here, unilateral politics tend toward the mundane—all of the action is buried in the details of line-item appropriations, reporting requirements, and the flexibility of budgetary accounts. In the vast minutiae of budgets, Congress can tie executive initiatives up in knots while presidents search for loopholes that allow them to fund controversial projects. On the whole, as case studies and new data on agency creation will show, presidents experience net losses where appropriations are concerned. But even when Congress may have the upper hand, presidents are able to use their unilateral powers to meaningfully influence public policy.

Chapter 6 casts a critical eye at the courts. It explores how judges have adjudicated cases on presidential power and, more specifically, instances when the president has acted unilaterally. Here again there is good cause to believe that the courts will be sympathetic to the president. The reason for this has less to do with their internal organization and more to do with the place they hold in the American system of separated powers. Because the courts rely upon the executive branch to enforce their orders, judges have strong incentives not to rule against the president.

Judges must always be sensitive to politics, proceeding cautiously, if at all, when government officials are unlikely to carry out their orders. But when the defendants of a case are the very people charged with enforcing the court's ruling, the issue of enforcement becomes full-blown. Judges, in these instances, essentially have three choices, each of which is usually more attractive than the next: rule against the president and risk some form of retaliation from the executive branch, if not on the enforcement of this opinion, then on the enforcement of others; rule in favor of the president, winning the executive branch's favor, though sometimes damaging its public prestige; or dismiss the case outright and avoid the problem entirely.

To verify that theory matches with reality, I constructed a database of every challenge to an executive order heard in a federal court case (district, appellate, and Supreme Court) between 1945 and 1998. To assemble this list, research assistants and I read thousands of court opinions that mentioned executive orders to determine which actually constituted direct challenges to executive orders. We eventually pared the list down to 83 cases and compiled descriptive information on each. These data enabled us to systematically inventory presidents' success rates in court challenges, and in the process assess the threat that the judiciary poses when presidents contemplate exercising their powers of unilateral action.

To summarize then, this book consists of two main sections. The first (chapters 2–4) lays out a spatial model of unilateral action and then, using data on executive orders, tests the model's central propositions. The second section (chapters 5–6) steps back from the model and examines how effective Congress and the courts are at constraining the president—examining many of the features of politics not easily captured by game theoretic or spatial analyses. But while separate, the two sections are ultimately complementary. The end product joins game theory with insights coming out of the new economics of institutions to produce a theory of unilateral action, a sense for how presidents empirically have used their power in the modern era, and what obstacles they have met along the way.

Writing this book, I received invaluable support from colleagues and friends. Foremost among them is Terry Moe. As the chair of my dissertation committee, Terry highlighted many of the limitations of the unilateral politics model and demanded that theory play a central role in this book. But it was his example—his knack for making ideas come alive—that established the strongest inspiration and clearest guide to this book.

Portions of this book were presented at the political science departments at Stanford University, the University of Wisconsin, and Harvard University, the Stanford Institute for the Quantitative Study of Society, the American Politics Research Group at the University of North Carolina, the Legal Studies Workshop at the University of Wisconsin, and various annual meetings of the American Political Science Association and the Midwest Political Science Association.

I owe an intellectual debt of gratitude to a number of books that highlight how rational choice theory can be used to examine the strategic environment within which presidents influence public policy. Standouts include Charles Cameron's *Veto Bargaining*, Patricia Conley's *Presidential Mandates*, Keith Krehbiel's *Pivotal Politics*, and David Epstein and Sharyn O'Halloran's *Delegating Powers*. Thanks to these scholars' path-breaking work, students of the presidency need no longer be defensive about using game theory to explain presidential behavior.

Alison Alter, Matthew Dickinson, Charles Franklin, Dan Gitterman, Elizabeth Katz, Doug Krines, and Sean Theriault all read drafts of this manuscript and offered critical advice. I am particularly thankful to Ken Mayer, who has written an original, thought-provoking book on the history of executive orders, and who has carved out a niche for subsequent scholars to construct new theories of unilateral policy making. Collaborations with David Lewis were particularly rewarding, yielding many of the ideas presented in this book.

David Brady and John Ferejohn both drew helpful connections to historical and legal literatures. Keith Krehbiel's influence, through both his reactions to early drafts of this manuscript and his own scholarly work, is pervasive. David Canon's support, both intellectual and personal, had a tangible bearing on both the content of this book and the spirits of the author while writing it. I am thankful for the friendship and insight that Brandice Canes-Wrone offered throughout this book's development. Gary King and Lynn Ragsdale kindly provided their data on executive orders issued between 1947 and 1983. Anonymous reviewers for Princeton University Press offered excellent suggestions on how to tighten and strengthen the arguments in this book. Among the many research assistants who worked on this project, Paul Schlomer stands out for his exceptional diligence and much-appreciated humor.

Richard Neustadt provided extensive feedback, for which this manuscript is much improved. Neustadt highlighted key distinctions between the creation and implementation of public policy, as well as important differences between what he intended to accomplish in *Presidential Power* (1991 [1960]) and the objectives of much of the social scientific research on the American presidency that followed. Neustadt does not agree with all of my interpretations of his work. His scholarly writings and personal correspondence, however, continue to shape my thinking about the foundations of presidential power.

I end my thanks where the book began—with Paul Peterson, whose friendship, generosity, and guidance have made an indelible imprint on my life.

I dedicate this book to my wife, Marcy. For her love and companionship, Roy and Sally by our sides, is really what it's all about.

POWER WITHOUT PERSUASION

1

Presidential Power in the Modern Era

WITH box cutters and knives, nineteen hijackers took control of four commercial jets on the morning of September 11, 2001, and flew the planes into the towers of the World Trade Center, the Pentagon, and Shanksville, Pennsylvania. The South and North Towers in New York collapsed at 10:05 and 10:28 A.M., respectively. Fires in the Pentagon burned for another seventy-two hours. In all, over three thousand civilians (including several hundred New York City fire fighters and police) died in the attacks. The greatest terrorist act in U.S. history sent politicians scrambling. Not surprisingly, it was the White House that crafted the nation's response, little of which was formally subject to congressional review.

In the weeks that followed, President Bush issued a flurry of unilateral directives to combat terrorism. One of the first was an executive order creating a new cabinet position, Secretary of Homeland Security, which was charged with coordinating the efforts of forty-five federal agencies to fight terrorism. Bush then created a Homeland Security Council to advise and assist the president "with all aspects of homeland security." On September 14, Bush issued an order that authorized the Secretaries of the Navy, Army, and Air Force to call up for active duty reservists within their ranks. Later that month, Bush issued a national security directive lifting a ban (which Gerald Ford originally instituted via executive order 11905) on the CIA's ability to "engage in, or conspire to engage in, political assassination"—in this instance, the target being Osama bin Laden and his lieutenants within al Qaeda, the presumed masterminds behind the September 11 attacks. On September 23, Bush signed an executive order that froze all financial assets in U.S. banks that were linked to bin Laden and other terrorist networks. In early October, when a bill to federalize airport security appeared doomed in the Senate, Bush threatened to issue an executive order accomplishing as much.

The most visible of Bush's unilateral actions consisted of retaliatory military strikes in Afghanistan. Though Congress never passed a formal declaration of war, in the fall of 2001 Bush directed the Air Force to begin a bombing campaign against Taliban strongholds, while Special Forces conducted stealth missions on the ground. Though these commands did not come as executive orders, or any other kind of formal directive, they nonetheless instigated some of the most potent expressions of executive power.[1] Within a year Bush's orders resulted in the collapse of the Taliban regime, the flight of tens of thousands of Afghani refugees into Pakistan, the destruction of Afghanistan's social and economic infrastructures, and the introduction of a new governing regime.

It was Bush's unilateral decision to create a new court system, however, that generated the most public controversy. On November 13, 2001, the president signed an order allowing special military tribunals to try any noncitizen suspected of plotting and/or committing terrorist acts or harboring known terrorists. The trials need not be public, Bush declared, and might be held in the United States or abroad. The tribunals can hand down death sentences with only two-thirds support on the panel of five judges, of whom only a majority need be in attendance. Further, the order lifted many of the constitutional protections afforded most individuals accused of crime, such as a guarantee of a trial by a jury of one's peers. According to the order, suspected terrorists "shall not be privileged to seek any remedy or maintain any proceeding, directly or indirectly, or to have any such remedy or proceeding sought on the individual's behalf, in (i) any court of the United States, or any State thereof, (ii) any court of any foreign nation, or (iii) any international tribunal." Bush effectively designed an entirely new court system to mete out justice in its efforts to hunt down and punish suspected terrorists, however they may be identified, and wherever they may be found.

During the proceeding weeks, denunciations of Bush's "sudden seizure of power"[2] ricocheted across the nation's editorial pages. Consider just a handful of the opinions expressed in the *New York Times*. William Safire protested that the "president of the United States has just assumed what amounts to dictatorial power to jail or execute aliens. Intimidated by terrorists and inflamed by a passion for rough justice, we are letting George W. Bush get away with the replacement of the American rule of law with military kangaroo courts." According to Safire, the order dismissed "'the principles of law and the rules of evidence' that undergird America's system of justice." By Anthony Lewis's account, the order represented an "act of executive fiat, imposed without even consulting Congress. And it seeks to exclude the courts entirely from a process that may fundamentally affect life and liberty." Several days later, Stephen Gillers condemned a "sham process that mocks [lawyers'] constitutional role in ensuring fair trials for their clients."[3]

Constitutional law scholars quickly followed suit. According to

Georgetown and Harvard University professors Neal Katyal and Laurence Tribe, the unilateral creation of military tribunals effectively blends executive, legislative, and judicial powers in one person in ways that are "ordinarily regarded as the very acme of absolutism." Worse still, Bush's actions were emblematic of an alarming trend in American politics—a propensity of presidents, especially during times of crisis, to unilaterally impose their will on the American public. As Katyal and Tribe note, "For the President to proceed on his own to alter the jurisdiction of the federal courts, redesigning the very architecture of justice, without any colorable claim that time is too short for Congress to act, is to succumb to an executive unilateralism all too familiar in recent days" (2002, 1260).

In January 2002, the United States began to ship captured members of al Qaeda and the Taliban to the U.S. Naval Base at Guantanamo Bay, Cuba. Public criticism proceeded unabated as pundits debated whether the rights and privileges generally afforded to prisoners of war, as detailed in the 1949 Geneva Convention, should extend to the roughly five hundred Afghani detainees. The United States' closest ally, Britain, began to express concerns over the detainees' legal status. The *London Guardian*, for instance, called upon the Bush administration "to process its prisoners as quickly as possible in line with the Geneva Convention. Those whose countries will accept them should in due course be returned there by agreement. Others will take more time, but the captives cannot stay indefinitely where they are." By late spring of 2002, public support for Bush's original order, measured both domestically and abroad, began to wane.

No matter, Bush carried onward. The U.S. military continued to interrogate its captives without settling their formal status, refusing even to release their names. Bush suspended the attorney-client privilege for certain suspects. He set additional restrictions on the right of detainees to appeal their cases. And critically, he never bothered to secure legislative authorization before taking any of these actions.[4]

Publicly, members of the Bush administration went to great lengths to stress the privileges and luxuries afforded to the detainees, noting that the military served culturally sensitive meals and that time was set aside daily for prayer and meditation. Bush also backtracked on some matters of dispute. To hand down a death sentence, Bush conceded, a panel's ruling would have to be unanimous. Furthermore, trials would not be held entirely in secret; under specific circumstances, members of the press and public would be allowed to attend.

Still, on most matters Bush gave little ground. The administration refused to capitulate to demands that the captives be granted POW status and, in due course, returned to their countries of origin. To the contrary, Secretary of Defense Donald Rumsfeld repeatedly insisted that the military planned to hold the nameless captives "indefinitely" and that the war on terrorism could proceed for the better part of a decade. As of this writing, the U.S. federal courts have dismissed every case brought before them that directly challenged the detention of prisoners from the Afghan conflict, insisting that they lacked any jurisdiction over military bases in Cuba.[5] Congress, too, continues to stand idly by, holding hearings but never taking formal action to either release the detainees or resolve their formal status as prisoners of war.

A war on terrorism obviously gave the president license to exercise his unilateral powers. Bush is not unique in this regard. Throughout the history of the Republic, the public, Congress, and the courts have looked to the president to guide the nation through foreign and domestic crises. And with few exceptions—Hoover?—presidents have met the call.

National crises, however, are not the only opportunity presidents have to unilaterally dictate public policy. Before there was a war on terrorism, Bush unilaterally instituted a wide array of important policy changes. During the first months of his administration, he issued an executive order that instituted a ban on all federal project labor contracts, temporarily setting in flux Boston's $14 billion "Big Dig" and dealing a major blow to labor unions. He later required federal contractors to post notices advising employees that they have a right to withhold the portion of union dues that are used for political purposes. Bush created the White House Office of Faith-Based and Community Initiatives, which was charged with "identify(ing) and remov(ing) needless barriers that thwart the heroic work of faith-based groups." In August 2001, he set new guidelines on federal funding of stem cell research.

Many of Bush's actions overturned Clinton orders passed in the waning days (and, in some instances, hours) of the Democrat's administration. As soon as he took office, Bush instructed the Government Printing Office to halt publication in the Federal Register of any new rules "to ensure that the president's appointees have the opportunity to review any new or pending regulations."[6] The new administration then issued a sixty-day stay on regulations that were published in the register but had not yet taken effect. Shortly thereafter, Bush undid a number of Clinton environmental orders that extended federal protections to public lands, tightened restrictions on pollution runoff in rural areas, established new pollution-reporting requirements for manufacturers of lead compounds, and decreased the percentage of arsenic allowed in drinking water. In addition, Bush reinstituted the ban on federal funding for international agencies that provide abortion counseling, a ban that Clinton had lifted eight years prior.

To effect policy change, Clinton relied just as heavily on his unilateral powers. For much of his tenure, Clinton confronted Republican majorities in Congress who repeatedly killed his legislative initiatives. The list is long, with health care and tobacco legislation ranking near the top. But rather than concede defeat, Clinton "perfected the art of go-alone governing" (Kiefer 1998). After losing major legislative battles, Clinton repeatedly rebounded with a series of steady, incremental reforms, each unilaterally imposed.

> Bill Clinton is often perceived as a weak President—a lame duck dogged by scandal, thwarted at many turns by a hostile Republican Congress. . . . But the perception of weakness is belied by a largely unnoticed reality. Mr. Clinton is continually stretching his executive and regulatory authority to put his stamp on policy. He has issued a blizzard of executive orders, regulations, proclamations and other decrees to achieve his goals, with or without the blessing of Congress. (Pear 1998, K3)

Nor did this activity decline in the waning years of his administration. Instead, Clinton "engaged in a burst of activity at a point when other presidents might have coasted. . . . Executive orders have flown off Clinton's desk, mandating government action on issues from mental health to food safety" (Ross 1999). Rather than wait on Congress, Clinton simply acted, daring his Republican opponents and the courts to try to overturn him. With a few notable exceptions, neither did.

Though Republicans effectively undermined his 1993 health care initiative, Clinton subsequently managed to issue directives that established a patient's bill of rights, reformed health care programs' appeals processes, and set new penalties for companies that deny health coverage to the poor and people with preexisting medical conditions. During the summer of 1998, just days after the Senate abandoned major tobacco legislation, Clinton imposed smoking limits on buildings owned or leased by the executive branch and ordered agencies to monitor the smoking habits of teenagers, a move that helped generate the data needed to prosecute the tobacco industry. While his efforts to enact gun-control legislation met mixed success, Clinton issued executive orders that banned numerous assault weapons and required trigger safety locks on new guns bought for federal law enforcement officials.

While Congress considered impeaching him, Clinton still managed to issue executive orders that expanded the government's role in fighting software piracy, established agencies to declassify all information held by the United States relating to Nazi war criminals, and increased sanctions against political factions within Angola. And during the waning months of his presidency Clinton turned literally millions of acres of land in Nevada, California, Utah, Hawaii, and Arizona into national monuments. Though Republicans in Congress condemned the president for "usurping the power of state legislatures and local officials" and vainly attempting to "salvage a presidential legacy," in the end, they had little choice but to accept the executive orders as law.[7]

Clinton and Bush are not aberrations. Throughout the twentieth century, presidents have used their powers of unilateral action to intervene into a whole host of policy arenas. Examples abound:

- During World War II, Roosevelt issued dozens of executive orders that nationalized aviation plants, shipbuilding companies, thousands of coal companies and a shell plant—all clear violations of the Fifth Amendment's "taking" clause. The courts overturned none of these actions.
- With executive order 9066, Roosevelt ordered the evacuation, relocation, and internment of over 110,000 Japanese Americans living on the West Coast.
- In 1948, Truman desegregated the military via executive order 9981.
- After congressional efforts to construct a program that would send American youth abroad to do charitable work faltered three years in a row, Kennedy unilaterally created the Peace Corps and then financed it using discretionary funds.
- Johnson instituted the first affirmative action policy with executive order 11246.
- Preempting Congress, Nixon used an executive order to design the Environmental Protection Agency not as an independent commission, as Congress would have liked, but as an agency beholden directly to the president.
- By subjecting government regulations to cost-benefit analyses with executive order 12291, Reagan centralized powers of regulatory review.
- In 1992, George Bush federalized the National Guard and used its members to quell the Los Angeles riots.

While the majority of unilateral directives may not resonate quite so loudly in the telling of American history, a growing proportion involve substantive policy matters. Rather than being simply "daily grist-of-the-mill diplomatic matter," presidential directives have become instruments by which presidents actually set all sorts of consequential domestic and foreign policy (Paige 1977). As Peter Shane and Harold Bruff argue in their casebook on the presidency, "presidents [now] use executive orders to implement many of their most important policy initiatives, basing them on any combination of constitutional and statutory powers that is thought to be available" (1988, 88).

Between 1920 and 1998, presidents issued 10,203 executive orders, or roughly 130 annually. As might be expected, presidents issued more civil service orders than orders in any other policy arena. On average, presidents issued thirty-three such orders, most of which dealt with the management of government personnel. This proportion, however, declined precipitously after World War II, when executive orders were no longer used to perform such trivial administrative practices as exempting individuals from mandatory retirement requirements.

Outside of those orders relating directly to the civil service, each year presidents issued on average thirty-two orders in foreign affairs, another eight on social welfare policy, sixteen on regulations of the domestic economy, and fully thirty-three that concerned the management of public lands and energy policy, though the number in this last category has declined markedly over the past few decades. The majority of orders, it seems, have substantive policy content, both foreign and domestic.[8]

These figures only concern executive orders, which represent but one tool among many that presidents have at their disposal. When negotiating with foreign countries, presidents can bypass the treaty ratification process by issuing executive agreements; not surprisingly, the ratio of executive agreements to treaties, which hovered between zero and one in the nineteenth century, now consistently exceeds thirty (King and Ragsdale 1988). If presidents choose to avoid the reporting requirements Congress has placed on executive orders, they can repackage their policies as executive memoranda, determinations, administrative directives, or proclamations. And if they prefer to keep their decisions entirely secret, they can issue national security directives, which neither Congress nor the public has an opportunity to review (Cooper 2002).

The U.S. Constitution does not explicitly recognize any of these policy vehicles. Over the years, presidents have invented them, citing national security or expediency as justification. Taken as a whole, though, they represent one of the most striking, and underappreciated, aspects of presidential power in the modern era. Born from a truly expansive reading of Article II powers, these policy mechanisms have radically impacted how public policy is made in America today. The president's powers of unilateral action exert just as much influence over public policy, and in some cases more, than the formal powers that presidency scholars have examined so carefully over the past several decades. As Kenneth Mayer notes,

Working from their position as Chief Executive and Commander in Chief, Presidents have used executive orders to make momentous policy choices, creating and abolishing executive branch agencies, reorganizing administrative and regulatory processes, determining how legislation is implemented, and taking whatever action is permitted within the boundaries of their constitutional or statutory authority. (2001, 4–5)

If we want to account for the influence that presidents wield over the construction of public policy, we must begin to pay serious attention to the president's capacity to create law on his own.

"Presidential Power Is the Power to Persuade"

The image of presidents striking out on their own to conduct a war on terrorism or revamp civil rights policies or reconstruct the federal bureaucracy stands in stark relief to scholarly literatures that equate executive power with persuasion and, consequently, place presidents at the peripheries of the lawmaking process.

Richard Neustadt sets the terms by which every student of American politics has come to understand presidential power in the modern era. When thinking about presidents since FDR, Neustadt argues, "weak remains the word with which to start" (1991 [1960], xix). Presidents are much like Shakespearean kings, marked more by tragedy than grandeur. Each is held captive by world events, by competing domestic interests and foreign policy pressures, by his party, his cabinet, the media, a fickle public and partisan Congress. To make matters worse, the president exercises little control over any of these matters—current events and the political actors who inhabit them regularly disregard his expressed wishes. As a result, the pursuit of the president's policy agenda is marked more by compromise than conviction; and his eventual success or failure (as determined by either the public at the next election or historians over time) ultimately rests with others, and their willingness to extend a helping hand.

The public now expects presidents to accomplish far more than their formal powers alone permit. This has been especially true since the New Deal, when the federal government took charge of the nation's economy, commerce, and the social welfare of its citizens. Now presidents must address almost every conceivable social and economic problem, from the impact of summer droughts on midwestern farmers to the spread of nuclear weapons in the former Soviet Union. Armed with little more than the powers to propose and veto legislation and recommend the appointment of bureaucrats and judges, however, modern presidents appear doomed to failure from the very beginning. As one recent treatise on presidential "greatness" puts it, "modern presidents bask in the honors of the more formidable office that emerged from the New Deal, but they find themselves navigating a treacherous and lonely path, subject to a volatile political process that makes popular and enduring achievement unlikely" (Landy and Milkis 2000, 197).

If a president is to enjoy any measure of success, Neustadt counsels, he must master the art of persuasion. Indeed, according to Neustadt, power and persuasion are synonymous. The ability to persuade, to convince other political actors that his interests are their own, defines political power and is the key to presidential achievement. Power is about bargaining and negotiating; about brokering deals and trading promises; and about cajoling legislators, bureaucrats, and justices to do things that the president cannot accomplish on his own. As Matthew Dickinson notes, "Neustadt's core argument in *Presidential Power* is that a president's bargaining exchanges with other actors and institutions constitute the primary means by which he (someday she) exercises influence" (2000, 209). The president wields influence when he manages to enhance his bargaining stature and build governing coalitions; and the principal way to accomplish as much, Neustadt claims, is to draw upon the bag of experiences, skills, and qualities that he brings to the office.

Intentionally or not, Neustadt set off a behavioral revolution. Subsequent generations of scholars posited skill, personality, style, and reputation as the ingredients of persuasion and thus the keystones of political power (Barber 1972; George 1974; Greenstein 2000; Hargrove 1966; Pfiffner 1989). Self-confidence, an instinct for power, an exalted reputation within the Washington community, and prestige among the general public were considered the foundations of presidential success. Without certain personal qualities, presidents could not hope to build the coalitions necessary for action. Power was contingent upon persuasion, and persuasion was a function of all the personal qualities individual presidents bore; and so, the argument ran, what the presidency was at any moment critically depended upon who filled the office.

By these scholars' accounts, a reliance on formal powers actually signals weakness. What distinguishes great presidents is not a willingness to act upon the formal powers of the presidency but an ability to rally support precisely when and where such formal powers are lacking. As Neustadt argues, formal powers constitute a "painful last resort, a forced response to the exhaustion of other remedies, suggestive less of mastery than of failure—the failure of attempts to gain an end by softer means" (1991 [1960], 24). Presidents who veto bill after bill (think Ford) do so because their powers to persuade have faltered. The presidents who effectively communicate (Reagan) or who garner strong professional reputations (Roosevelt) stand out in the eyes of history.

Although the notion of the personal presidency dominated the field for decades, its influence is on the decline. The principal reason is that it no longer matches up with the facts. The personal presidency became a popular theoretical notion just as the American presidency was experiencing tremendous growth and development as an institution: in its staffing, its budget, and the powers delegated to it by Congress. As time went on, it became increasingly clear that the field needed to take more seriously the formal structures and powers that define the modern presidency.

If the personal presidency literature is correct, executive power should rise and fall according to the personal qualities of each passing president. Presidential power should expand and contract according to the individual skills and reputations that each president brings to the office. The constituent elements of the personal presidency may be important. Prestige and reputation may matter. But if we are to build a theory of presidential power, it seems reasonable to start with its most striking developments during the modern era. And these developments have little to do with the personalities of the men who, since Roosevelt, have inhabited the White House.

By virtually any objective measure, the size and importance of the "presidential branch" has steadily increased over the past century (Hart 1995). According to Thomas Cronin, "for almost 150 years the executive power of the presidency has steadily expanded" (1989, 204). Edward Corwin echoes this sentiment, arguing that "taken by and large, the history of the Presidency is a history of aggrandizement" (1957, 238). How can such trends persist if presidential powers are fundamentally personal in nature? It cannot be that the caliber of presidents today is markedly higher than a century ago, and for that reason alone presidents have managed to exert more and more influence. Does it really make sense to say that successful twentieth-century presidents (e.g., the Roosevelts or Reagan) distinguish themselves from great nineteenth-century presidents (e.g., Jackson, Polk, or Lincoln) by exhibiting stronger personalities? And if not, how can we argue that the roots of modern presidential power are fundamentally personal in nature? While Neustadt may illuminate short-term fluctuations at the boundaries of presidential influence—skill in the art of persuasion surely plays some part in political power—he cannot possibly explain the general growth of presidential power.

During the past twenty years, scholars have revisited the more formal components of presidential power. Work on the institutional presidency has regained the stature it held in political science during the first half of the twentieth century (Bond and Fleisher 1990, 2000; Burke 1991; Hargrove 1974; Jones 1994; Moe 1985, 1999; Nathan 1983; Peterson 1990). This work is far more rigorous than the personal presidency literature and, for that matter, the institutional literature's earlier incarnations (Corwin 1957; Rossiter 1956). A science of politics is finally taking hold of presidential studies: empirical tests now are commonplace; theoretical assumptions are clearly specified; and hypotheses are subject to independent corroboration. Perhaps more important than its methodological contributions, though, the institutional literature has successfully refocused scholarly attention on the office of the presidency and the features that make it distinctly modern: its staff and budget, the powers and responsibilities delegated to it by Congress, and the growth of agencies and commissions that collect and process information within it.

Nothing in the institutional literature, however, fundamentally challenges Neustadt's original claim that "presidential power is the power to persuade" (1991 [1960], 11). Scholars continue to equate presidential power with an ability to bargain, negotiate, change minds, turn votes, and drive legislative agendas through Congress. Not surprisingly, the president remains secondary throughout this work. He continues to play second fiddle to the people who make real policy decisions: committee members writing bills, congressional representatives offering amendments, bureaucrats enforcing laws, judges deciding cases.

To legislate, to build a record of accomplishments about which to boast at the next election, and to find their place in history, presidents above all rely upon Congress—so the institutional literature argues. Without Congress's active support, and the endorsement of its members, presidents cannot hope to achieve much at all.

> Under the Americans system, you [the president] need [congressional] votes all the time and all kinds of votes; votes for and against bills, votes for and against amendments, votes to appropriate funds, votes not to appropriate funds, votes to increase the budget, votes to cut the budget, votes to enable you to reorganize the executive branch, votes to strengthen you (or not to weaken you) in your dealings with administrative agencies, votes to sustain your vetoes, votes to override legislative vetoes, votes in the Senate to ratify the treaties you have negotiated and to confirm the nominations you have made, votes (every century or so) in opposition to efforts to impeach you. (King 1983, 247)

The struggle for votes is perennial; and success is always fleeting. Should Congress lock up, or turn away, the president has little or no recourse. Ultimately, presidents depend upon Congress to delegate authority, ratify executive decisions, and legislate when, and where, presidents cannot act at all.

Almost uniformly, the institutional literature measures presidents' power by their ability to drive through Congress a legislative agenda (Bond and Fleisher 1990, 2000; Goldsmith 1974; Haight and Johnston 1965; Light 1999; Peterson 1990; Rudalevige 2002; Spitzer 1993; Wayne 1978). The signature of strong presidents is a high legislative success rate in Congress, of weak presidents, the sight of legislative proposals repeatedly dying in committees and on floors. While its form is no longer personal in nature, presidential power very much remains tied to persuasion and bargaining.

Consider, by way of example, the work on the "two presidencies" hypothesis. In 1966, Aaron Wildavsky proposed that there are two-presidencies, one foreign, the other domestic. In the former, presidents dominate policy making; in the latter, Congress does.

Since its publication, Wildavsky's argument has received consider-able attention, much of it critical (Edwards 1986, 1989; Fleisher and Bond 1988; Pepper 1975; Sigelman 1979; Zeidenstein 1981). Still, there remains one point that all parties agree upon, if only tacitly. Presi-dents are powerful to the extent that they can influence the legislative process; the ability to turn congressional votes, amend bills, and push policies through committees and chambers is the mark of success. This theoretical assumption lays the foundation for all of the empiri-cal work on the two-presidencies hypothesis. Every scholar attempts to answer the same question: whether presidents' foreign policy ini-tiatives enjoy a greater measure of congressional support than do do-mestic initiatives.

Like the rest of the institutional literature, this work examines pres-idential success *in* Congress rather than presidential success *versus* Congress (Lindsay and Steger 1993). Scholars rely exclusively on roll call votes and variations of presidential success scores to determine whether presidential success in Congress varies across policy do-mains. The president, it is supposed, exercises and defines his power through deliberations with Congress. What presidents do outside of these deliberations, presumably, either perfectly reflects the underlying wishes of congressional majorities or lacks substantive importance.

Empirically motivated institutional studies are not alone in this re-gard. Game theoretic models, for the most part, also gauge executive power by the president's ability to influence legislative affairs. In-deed, to the extent that presidents play any role whatsoever in most models of lawmaking, they almost always act as a veto player. These models do an excellent job of delineating the precise conditions under which the president's power to veto legislation impacts public policy

(Cameron 2000; Krehbiel 1998; Matthews 1989; McCarty 1997). Not surprisingly, however, presidents appear remarkable only because they are so feeble. As represented in these models, presidents appear only slightly more important than members of Congress who can credibly threaten to filibuster a bill. Rather than having to assemble a super-majority of sixty in the Senate, enacting coalitions now must occasionally win the votes of sixty-seven. The technical impact of the president within these models of lawmaking is to replace the three-fifths cloture point with the two-thirds veto override player as the veto-pivot—not exactly the stuff of a modern, ascendant presidency.

While they provide important insights into the strategic uses of the veto power, these models remain almost completely Congress-centered. As such, they largely ignore the ability of presidents to set policy on their own. The fact of the matter is that presidents have always made law without the explicit consent of Congress, sometimes by acting upon general powers delegated to them by different congresses, past and present, and other times by reading new executive authorities into the Constitution itself.

Presidents regularly effect policy change outside of a bargaining framework. Because of his unique position within a system of separated powers, the president has numerous opportunities to take independent action, with or without the expressed consent of either Congress or the courts. Sometimes he does so by issuing executive orders, proclamations, or executive agreements; other times by handing down general memoranda to agency heads; and still other times by dispensing national security directives. The number of these unilateral directives, and of opportunities to use them, has literally skyrocketed during the modern era (Moe and Howell 1999a, 1999b). While presidents freely exercise these powers during periods of national crises, as the events following September 11th have made clear, they also rely upon executive orders and executive agreements during periods of relative calm, effecting policy changes that never would survive the legislative process. And to the extent that presidents use these "power tools of the presidency" more now than they did a century ago, the ability to act unilaterally speaks to what is distinctively "modern" about the modern presidency (Cooper 1997, 2002).

Rather than hoping to influence at the margins what other political actors do, the president can make all kinds of public policies without the formal consent of Congress. While the growth of the presidency as an institution (its staffs, budgets, departments, and agencies) augments presidential power, it is the ability to set policy unilaterally that deserves our immediate and sustained attention.

This book critically examines how the power of unilateral action, which the Constitution nowhere mentions and even lackluster presidents can exercise, augments the chief executive's influence in the push and scuffle of public policy making. As such, this book represents an important break from our previous understanding of presidential power. Modern presidential power does not strictly involve persuasion as Neustadt insists and the institutional literatures assent. The lessons of legislators' successes do not apply, in equal measure, to the presidency. Bargaining does not define all aspects of presidential policymaking. Rather, modern presidents often exert power by setting public policy on their own and preventing Congress and the courts— and anyone else for that matter—from doing much about it.

Thinking about Unilateral Powers

From the beginning, it is worth highlighting what makes unilateral powers distinctive. For the ability to act unilaterally is unlike any other power formally granted the president. Two features stand out.

The most important is that the president moves policy first and thereby places upon Congress and the courts the burden of revising a new political landscape. Rather than waiting at the end of an extended legislative process to sign or veto a bill, the president simply sets new policy and leaves it up to Congress and the courts to respond. If they choose not to retaliate, either by passing a law or ruling against the president, then the president's order stands. Only by taking (or credibly threatening to take) positive action can either adjoining institution limit the president's unilateral powers.

While it has yet to apply the lesson to the presidency, the formal literature on agenda setting and coalition formation pays fair tribute to the strategic advantages associated with moving first (Baron 1991, 1996). By moving first, and anticipating the moves of future actors, legislators of all stripes and in very different political systems influence the kinds of policies governments produce. Indeed, an entire public choice literature argues that if preferences are multidimensional—that is, preferences cannot be represented along a single, usually liberal-conservative, continuum—then it is possible to manipulate the agenda so that any conceivable public policy can be enacted (McKelvey 1976). But gains to the president are twice over. While agenda setters in Congress only propose bills, the president moves first and creates legally binding public policies. And he does so without ever having to wait on coalitions subsequently forming, committee chairs cooperating, or party leaders endorsing.

The second important feature of unilateral powers is that the president acts alone. There is no need to rally majorities, compromise with adversaries, or wait for some interest group to bring a case to court. Rather than depending upon Congress to enact his legislative agendas, the president frequently can strike out on his own, occasionally catching even his closest advisors off guard (recall Clinton's unilateral decision to bomb Iraq in the fall of 1998, the day before his scheduled impeachment hearing in the House Judiciary Committee). As the chief of state, the modern president is in a unique position to lead, to define a national agenda, and to impose his will in more and more areas of governance.

To be sure, the executive branch does not reduce to the president himself. Should they vehemently disagree with a president, subordinates can set up roadblocks, as Clinton learned early in his first term when he threatened to unilaterally lift the ban on gays in the military and subsequently bumped up against the fierce opposition of the Joint Chiefs of Staff (more on this in chapter 5). The relationship between a president who stands atop his governing institution and subordinates who ultimately are responsible to him, however, is fundamentally different from that of a legislator who stands on roughly equal footing with 534 colleagues across two chambers. Hierarchies reside in both the legislative and executive branches. In the former, party leaders and committee chairs exert disproportionate influence in the House and Senate. No single member, however, has the final word on which bills are introduced and which amendments are considered. In the executive branch, however, ultimate authority resides with a president who (fairly or not) is given credit or blame for the success or failure of public policies. While bureaucrats certainly retain a significant amount of discretion to do as they please, the lines of authority generally converge upon a single individual, the president.[9]

The ability to move first and act alone, then, distinguishes unilateral powers from all other sources of influence. In this sense, Neustadt is turned upside-down, for unilateral action is the virtual antithesis of bargaining and persuading. Here, presidents just act; their power does not hinge upon their capacity to "convince [political actors] that what the White House wants of them is what they ought to do for their sake and for their authority" (Neustadt 1991 [1960], 30). To make policy, presidents need not secure the formal consent of Congress, the active support of bureaucrats, or the official approval of justices. Instead, presidents simply set public policy and dare others to counter. For as long as Congress lacks the votes (usually two-thirds of both chambers) to overturn him, the president can be confident that his policy will stand.

The presidency literature's traditional distinction between formal and informal powers does not contribute much insight here. Because the Constitution does not mandate them, powers of unilateral action cannot be considered formal. It is by reference to what presidents have done (or gotten away with) that these powers take form. But nor are these discretionary powers informal. They are not rooted in personal qualities that vary with each passing president. Rather, these powers emerge from specific institutional advantages within the office of the presidency itself: its structure, resources, and location in a system of separated powers. The promise of a sustained analysis of unilateral powers, then, is great. To the extent that presidents act unilaterally with increasing frequency and effect in the postwar era, an institutional theory of unilateral action enables scholars to see beyond Neustadt's original conception of presidential influence in the modern era.

The Tool Chest

John Locke first spoke of "prerogative powers." According to Locke, certain public officials ought to enjoy the "power to act according to discretion, for the publick good, without the prescription of the law and sometimes even against it" (1988 [1689], 237). These powers are necessary, Locke argued, because the designers of any constitution cannot foresee all future contingencies and therefore must permit certain discretionary allowances. "There is a latitude left to the Executive power, to do many things of choice, which the Laws do not prescribe" (375). In order to meet new expectations, and serve the public when laws cannot, the president may act unilaterally, even when neither the legislature nor the Constitution has mandated appropriate powers.

Presidents in more modern times have manufactured a number of policy instruments that give shape and meaning to these prerogative powers. The most common include executive orders, proclamations, national security directives, and executive agreements. There are few hard and fast rules about how policies are classified, affording presidents a fair measure of liberty to select the instrument that best serves their objectives. Still, some basic distinctions generally apply.

Among all unilateral directives, "executive orders combine the highest levels of substance, discretion, and direct presidential involvement" (Mayer 2001, 35). Executive orders, for the most part, instruct government officials and administrative agencies to take specific actions with regard to both domestic and foreign affairs. "Executive orders are directives issued by the president to officers of the executive branch, requiring them to take an action, stop a certain type of activity, alter policy, change management practices, or accept a delegation of authority under which they will henceforth be responsible for the implementation of law" (Cooper 2002, 16). But while presidents direct executive orders to subordinates within the executive branch, the impact of these orders is felt well beyond the boundaries of the federal government. Terry Eastland, who worked in the Justice Department during the Reagan Administration, cautions, "In theory executive orders are directed to those who enforce the laws but often they have at least as much impact on the governed as the governors" (1992, 351). Through executive orders, presidents have dictated the terms by which government contractors hire and fire their employees, set restrictions on where American citizens can travel abroad, frozen the financial holdings of private parties, reset trade tariffs, and determined the kinds of recreational activities that are allowed on public lands.

If executive orders are typically directed to officials within the federal government, presidential proclamations almost always target individuals and groups outside of the government. Because Article II of the Constitution does not endow the president with clear and immediate authority over private parties (as it does over the federal bureaucracy), it is not surprising that proclamations tend to be less consequential than executive orders, most involving ceremonial and commemorative affairs. There are, however, numerous exceptions, such as Nixon's 1971 proclamations and orders temporarily freezing all wages, rents, and prices as part of the national economic stabilization program; Ford's 1973 proclamation granting pardons to draft dodgers; and Carter's 1980 proclamations imposing new surcharges on imported oil.

Beyond the 1937 Federal Register Act's publication requirements, presidents need not abide by any fixed requirements when developing, issuing, or circulating an executive order or proclamation. There are occasions, however, when presidents would prefer not to alert Congress, the courts, or the public as to their actions, and then presidents often turn to national security directives (also known as national security decision directives or presidential decision directives). Issued through the National Security Council, most national security directives remain classified, and hence beyond the purview of political opponents. While presidents presumptively use these directives to safeguard the nation's security, in practice presidents may repackage a particularly controversial executive order as a national security directive and thereby avoid the scrutiny of Congress and interest groups. As Phillip Cooper notes,

It is tempting to employ NSDs because they cloud actions the president wishes to take with the mantle of national security and hold out the threat of security laws for violation. Although it happens, it is more dangerous for employees to leak or discuss these devices, and Congress has difficulty getting into documents it cannot see. It is even tempting to use NSDs in ways that help the president domestically. (1997, 547)

Though precise figures are impossible to obtain, the General Accounting Office (GAO) estimated that from 1961 to 1988 presidents issued over one thousand national security directives. Of those the GAO was able to review, 41 percent directly affected military policy, 63 percent foreign policy, and 22 percent domestic policy.[10] A sample of recently declassified national security directives includes orders to the CIA to support and recruit Nicaraguan Contras; the funding of covert operations to prevent nations from replicating the "Cuban model"; the authorization to execute preemptive and retaliatory strikes against confirmed and suspected terrorists; the establishment of new classified information rules for the National Security Agency; the approval of the invasion of Grenada in 1983. According to Harold Relyea, the content of national security directives "is not only imaginatively diverse, but also often highly controversial, if not dangerous. Indeed, they appear to be an attempt by the President to make a determination unilaterally about matters better decided with congressional comity" (1988, 108).

Even the advent of the Cold War can be traced back to a national security directive. Issued in April 1950, N.S.C. 68 emphasized the historical importance of the mounting conflict between the United States and Soviet Union. The document, drafted by the director of the State Department's policy-planning staff, Paul Nitze, was a call to arms and defined the nation's military and political objectives as it waged an ongoing struggle against the world's only other superpower. Calling for a massive expansion of military capabilities, N.S.C. 68 concluded that

we must, by means of a rapid and sustained build-up of the political, economic, and military strength of the free world, and by means of an affirmative program intended to wrest the initiative from the Soviet Union, confront it with convincing evidence of the determination and ability of the free world to frustrate the Kremlin design of a world dominated by its will. . . . The whole success of the proposed program hangs ultimately on recognition by this Government, the American people, and all free peoples, that the cold war is in fact a real war in which the survival of the free world is at stake.[11]

While it met some initial resistance within the Truman and Eisenhower administrations, N.S.C. 68, more than any other document, established the guiding doctrine for successive presidents' Cold War foreign policy.

Executive agreements stand apart from these other directives. While executive orders, proclamations, and (to a lesser degree) national security directives all are unilateral counterparts to legislation, executive agreements provide presidents with an alternative to the treaty ratification process. Rather than having to secure the consent of two-thirds of the Senate before entering into a bi- or multilateral agreement with foreign nations, presidents can use executive agreements to unilaterally commit the United States to deals involving such issues as international trade, ocean fishing rights, open air space, environmental standards, and immigration patterns. While most of these agreements concern very specific (and often technical) matters, the sheer number issued during the modern era has increased at such an astronomical rate that collectively they now constitute a vital means by which presidents unilaterally affect public policy.

When setting public policy, presidents frequently issue combinations of these various policy directives. To force the integration of schools in Little Rock, Arkansas, Eisenhower simultaneously issued a proclamation and an executive order. Carter relied upon a series of executive orders and executive agreements to negotiate the Iran Hostage Crisis. Presiding over World War II, the Korean War, and the Vietnam War, Roosevelt, Truman, Johnson, and Nixon all issued a wide array of secretive orders, national security directives and otherwise. Presidents frequently use executive orders, secretarial orders, and reorganization plans to create administrative agencies and then turn to other kinds of unilateral directives—for example, administrative directives, findings and determinations, and regulations—to monitor their behavior. The ease with which presidents can mix and match these unilateral directives to advance their policy goals is considerable.

The Legality of Unilateral Powers

The first Court challenge to a presidential order, *Little v. Barreme* (1804), concerned the legality of a seizure of a Danish ship, the *Flying Fish*.[12] George Little, the captain of the *U.S.S. Boston*, had intercepted the ship at sea. At the time, Captain Little was complying with a John Adams presidential order that the Navy seize any and all ships sailing to or from French ports. Previously, however, Congress had only authorized the seizure of frigates sailing to French ports. Because the Danish brig was sailing *from* a French port and not *to* one (it was headed from Jérémie to St. Thomas), the Court for the first time had to resolve a discrepancy between a presidential order and congressional statute.

In a unanimous ruling written by Chief Justice John Marshall, the Court declared that had Adams' order stood alone, the Navy's actions would be constitutional. Because Congress had enacted a more restrictive statute, however, the Court was forced to rule in favor of the Danish captain. "Congressional policy announced in a statute necessarily prevails over inconsistent presidential orders. . . . Presidential orders, even those issued as Commander in Chief, are subject to restrictions by Congress." Marshall subsequently ordered Captain Little to pay damages. More importantly, though, Marshall established the clear principle that when an executive order blatantly conflicts with a law, the law prevails.

During the rest of the nineteenth century, the federal courts considered a host of challenges to unilateral directives issued by presidents, most of which involved military orders.[13] It was not until the 1930s that the Supreme Court formally recognized the president's power to act unilaterally. Three cases—United States v. Curtiss-Wright (1936);[14] United States v. Belmont (1937);[15] and United States v. Pink (1942)[16]— made the difference (Schubert 1973, 107).

Curtiss-Wright centrally involved the constitutionality of an executive agreement that forbade the sale of arms to countries involved in armed conflict. When it sold fifteen machine guns to the government of Bolivia, Curtiss-Wright Export Corporation was charged with violating the agreement. As part of its defense, the company argued that Congress had "abdicated its essential functions and delegated them to the Executive," and for that reason, the Court should overturn the executive agreement. Instead, the Supreme Court, in an oft-cited phrase, deemed the president the "sole organ of the federal government in the field of international relations" and upheld the constitutionality of this particular delegation of authority. Doing so, it formally recognized his legal right to issue executive agreements.

In United States v. Belmont, the Supreme Court extended this right to executive orders. When Russia reneged on debts owed to the United States in the 1930s, President Roosevelt seized Russian financial assets held in American banks. Arguing that Roosevelt's actions violated New York State law, a Russian investor asked the Court to overturn the executive order and to award compensation for his losses. The Court, however, refused. Doing so, it equated an executive order with federal law and reaffirmed its preeminence over state law.

The Supreme Court extended this reasoning to executive agreements in United States v. Pink, which again involved the seizure of

Russian assets in American banks. This time, however, the focus concerned an exchange between the president and the Russian government known as the Litvinov Assignment. In a letter to Roosevelt, People's Commissar for Foreign Affairs Maxim Litvinov relinquished certain Russian claims to assets of Russian companies in New York banks. Roosevelt subsequently acknowledged the reassignment of property claims. In *Pink*, the question before the Court centered on the legal authority of this exchange. Ultimately, the Court ruled that because executive agreements have the same status as treaties, and because both override state laws, the plaintiffs could not use New York State law to try to recover their lost assets.

Collectively, *Curtiss-Wright*, *Belmont*, and *Pink* firmly established the president's authority to issue directives involving "external affairs." Their distinction between foreign and domestic policy, however, subsequently blurred. And for good reason. The list of exceptions to any definition of "foreign" or "domestic" policy is sufficiently long as to make the definitions themselves unworkable as elements of jurisprudence. "The original constitutional understanding that in domestic affairs Congress would make the law and presidents would see to its enforcement had never worked in practice and by the early 1990s it had largely been abandoned" (McDonald 1994, 314). The courts now fully recognize the president's power to issue executive orders and agreements that concern both foreign and domestic policy. Indeed, powers of unilateral action have become a veritable fixture of the American presidency in the modern era.

Writing Public Policy

Much can happen between the issuance of a presidential order and its implementation. Opportunities for shirking abound. Administrative agencies may read their mandates selectively; they may ignore especially objectionable provisions; they may report false or misleading information about initiatives' successes and failures. As we have already noted, the executive branch assuredly does not reduce to the president himself. Bureaucrats enjoy a fair measure of autonomy to do as they please.

Demanding a policy change does not make it so. As Neustadt himself forcefully argued, orders handed down from on high are not always self-executing (1991 [1960], 10–28). In 1948, for instance, Truman issued an executive order demanding the desegregation of the military, but decades passed before the outcome was finally realized. Presidents are engaged in a constant struggle to ensure compliance

among members of the executive branch, and to advance the realization of their policy interests. Presidents appoint high-ranking officials
who share their worldview, and whenever possible, presidents try to
rally the support of their subordinates. This has important consequences for our understanding of presidential power; for when it
comes to the implementation of public policy (whether enacted as a
federal statute or issued as a unilateral directive), the power modern
presidents wield very much depends upon their ability to persuade.

This book, though, is principally concerned with how policy is
made, not with how it is carried out. For how laws are written (if they
are written at all) matters greatly. As chapter 3 shows, Truman ordered that the military be desegregated at a time when congressional
action on the matter was unthinkable. His ability to act unilaterally
had an immediate and profound impact on the growth and development of federal civil rights policy. Further, it set in motion societal
changes much earlier than would have occurred had the president's
only opportunity to exercise power been to persuade Congress to act
on his behalf.

This book sets presidential policy-making aside from the traditional
legislative process; for while presidents must build and sustain coalitions to pass laws, they can unilaterally issue policy directives over
the vocal objections of congressional majorities. As one political ob-
server instructs, "Forget Capitol Hill deliberations and back-room negotiations with industry titans. No need for endless debate and deal-
making. For a president, an executive order can be as powerful as a
law—and considerably easier to achieve."[17] In the political fight over
the content of public policy, presidents regularly exert power without
persuasion. This book shows how.

Institutional Foundations

Unilateral powers are always available to all presidents. That does not
mean, however, that all presidents will choose to use them with equal
frequency. Some, for example Eisenhower, may not take advantage of
these powers for lack of a clear domestic agenda; others, such as Clinton, may back off from threats to exercise them because they fear the
political fallout. An examination of unilateral powers is not entirely
inimical to the kinds of personal concerns Neustadt and his suc-
cessors highlight.

Nonetheless, this book focuses on the institutional factors—the
ideological composition of Congress and the courts, divided government, presidential elections, budgetary processes, delegated author-

ity—that affect presidents' ability to exercise their powers of unilateral action. Just as the skills and dispositions of individual presidents vary with each administration, so, too, does the institutional environment within which each must operate. The relative importance of these realms is in dispute, as they shall likely always be. I, for one, am basically agnostic on the matter. But to the extent that institutions are more tractable than personalities, and the defining characteristics of the modern presidency are institutional rather than personal, an institutional approach appears more promising than previous efforts to specify and empirically measure the personal foundations of presidential influence.

To account for this institutional environment, we really need only ask a single question: how well can Congress and the courts constrain a president who has incentives to continually, albeit strategically, press out on the boundaries of his power? This gets to the heart of the matter. The limits of unilateral powers are as wide or narrow as Congress and the courts permit. Presidents may opt not to exercise their unilateral powers to the maximum extent possible—there will certainly be occasions when Congress and the courts afford a president more discretion than he chooses to utilize. This, however, is a separate matter. My concern is the fundamentally institutional question (what can the president do) rather than the more personal one of what he will choose to do in different circumstances.

When do presidents have the strongest incentives to set policy unilaterally? When will they be able to do so? Do these occasions always coincide? When can Congress rein in an imperial president? Will its members necessarily want to? How are the courts likely to respond to the president's use of these powers? These are the kinds of considerations a theory of direct presidential action must address. They take center stage in the chapters that follow.

2

A Formal Representation of Unilateral Action

In 1993, George Edwards, John Kessel, and Bert Rockman commissioned papers on the state of research on the American presidency. In the resulting edited volume, many of the authors extolled the benefits of rational choice theory. Terry Moe argued most forcefully: "Unlike at any time in the past, a powerful theoretical framework is now available to help us work our way toward an institutional theory of the presidency. This is an extraordinary opportunity for a field that has long found theory so elusive, an opportunity that presidential scholars should welcome and exploit" (1993, 356).

A new generation of presidency scholars has heeded Moe's call, using rational choice to explain topics as varied as the vetoes, public appeals, pandering, mandates, and honeymoon effects (Cameron 2000; Canes-Wrone 2001, forthcoming; Canes-Wrone, Herron, and Shotts 2001; Conley 2001; McCarty 1997).[1] It is not an overstatement to say that rational choice is revolutionalizing the presidency subfield, much as it did the congressional subfield in the 1970s and 1980s and the judicial subfield in the 1990s.

The introduction of rational choice to the presidency literature has two immediate consequences. The first involves a change in the dependent variable. Rational choice shifts the analytic focus away from the president and toward the decisions that presidents regularly make. We will never build theories (formal or otherwise) of individual presidents. But we can construct theories of the actions they take: the vetoes they issue, the judges and justices they nominate, the legislation they propose, the treaties they negotiate, the unilateral directives they issue. Rather than probing who presidents are, rational choice strictly examines what presidents do.

The second change concerns the status of what Nigel Bowles refers to as "nuance, complexity, contingency, and discounting for the future" (1999, 2). While much of the presidency literature examines the exceptional qualities of individual presidents making decisions that are time-bound and context-driven, rational choice emphasizes the things that all presidents have in common. It treats presidents as generic types, intentional actors who seek policy objectives within well-defined institutional settings. Presidents are differentiated not by their personalities, personal histories, or leadership styles. Rather, presidents distinguish themselves by the policy positions they take relative to those assumed by Congress, the courts, and the bureaucracy, and by their respective abilities to impose those preferences either in concert with, or over the objection of, other political actors.

Sacrifice is unavoidable, as rational choice strips presidential narratives of much that makes them so compelling: firsthand observations about a president's character flaws, reflections on his personal relations with trusted cabinet members, speculations on how his childhood affected the man, the leader, he grew up to become. FDR's mother, Johnson's nagging insecurities about Eastern intellectuals, Nixon's ghosts, Reagan's dementia, and Clinton's reckless libido have no place in formal models of the American presidency, even though each obviously impacted their presidencies. Who presidents are assuredly affects what they accomplish, but rational choice consciously and deliberately sets these matters aside and focuses instead on the strategic environments in which presidents govern.

At first blush, the prospect of using rational choice to predict when presidents will unilaterally change public policy appears rather bleak. Rational choice has proved most successful in explaining strategies and choices that political elites regularly make in highly structured environments: congressional committees interacting with floors, judges deciding whether to grant certiorari, presidents issuing vetoes. In each of these instances, the participants involved, the rules of the game, and the order of play are quite clear. But to issue a unilateral directive, presidents need not secure anyone's formal authorization; and they need not wait on Congress to first pass a bill or parties to bring a suit. They can simply act, whenever they like, on whichever policy matter they choose. As such, personalities and chance may matter more than the sorts of institutional dynamics with which rational choice is preoccupied.

But things are not as hopeless as they seem. If we accept that presidents care about the long-term integrity of their policy initiatives, and that presidents act strategically to minimize the chances that other branches of government will undermine their efforts, rational choice appears quite valuable. And there is good cause to believe as much. Presidents do not blindly pronounce any sort of policy initiative—come what may! They monitor politics, anticipating the likely reception that their actions will receive in Congress and the courts. Whether presidents detect organized or ineffectual opposition from the aligning branches of government critically affects their willingness to issue a unilateral directive.

The logic of unilateral action emerges not from a constitutionally mandated sequence of exchanges between political actors, each with some formal say about the content of the president's order. Instead, it arises from the checks that aligning branches of government place on presidential power. Because they can overturn his directives post hoc, Congress and the courts constrain the ability of presidents to unilaterally impose their policy preferences. The tools of rational choice, in such a context, help delineate precisely when Congress and the courts will overturn the president and when the president enjoys a measure of discretion to strike out on his own.

Modeling Presidential Policy Making

During the 1980s, formal models of lawmaking routinely omitted the president (see, e.g., Baron 1989; Baron and Ferejohn 1989; Gilligan and Krehbiel 1987; Shepsle 1986; Weingast and Marshall 1988). Which bills were enacted and how they were crafted remained the exclusive purview of Congress. More recently, however, positive theorists have begun to examine the president's capacity to influence the legislative process through the veto. By strategically threatening vetoes, and occasionally exercising them, these models identify the conditions under which presidents can exact legislative concessions from Congress (Cameron 2000).

The veto, however, is not the only opportunity that presidents have to influence public policy. When considering how to enact their legislative agendas, presidents can either engage the legislative process, and all of the uncertainties that come along with it, or, by issuing some kind of directive, they can just act on their own. Both processes yield policies that carry the weight of law. The issue, then, revolves around which bears the greatest benefit.

There are clear advantages associated with acting alone. When presidents decide to unilaterally set policy, they present Congress (and the courts) with a fait accompli. Rather than proposing legislation, and hoping Congress enacts it, or vetoing legislation, and hoping that Congress does not override, here presidents can independently shift policy in any way they wish, and there it will stay, until and unless either Congress or the courts effectively respond.

Under what conditions will presidents decide to exercise this option? And when they do, how far can they shift policy? This chapter introduces a simple model of the law-making process that is designed to answer precisely these questions. The unilateral politics model takes seriously the fact that the president can choose between administrative and legislative routes to enact his policy initiatives. Consequently, we can compare what Congress and the president can accomplish together, through the traditional legislative process, with what the president can accomplish alone, by exercising his unilateral powers.

I explore several representations of the model, each of which yields the same conclusion: the power to act unilaterally significantly expands the president's influence over public policy. The president *is* fundamentally constrained by Congress, the judiciary, and the previous implementation of status-quo policies. But as we shall soon see, there are clear instances when acting unilaterally generates preferable outcomes to those laws that would exist if the president's only power was to veto legislation he did not like. The lesson here is plain. To the extent that scholars have almost singlemindedly focused on the traditional legislative process, they have underestimated the president's influence over policy outcomes, and, as a result, presidential power generally.

In the final analysis, the unilateral politics model is meant to provide insight into real-world politics—its value is not intrinsic. The purpose of this chapter is to provide a framework for thinking about the politics of unilateral action—not to capture every aspect of lawmaking—and show how this framework relates to the power of the presidency. This chapter, then, sets a stage for discussions in future chapters on how presidents have utilized their powers of unilateral action and how effectively Congress and the courts have responded.

The Unilateral Politics Model

A theory of unilateral action should have two characteristics. First, it should account for the president's first-mover advantage (Mayer 1999; Moe 1999). Unlike Congress, which is a collective decision-making body, or the judiciary, which is highly fragmented and depends upon external parties to bring suits, the president is uniquely equipped to act, as the Founders noted, "with energy and dispatch." In those areas where presidents have carved out some discretion of their own, either by reference to congressional delegations of power, their own constitutional authority, or historical precedent, they often engage the policy making process at its onset.

Second, whenever presidents contemplate a unilateral action, they anticipate how Congress and the judiciary will respond. The limits to unilateral powers are critically defined by the capacity, and willingness, of Congress and the judiciary to overturn the president. Rarely will presidents issue a unilateral directive when they know that other branches of government will subsequently reverse it.

TABLE 2.1
Notation Used in the Unilateral Politics Model

Parameters	
q	An exogenously determined status-quo policy
d	An exogenously determined quantity of legal discretion that the president has to change the original status quo (q)
Players	
P	The president
M	The median legislator in Congress
V	The veto-pivot in Congress
F	The filibuster-pivot in Congress
J	The judiciary
N	Nature[1]
Players' Preferences	
p	The president's ideal point
m	The ideal point of the median legislator in Congress
v	The ideal point of the veto-pivot in Congress
f	The ideal point of the filibuster-pivot in Congress
j	The ideal point of the judiciary (only relevant for select versions of the unilateral politics model)
Policy Outcomes	
$p(q, d)$	A unilateral directive set by the president that revises the original status quo (q)
$c(p)$	A law enacted by Congress that revises a unilateral directive $p(q, d)$ previously set by the president
$c(q)$	A law enacted by Congress that revises the original status quo (q)—this outcome only occurs when the president opts not to issue a unilateral directive.

[1] "Nature" is a convention used in game theory to assign values to exogenous parameters.

The unilateral politics model incorporates both of these fundamentals. The model assumes that presidential decisions are part of a finite, noncooperative game, in which actors have complete information about the order of the game and one another's preferences. The president and members of Congress have Euclidean, and hence single-peaked, preferences along a unidimensional continuum, typically understood as measuring liberalism and conservatism. There exists an exogenously determined status quo (q), and associated with that status quo, a certain amount of discretion afforded to the president, denoted by the parameter d. This parameter defines the distance (and hence is always positively signed) over which the president may uni-

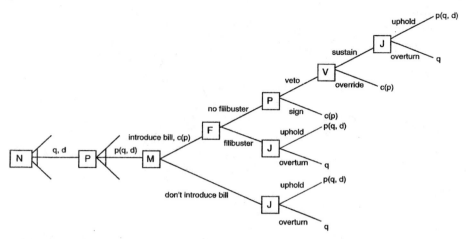

2.1 Sequence of Play in the Unilateral Politics Model

laterally shift policy without being overturned by the judiciary. As a point of reference, Table 2.1 lists all of the notation used in the unilateral politics model.

Figure 2.1 displays the game's form. Because the president acts first, this game differs from other legislative models. Rather than being a veto player, the president may shift q to any point along the policy dimension. It is then up to Congress and the judiciary to respond to a new reversion point, $p(q, d)$. The president may choose not to move q at all, in which case $p(q, d) = \emptyset$.[2] Conditions under which this is an optimal strategy are discussed below.

A unicameral Congress moves next.[3] Congress can overturn $p(q, d)$ by simply passing a new law, $c(p)$, which the median legislator introduces under an open rule.[4] The filibuster-pivot (f) then may choose to filibuster the bill. (The filibuster pivot is simply the sixtieth legislator required to invoke cloture). If there are not enough votes to invoke cloture, $c(p)$ dies and the reversion policy, $p(q, d)$, moves on to the judiciary. If the filibuster-pivot does not filibuster, or if cloture is invoked, then the bill passes Congress and the president either signs it, in which case the game ends, or he vetoes it, in which case Congress has the opportunity to override. If the veto-pivot (v) prefers $c(p)$ to $p(q, d)$, then $c(p)$ becomes law and the game ends. (Likewise, the veto pivot is the sixty-seventh legislator required to override a presidential veto). If the veto-pivot prefers $p(q, d)$ to $c(p)$, however, then $c(p)$ dies and $p(q, d)$ moves on to the judiciary.

As Figure 2.1 makes clear, the judiciary (a single body, which means to represent the federal court system generally) is the final actor in all scenarios except where Congress passes a new law, $c(p)$.[5] The judiciary may choose either to uphold the president's action, in which case the final policy is $p(q, d)$, or overturn the president, in which case the final policy reverts to the original status quo (q). The judiciary has the following decision rule:

Definition 1: *Judiciary's Decision Rule*

If $| q - p(q, d) | \leq d$, then the judiciary rules in favor of the president.

If $| q - p(q, d) | > d$, then the judiciary rules against the president.

To interpret the constitutionality of, or statutory basis for, the president's actions, the judiciary needs only know the status quo (q), the amount of discretion this status quo accords the president (d), and the location of the new policy, $p(q, d)$, set by the president. When the president shifts a status-quo policy within the bounds defined by d, then the judiciary upholds the action. When the president overextends his authority, however, the judiciary overturns him and policy reverts to the original status quo (q). (Later in the chapter we consider instances when the judiciary has actual preferences over policy outcomes.)

In the real world, of course, Congress assigns and the courts interpret the amount of discretion presidents have to change public policy. For our purposes, though, it is perfectly acceptable to assume the discretionary parameter (d) is exogenous: plenty of other models specify conditions under which Congress delegates powers to the president (Epstein and O'Halloran 1999; Sala 1998). The unilateral politics model represents an extension of these models. It assumes that the president inherits a status-quo policy and a certain amount of discretionary authority, and then assesses his ability to unilaterally change the policy given legislative and judicial constraints.

The value of the discretionary parameter (d) obviously varies from policy to policy. For certain policies, such as minimum wage legislation, d is negligible; the president cannot unilaterally change the minimum wage by even the smallest margin without being overturned by the judiciary. In these instances, the unilateral politics model resembles other formal representations of lawmaking that incorporate only the president's veto power (e.g., Krehbiel 1996). When setting affirmative action guidelines, classifying secret information, or revising standards for regulatory review, d is much larger, and the president therefore has greater discretion to set policy on his own.[6] Here, as we shall soon see, presidents often influence final policy outcomes by acting unilaterally.

Note that the discretionary parameter (d) does not constrain Congress's behavior. Because d represents the discretion that a particular law or constitutional power *affords the president*—either because of the ambiguity of the law itself or because of powers it explicitly grants to the president—it has no bearing on Congress's freedom to legislate. Thus, when Congress enacts a law, the game ends.

There clearly are numerous ways d, and the courts generally, may be represented. To begin, I examine the most restrictive case possible for presidents: the president can only change policy in ways that maintain or enhance Congress's utility. Consequently, d points in the direction of the median legislator of the enacting Congress and is fixed in length, such that $0 \le d \le 2 \mid m - q \mid$.[7] To keep things as simple as possible, assume for now that the preferences of the enacting and current Congress are identical; thus, $m_{enacting} = m_{current}$. Later in the chapter we will consider alternative specifications of the d parameter and solve the game when the preferences of the enacting and current congresses differ.

While fixing d to be unidirectional and fixed in length presents the president with a hard case, it is more than just an analytic device. Empirically, when deciding challenges to presidential actions, judges consult the legislative history of the original law that delegates authority to the president. It is on the basis of this history, rather than the preferences of the current Congress, that judges try to decipher the "intent," "will," or "purpose" of Congress and thus render a decision (Bruff 1982; Eskridge 1994; Eskridge and Frickey 1988). Congresses delegate powers to the president so that final policy will reflect their interests, not those of future congresses. Judges, meanwhile, "pay substantial deference to the words of the enacting legislature as opposed to the preferences of the current one" (Ferejohn and Weingast 1992, 573). According to this logic, then, it makes sense to limit possible values of d so that the president can only shift q closer to the median legislator of the enacting Congress.[8]

These are strong assumptions. And each obviously is open to question:

- The federal courts surely constrain Congress's ability to legislate, just as they do the president's. The constitutional rights of individuals and states certainly limit Congress's ability to shift the status quo (q).
- To ascertain the amount of discretion a status-quo policy affords the president, judges rely upon a whole host of concerns beyond a particular law's legislative history. Their own preferences, the preferences of

the current Congress, the plain meaning of the statutory text all can play important roles. Indeed, "the existing literature [on statutory interpretation] strongly suggests . . . that the Court rarely just implements some preexisting 'original legislative intent' when it interprets statutes" (Eskridge 1991).

• Under some circumstances (e.g., war or economic depression), the judiciary may well permit broad shifts in policy, even when these shifts clearly defy the "will of Congress," however one might like to define it. In the real world, the parameter d is not fixed forever, locked in until some future Congress renegotiates its value.

These parameters, nonetheless, provide a useful starting point. Indeed, they fit nicely within the broader class of discretionary agency models (Ferejohn and Shipan 1990; McCubbins, Noll, and Weingast 1989). And should we relax these assumptions, by, say, permitting larger values of d that point in both directions of q, we will only grant greater latitude for presidents to act unilaterally. We will examine just such a scenario later in this chapter. But for now, we present the president with a hard case. If the president can shift q closer to his ideal point than would occur through a strictly legislative process in this model, then surely he can do so under more permissive conditions.

Using backwards induction, we can solve the subgame perfect equilibrium strategies of the median legislator and president. The solution concept of a Nash equilibrium refers to the situation(s) in which no player in a game will unilaterally deviate from his strategy given the strategies of all other players; because no player can independently improve his utility, strategies are self-enforcing. As such, behaviors of the president and key members of Congress should converge toward the equilibrium strategies defined below.

To begin, we need to define the preference sets of the veto- and filibuster-pivots. Because players have Euclidean preferences, this task is straightforward.

Definition 2: *Veto-pivot's override set*

$$O[p(q,d),v] = \begin{cases} [p(q,d), 2v - p(q,d)] & \text{if } p(q,d) < v \\ [2v - p(q,d), p(q,d)] & \text{if } p(q,d) \geq v \end{cases}$$

Definition 3: *Filibuster-pivot's no-filibuster set*

$$N[p(q,d),f] = \begin{cases} [p(q,d), 2f - p(q,d)] & \text{if } p(q,d) < f \\ [2f - p(q,d), p(q,d)] & \text{if } p(q,d) \geq v \end{cases}$$

Each of these sets is defined by the player's ideal points and the new reversion policy, $p(q, d)$, which was set by the president in the second period of the game. The veto-pivot's override set simply consists of all those policies that yield the veto-pivot at least as much utility as

$p(q, d)$. For these policies, the veto-pivot will vote to override. The filibuster-pivot's no-filibuster set, likewise, consists of those policies that provide the filibuster-pivot with at least as much utility as $p(q, d)$.

Given these preference sets, where will the median legislator set $c(p)$? An optimal bill, $c^*(p)$, withstands a possible filibuster and presidential veto *and* is at least as close to the median legislator's ideal point as the reversion point, $p(q, d)$. If either the veto- or filibuster-pivot opposes $c(p)$, then $c(p)$ will die. Under certain circumstances, there are no $c(p) \neq p(q, d)$ that can be introduced that gain the support of both pivots.

This segment of the unilateral politics model virtually replicates Keith Krehbiel's pivotal politics model (1996, 1998). It is worth noting, however, that in the pivotal politics model, the court are absent, the president acts only as a veto player, and Congress's reversion policy, rather than being set by the president, is assumed exogenous. Nonetheless, the subgame perfect equilibrium Krehbiel derives carries over fully to the unilateral politics model.

Figure 2.2 illustrates how far the median legislator can shift the status quo, $p(q, d)$, given the constraints presented by the veto- and filibuster-pivots. The horizontal axis represents possible locations of status-quo policies and the players' preferences along a unidimensional continuum; the vertical axis represents the optimal values of $c(p)$ that the median legislator can set given these locations. For extreme $p(q, d)$, located in intervals I and V, the median legislator will set $c(p)$ at her ideal point, for both pivots will prefer $c(p)$ to the reversion policy, $p(q, d)$. For less extreme values of $p(q, d)$, located in intervals II and IV, the median legislator cannot set $c(p)$ at her ideal point without losing the support of one of the pivots. Under these conditions, only partial convergence to her ideal point occurs. Finally, when $p(q, d)$ is in interval III, gridlock prevails. If the median legislator shifts $p(q, d)$ slightly to the left, the president will veto the bill and Congress will not be able to override. A slight shift to the right will provoke a filibuster for which cloture cannot be invoked. Krehbiel aptly labels III the "gridlock interval."[9]

There is a strange logic to this. The further away the president sets $p(q, d)$, the greater the ability of the median legislator to set $c(p)$ at her ideal point, (m). As $p(q, d)$ moves into intervals II and IV, the veto– and filibuster-pivots act as constraints and only partial convergence can be achieved. Finally, when the president sets $p(q, d)$ within the gridlock interval, the median legislator cannot move policy at all. In this sense, the median legislator is most advantaged by a president who unilaterally shifts policy far away from the preferences of more moderate legislators, for only then can she set $c(p)$ right at her most preferred policy, (m).

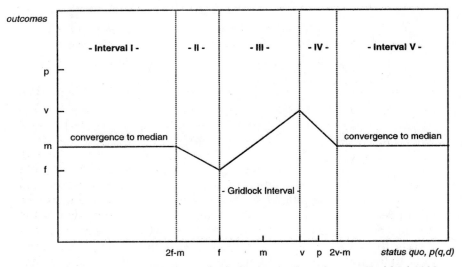

2.2 Median Legislator's Ability to Shift the Status Quo. Source: Krehbiel 1998, p. 35.

The median legislator's equilibrium behavior is summarized as follows:

Definition 4: *Assuming $p > m$,[10] then in equilibrium the median legislator will propose*

$$c(p) = \begin{cases} m, & \text{if } p(q, d) \leq 2f - m \text{ or } p(q, d) \geq 2v - m \\ 2f - p(q, d), & \text{if } 2f - m \leq p(q, d) \leq f \\ 2v - p(q, d), & \text{if } v \leq p(q, d) \leq 2v - m \\ \varnothing, & \text{if } f \leq p(q, d) \leq v \end{cases}$$

How does this behavior affect the president's calculation of where to set $p(q, d)$? The optimal choice $p^*(q, d)$ for the president minimizes the distance between the final policy, be it a unilateral directive $p(q, d)$ or a statute $c(\cdot)$, and the president's ideal point (p). Under certain circumstances along the equilibrium path of play Congress will overturn the president. It is never to the benefit of the president, however, that the courts overturn his unilateral directive $p(q, d)$.

The president's equilibrium strategy is as follows. (Appendix 2 proves all propositions.)

Proposition 1A: *Assuming $q < v, p > m$, and d points in the direction of m, then in equilibrium,*

$$p^*(q,d) = \begin{cases} q+d, & \text{if } q < m, q+d \le v \ \& \ |c(q)-p| \ge |p(q,d)-p| \\ v, & \text{if } q < m, q+d \ge v \ \& \ |c(q)-p| \ge |p(q,d)-p| \\ \varnothing, & \text{if } m \le q \le v \text{ or } |c(q)-p| \ge |p(q,d)-p| \end{cases}$$

Here, the president will shift q as far as $(q + d)$, provided that $q < m$ and the median legislator will not introduce a new policy $c(p) <$ $(q + d)$ that will gain the support of the veto-pivot. Thus, if $(q + d)$ is outside of the "gridlock interval" (that is, the set of status-quo policies that Congress cannot change due to super-majoritarian constraints), the president will settle for setting his directive $p(q, d)$ at the veto pivot's ideal point, (v). If $m \le q \le v$, then both the president and Congress are deadlocked, and no action will be taken. And similarly, if the status quo q is located to the left of f and the constraint of the discretionary parameter (d) on the president is greater than the constraint of the filibuster-pivot on the median legislator, then the president will not act unilaterally, preferring that Congress shift policy instead.

Proposition 1B: *If $q \ge v$, $p \ge m$, and d points in the direction of m, then in equilibrium,*

$$p^*(q,d) = \begin{cases} v, & \text{if } v \ge q-d \\ q-d, & \text{otherwise} \end{cases}$$

In this scenario, rather than leaving $p(q, d)$ at q, the president's equilibrium strategy is to undermine Congress's ability to set policy at or near the ideal point of its median member. When the president can set $p(q, d)$ at v, without being overturned by the judiciary, then there final policy will rest. If the president's ability to set $p(q, d)$ at v is constrained by the value of d, then $p^*(q, d) = q - d > v$, and the final policy will be $2v - (q - d) \ge c(q)$.

For most preference assignments, values of d, and locations of q, these equilibrium strategies are remarkably intuitive. When q is located within the gridlock interval, the president may shift policy only as far as the judiciary will permit, even though the current Congress might allow even more extensive policy changes; for status-quo policies to the right of the veto-override pivot, the president may issue a unilateral directive that shifts policy further away from his ideal point, but in so doing undermines Congress's bid to make even more dramatic policy changes; and for status-quo policies to the left of the filibuster-pivot, the president's optimal strategy usually involves stepping aside and letting the current Congress legislate.

Figure 2.3 summarizes how these equilibrium strategies translate

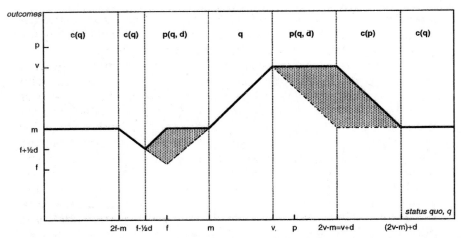

2.3 Equilibrium Outcomes, Fixing Discretionary Parameter. $c(q)$ indicates that Congress alone moves q; $p(q)$ indicates that the president alone moves q; $c(p)$ indicates that the president first moves q and then Congress moves the new reversion point $p(q, d)$; and $\emptyset$ indicates that neither the president nor Congress moves q. The length of d is fixed to equal $|v - m|$, with the one restriction being that for $m - |v - m| \leq q \leq m + |v - m|, d = |m - q|$.

into policy outcomes. The horizontal axis represents the locations of actors' preferences and possible locations of status-quo policies; the vertical axis denotes policy outcomes. The thick line, then, tracks the equilibrium outcomes.[11] Along this line, policy outcomes may be the result of presidential action alone, $p(q, d)$, congressional action alone, $c(q)$, or successive policy changes first by the president and then by Congress, $c(p)$. Between m and v, the original status quo (q) remains the prevailing public policy; gridlock remains a very real possibility even in a world where the president can unilaterally set public policy. Depending upon the location of status-quo policies and the size of d, all of these sequences are possible along the equilibrium path of play.

The two shaded regions in Figure 2.3 represent the policy gains delivered to the president by having the option to act unilaterally, rather than always relying upon members of Congress to legislate. While the equilibrium outcomes of the pivotal politics model and the unilateral politics model are the same for status-quo policies to the left of $f - \frac{1}{2}(d)$, between m and v, and to the right of $(2v - m) + d$, in two intervals the president is able to shift status-quo policies significantly closer to his ideal point. Between $f - \frac{1}{2}(d)$ and m, and between v and $(2v - m) + d$, the distance between the dashed line (which identifies the equilibrium outcomes of the pivotal politics model) and the solid line (which identifies the equilibrium outcomes of the unilateral politics model) represents the gains afforded the president by having the option to unilaterally set policy.

In the shaded region to the left, the president exercises the greatest amount of influence (i.e., the distance between the dashed and solid lines are longest) when the status-quo policy lies at f. Here, Congress on its own cannot enact an alternative to q, and the president uses the full measure of his discretionary authority to shift policy closer to his ideal point. Subject to the constraining effect of the filibuster-pivot, Congress is able to shift on its own policies slightly to the left of f, and therefore the residual influence afforded the president is slightly smaller. While Congress cannot shift policies to the right of the fili-buster-pivot's ideal point (f), by assumption the value of the discre-tionary parameter (d) diminishes the closer the status quo (q) lies to the median legislator's ideal point (m) (see chapter 2, note 7, above).

In the shaded region to the right, the president exercises the great-est amount of influence when the status quo lies at $2v - m = v + d$. At this point, the president uses all of his discretionary authority to shift q to v, which keeps the median legislator from subsequently en-acting an alternative policy even further to the left. For status-quo policies to the left of $2v - m$, the president does not need to use the full value of d to tie the median legislator's hands; and for status-quo policies to the right of $2v - m$, the value of d is not large enough to keep the Congress from enacting an alternative policy to $p^*(q, d)$.[12]

Figure 2.4 fixes the value of d. It is clear, though, that the sizes of the shaded regions vary according to the amount of discretion af-forded the president. Figure 2.4 graphs the equilibrium outcomes of the unilateral politics model in three dimensions (status quo, out-comes, and d). As one backs into the figure, examining smaller values of d, the sizes of the shaded regions steadily diminish until $d = 0$, whereupon the president is stripped of his unilateral powers entirely, the shaded regions disappear, and the equilibrium outcomes match those of the pivotal politics model.

When the Preferences of the Enacting and Current Congresses Differ

Occasionally, the president will face a Congress whose preferences look very different from those of the enacting Congress that originally delegated authority. Congress, for reasons having to do with its insti-tutional capacity to legislate, cannot update every status-quo policy it inherits. While Congress may address those policies deemed partic-ularly salient to its members' reelection prospects, it will leave others

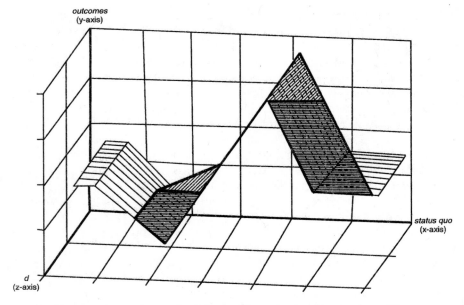

2.4 Equilibrium Outcomes, Allowing the Discretionary Parameter to Vary

untouched, even though these policies grant the president broad discretionary powers to do things the current Congress might not endorse. This raises an important issue. If what the president can legally
accomplish unilaterally is defined by the enacting Congress, but a
very different current Congress nonetheless can overturn his directive, what leverage does the president have to act unilaterally?

To answer this question, we need to consider the range of possible
cases when d points away from m, allowing the president to shift
policy away from the current median legislator without being overturned by the courts. Propositions 1A and 1B, as previously noted,
specify the president's optimal strategies when d points toward m,
presumably because the preferences of the enacting and current congresses coincide.

Before stating these strategies, let's quickly consider a few examples of presidential policy making when the preferences of the current
and enacting congresses differ significantly from one another. First,
look at Case A in Figure 2.5. Here the status quo (q) is located between
m and f within the gridlock interval, and the discretionary parameter
(d), which points away from m, is relatively large. The president cannot shift q closer to his ideal point without being overturned by the
judiciary. Congress, meanwhile, cannot introduce any new bill as

Case A: President and Congress Both Act

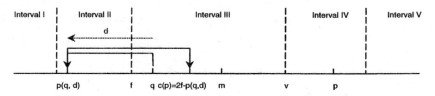

Case B: President Acts Alone

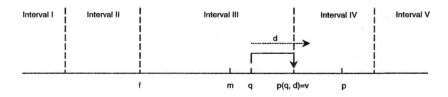

Case C: Congress Acts Alone

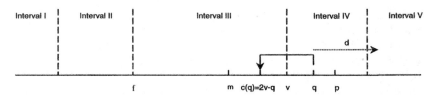

2.5 Divergent Preferences of Current and Enacting Congresses

long as q remains the reversion point. Thus, it appears, we have grid-lock. But take a closer look. If the president shifts q far enough to the left, in this instance to $q - d$, the median legislator will then have the leverage she needs to pass $c(p)$ closer to both her and the president's ideal points. The president's optimal strategy here is to set $p(q, d)$ further away from his ideal point in order to then enable Congress to swing it back even closer.[13]

Case B illustrates what happens when q remains in the gridlock interval, but is on the opposite side of m. Because d now points away from m, the president here can shift q closer to his ideal point without Congress or the courts overturning him. In this instance, d is suffi-ciently large that the president can set $p(q, d)$ right at v. He will not go any further, however, because doing so would enable the median legislator to shift this new policy back into the interior of the gridlock interval.

Given dramatic shifts in preferences, it is possible that q will be greater than v and that d will point away from the ideal point of the current Congress's median legislator. Case C shows how this situation leaves the president incapacitated. While the president would certainly like to move policy closer to his ideal point, something he could do without being overturned by the judiciary, doing so only gives the median legislator more flexibility to set $c(p)$ even further away from p. Simultaneously, however, if the president tries to preempt Congress by shifting q to the left, he invites a reversal by the judiciary. The president, then, has no choice but to step aside and let the median legislator set $c(p)$ back into the gridlock interval, and possibly even at her ideal point.

We now can complete the president's equilibrium strategies:

Proposition 2A: *Assuming $q < m$, $p > m$, and d points away from m, then in equilibrium,*

$$p^*(q, d) = \begin{cases} \varnothing, & \text{if } q \leq 2f - m \\ q - d, & \text{if } 2f - m \leq q \leq f \\ \varnothing \text{ or } q - d, & \text{if } f \leq q \leq v \end{cases}$$

Proposition 2B: *If $q \geq m$ and $p \geq m$, and d points away from m, then in equilibrium,*

$$p^*(q, d) = \begin{cases} v, & \text{if } f \leq q \leq v \text{ and } q + d \geq v \\ q - d, & \text{if } f \leq q \leq v \text{ and } q + d \leq v \\ \varnothing, & \text{if } q \geq v \end{cases}$$

The verdict for presidents is not unanimous. Under certain circumstances, for example when the status quo (q) is located to the left of f, allowing the discretionary parameter (d) to point away from m usually does not change any of the players' strategies or the final outcomes. When q is located in the gridlock interval and to the left of m, in equilibrium the president will not act except when d is extremely large, for then he can set $p(q, d)$ well outside of the gridlock interval so that Congress can set $c(p)$ even closer to p than q already is. In either case, however, the president is made worse off than if d pointed in the direction of m.

As Proposition 2B makes clear, when q is located to the right of m within the gridlock interval, then the president is given the upper hand. Whereas before the president could not shift q closer to his ideal point without being overturned by the judiciary, now he can set

$c(p)$ as far as v. When we move to the right of v, however, the president gets short shrift. When d pointed in the direction of m, the president could preempt Congress by setting $p(q, d)$ at, or slightly to the right of, v. Now that d points away from m, however, this action only invites a reversal by the judiciary. Thus, the president can do nothing, for shifting q further to the right will only give the median legislator greater leverage to swing the policy even deeper into the gridlock interval. And so the president is squeezed out of play, and here the equilibrium outcome is equivalent to that in the pivotal politics model.

This appears to be a mixed bag for presidents. In some circumstances, presidents are made better off, in others they are left noticeably worse off. But the president's position is not as weak as it may seem. Three points are worth highlighting:

1. The alignments of preferences depicted in some of these scenarios are rather contrived. For the most part, the preferences of the median legislator and veto-pivots shift very little across congresses. Save for an electoral realignment, we simply rarely witness the kind of turnover required to create these alignments of preferences.

2. If we allow for enacting and current congresses to differ, but still believe that d ought to point in both directions from q, rather than pointing in one direction or the other, then the president regains all of the advantages we discovered in the previous section.

3. It is rare that presidents ever have just one status-quo policy, and an associated quotient of discretion, to justify setting new policy. In the years that transpire between the passage of q and the shifting of preferences that create these particular scenarios, Congress may enact other laws that give the president the discretion he needs to set new policy. Indeed, at any given time there frequently are multiple laws on the book that conflict with one another, but from which presidents can strategically choose when deciding to act unilaterally. If one law is constraining, presidents, who are responsible for executing all laws, can often read into another law meanings that allow them to set new policy.

This final point suggests that presidents have even greater latitude to set policy than the unilateral politics model predicts, a theme we will return to in chapter 5. When multiple laws conflict with one another, presidents can choose among them when setting new policy. Unlike the unilateral politics model, or, for that matter, spatial models in general, presidents are rarely tethered to just one reversion point when they try to set new policy; frequently there are literally dozens of laws, new and old, that delegate some measure of discretion. And rather than interpret and implement them all, presidents can, and regularly do, strategically choose among them.

Model Expansions

There are any number of ways to tweak the unilateral politics model, each justified by different substantive concerns about the relationships between the president, Congress, and the judiciary. This section presents a handful of alternative specifications and solves their respective equilibrium outcomes.

Rethinking Discretion

Up until now, we have assumed that to avoid a court reversal, the president can only shift a status-quo policy in one direction. The reason is simple. Congress delegates powers to the president so that final policy outcomes better reflect its own majoritarian interests. It seems unlikely then, that Congress knowingly would pass a law that enabled the president to shift q further away from its own median legislator.

But this ignores an important source of discretion. The discretionary parameter (d) does not derive only from those powers expressly delegated by Congress to the president. Frequently, d is a function of a particular statute's language. Many laws do not explicitly grant formal powers to the president. Rather, these laws state broad objectives that are open to multiple interpretations. The president, then, charged with making sure that the laws of Congress are "faithfully executed," can choose among competing interpretations. And the more vague these laws are, the more options the president has before him.

To change policy, presidents do not rely exclusively on powers delegated to them by Congress. As the Commander in Chief and Chief Executive, the president, unlike bureaucratic agencies, enjoys broad constitutional powers to act in his own right. Congressional intent is not irrelevant, it is just not the only factor determining the scope of presidential involvement in the policy-making process. The president's discretion to unilaterally set public policy is much larger than what any given Congress, past or present, stipulates in a single law.

A slight modification to the unilateral politics model, then, may be in order. Given that the value of d may derive from the ambiguity of a given status-quo policy, and the fact that presidents have broad quasi-constitutional powers to intervene in different policy arenas on their own, presidents may well be able to justify setting $p(q, d)$ far to the right _or_ left of the status quo (q). In the context of the unilateral politics model, then, d ought to be symmetrically distributed around q.

How does this new representation of d affect the analysis? It only helps the president. Because d plays no role in calculations of the veto-override player, the filibuster-pivot, or the median legislator, the equilibrium strategies for these players do not change at all. Only the president's optimal choice of $p(q, d)$ requires modification.

Proposition 1B still characterizes the president's equilibrium strategy when $q \geq v$ and $p \geq m$. The president, under these circumstances, will always shift q to the left, in the direction of m. In these intervals, it is never to the president's benefit to set $p(q, d)$ to the right of q, and thus our new representation of d does not alter the president's equilibrium strategies.

In most respects, Proposition 1A remains intact as well. Recharacterizing d requires only two slight modifications to the president's strategy. Given q between m and v, the president now can shift policy closer to his ideal point without eliciting a response by either the judiciary or Congress. If $q + d < v$, then in equilibrium the president will set $p^*(q, d)$ at $q + d$—thus minimizing $| p - p(q, d) |$, while still making sure that the median legislator cannot introduce a bill, $c(p)$, which overturns $p(q, d)$. If $q + d \geq v$, then the president's optimal strategy is to set $p^*(q, d)$ right at v. In both of these instances, however, the same events occur: the president shifts q closer to his ideal point. Whereas before the branches remained deadlocked, now the president gains the upper hand.

A second, and far less intuitive, adjustment must also be made to Proposition 1A. Given our new representation of d, a new equilibrium strategy arises when q is located between $2f - m$ and f. Here the president is able to shift q considerably closer to his ideal point than before. He does so, however, by increasing the leverage of the median legislator to move q closer to her ideal point in subsequent rounds of the game.

Figure 2.6 illustrates this conclusion by showing the three possible moves the president may make when the status quo is located in interval II. In Case A, the president acts unilaterally to move policy toward his ideal point. His ability to do so, however, is hindered by the value of d—the threat of a reversal by the judiciary prevents the president from shifting policy past $q + d$. Because $p(q, d)$ is within the gridlock interval, where Congress cannot overcome super-majoritarian constraints, here policy will stay.

In Case B the president makes no move whatsoever. Because q is outside of the gridlock interval, Congress can shift q all the way to $2f - q$. This outcome is closer to the president's ideal point (p) than that of Case A, which seemingly makes doing nothing the most attractive presidential strategy. It is important to remember, however,

Case A: President Acts Alone

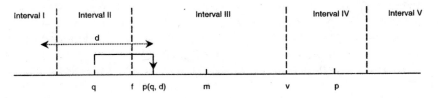

Case B: Congress Acts Alone

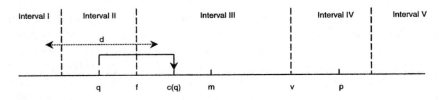

Case C: President & Congress Both Act

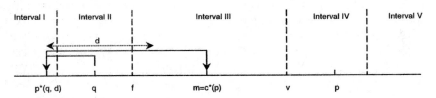

2.6 Interval II Strategies

that the median legislator may not set $c(q)$ at her ideal point because q is located within interval II, where the filibuster-pivot constrains policy shifts to m. But the further q is from f, the closer the median legislator can set $c(q)$ to her ideal point. And when q is all the way in interval I, the filibuster-pivot no longer acts as a constraint at all.

This suggests an alternative presidential strategy, one that is possible given our new characterization of d. Rather than simply ceding the initiative to Congress, the president can shift q to the left, *in the opposite direction of his ideal point*, and thereby give the median legislator greater leverage to shift the reversion policy back to the right. Examine the sequence of play mapped in Case C. Rather than not acting at all (as depicted in Case B), here the president shifts q to the left—in this instance all the way into interval I. The median legislator, then, proposes $c^*(p)$ right at m—which is greater than $c(q)$—and Congress and the president enact it.

The president will follow this strategy whenever he prefers $c(q)$ to $p(q, d)$, and Congress's ability to set $c(q)$ is constrained by the filibuster-pivot.[14] Again, which alternative he chooses depends upon the actual value of d. If d is extremely large, then the president may be able to unilaterally set $p(q, d)$ at or to the right of m, in which case this strategy is suboptimal. And for smaller values of d, the president may wish to follow the Case C strategy, but may not be able to move q all the way into interval I, which enables Congress to set $c(p)$ right at m. Still, there are times when the president's optimal strategy is to shift q further away from p, not in order to undermine Congress's ability to legislate even more extreme policy changes, but instead to enhance Congress's ability to set the final policy even closer to his ideal point. By exercising his unilateral powers, the president frees Congress to act in ways he alone cannot without being overturned by the judiciary.

Clearly, in practice this rarely happens, and for one simple reason. When Congress legislates, the policy game does not suddenly grind to a halt. Indeed, each new policy passed by Congress, $c(p)$, provides new opportunities for the president to intervene and unilaterally set policy—assuming that the new d associated with $c(p)$ is not zero. By representing the unilateral politics model as a one-shot game, when the world of policy making simply is anything but, we have stumbled across one rather peculiar equilibrium strategy, recommending a sort of bluffing as a means of overcoming super-majoritarian constraints. Later in this chapter we will explore what a multistage representation of the unilateral politics model might look like.

Recasting the Role of the Judiciary

Whether the discretionary parameter (d) points in one or both directions from the status quo (q), the essential function of the judiciary remains the same—to determine whether the president has shifted policy within the bounds of discretion afforded by congressional statute or his own independent authority. As such, the judiciary is a strictly procedural body, one that stands outside of the political haggling over where public policy should rest at any given time. This notion, for the most part, comports quite well with the legal literature on statutory interpretation (Choper 1980; Mikva and Lane 1997).

A number of judicial scholars and virtually all formal theorists cast the courts in an entirely different light (Eskridge and Ferejohn 1992a,

1992b; Segal and Spaeth 1993). Rather than deciphering either the will of the enacting Congress or the plain meaning of the statute itself, much of the game theoretic literature assumes that the courts have clear preferences over policy outcomes. "Courts, in this view, are not importantly different than legislatures and judges are no different than elected politicians" (Ferejohn and Weingast 1992, 55). Statutory interpretation, as such, is little more than a "convenient fiction" used to justify court policy making.

With a few slight adjustments, the unilateral politics model can easily accommodate this understanding of judicial behavior. Let's assume that the judiciary has some ideal point (j), located along the same ideological continuum as those of Congress and the president. This ideal point, rather than an exogenously determined quantity of discretion, will provide a basis for deciding whether or not to uphold the president's unilateral action, in which case final policy is $p(q)$, or to overturn it, in which case policy reverts back to q. Consequently, the judiciary adopts a new decision rule: if $| j - q | \geq | j - p(q) |$, then the judiciary rules in favor of the president; and if $| j - q | < | j - p(q) |$, then the judiciary rules against the president.[15] As long as the president sets $p(q)$ at least as close to the court's ideal point as is q, the judiciary will uphold his action; only when the president shifts policy further away from the judiciary's ideal point will the judiciary overturn him. The discretionary (d) parameter no longer plays any part in the judiciary's decision rule.[16]

Again, by design, the judiciary only constrains the president's ability to change public policy in the unilateral politics model. Hence, the judiciary's decision has no bearing on the strategies employed by the veto- and filibuster-pivots and median legislator, and we need only recalculate the president's equilibrium strategy, $p^*(q)$. Three scenarios require consideration, each involving different locations of the court's ideal point and the status quo. First, consider the case when the judiciary's ideal point (j), is to the left of the filibuster's (f). There are three segments of the continuum that require analysis. First, for status-quo policies to the right of v, the president will set policy right at v. For all status-quo policies between j and v, the president cannot set any $p(q) > q$ without being overturned by the judiciary; as a consequence, he does nothing. And finally, for $q < j$, acting unilaterally usually generates policy outcomes inferior to those of the legislative process. When q is extreme relative to j, however, the president can unilaterally set policy to the right of m.

What happens when the judiciary's ideal point is located within the gridlock interval? For all $q \leq f$, the president will compare $p(q)$ to $c(q)$. As we already have established, $c(q) = m$ for extreme status-quo policies and $c(q) = 2f - q$ for more moderate status-quo policies. So as not to be overturned by Congress, the president will set $p(q)$ either at $2j - q$ or, when $2j - q \geq v$, at v. Thus, when $p(q) \geq c(q)$, the president will act unilaterally; when $p(q) \leq c(q)$, then he will not act unilaterally, preferring that Congress shift policy on its own. Moving on, then, for $f \leq q \leq j$, the president will set $p(q)$ either at $2j - q$, or, when $2j - q \geq v$, he will set $p(q)$ right at v.

The third and final scenario we need to consider is when the judiciary's ideal point is to the right of the veto-pivot. Here, for all $q \leq v$, the president will set $p(q)$ right at v. Never is it to the president's advantage to let Congress legislate on its own. For $v < q < j$, the president will not act at all, for his only incentive is to shift q to the left, and thereby constrain Congress's subsequent ability to shift policy into the gridlock interval. For $j < q < 2q - j$, the president will set $p(q)$ either at $2j - q$, or, if $2j - q < v$, then right at v. Finally, for all $q > 2q - j$, the president will set $p(q)$ right at v.

Surely, judges must temper their own policy preferences with concerns for how the law is applied—and consequently, these equilibrium strategies probably overstate the court's influence on policy making. In reality, judges care about legislative intent, the actual meaning of the statute, *and* their own policy preferences. By casting them in each role independently, though, a clear lesson is learned. No matter how we represent the courts in the legislative process, and the constraint they pose for the president, there consistently arise occasions when it is to the president's advantage to act unilaterally, for, by doing so, he is able to set policy closer to his ideal point than would occur through a strictly legislative process.

The Presiding Relevance of Lawmaking

The unilateral politics model predicts that two factors increase the likelihood that policy change will proceed through legislation and not a unilateral directive: the relative extremity of the status quo, and the amount of discretion the president has to move it.

First, the model predicts that Congress and the president together, rather than the president alone, will shift relatively extreme status-quo policies. It is not that the president is incapable of acting on extreme status-quo policies. Rather, in some instances (policies in interval I), it is because both Congress and the president benefit from this arrangement—Congress can shift policy closer to p than can the president on his own. In other instances (policies in interval V), the president is sufficiently constrained by the discretionary parameter (d) to keep him from effectively moderating attempts by the median legislator to shift policy closer to her ideal point, and away from his. The logic of the unilateral politics model, therefore, supports the empirical regularity that landmark laws usually take the form of legislation, while policies of lower to intermediate importance fill the ranks of unilateral directives. To the extent that landmark legislation defines the scope and responsibilities of the federal government, assuredly "the president's success in solving the nation's problems . . . depends in large part on success in the legislative arena" (Bond and Fleisher 1990, 220).

Second, whenever the discretionary parameter (d) is quite small, presidents cannot influence public policy much at all, no matter where the status quo is located. In these instances, the unilateral politics model reverts back to Krehbiel's pivotal politics setup. When the president lacks any discretionary authority to change a public policy, he is effectively squeezed out of the game. Opportunities for influence then only emerge once Congress presents him with a bill to sign or veto.

Stepping Back

The central task of any theory is to "organize or 'explain' a range of empirical phenomena by finding the underlying principles or laws which account for them. Principles which are simpler, fewer, more general, or more precise are more valuable in this endeavor" (Kramer 1986, 12). It is, in part, their parsimony that makes theories powerful. Theories inform when they successfully uncover an underlying logic that explicates what otherwise appear to be idiosyncratic and disparate behaviors.

Theories of lawmaking, or any theory for that matter, are not meant to exactly reflect reality, to perfectly predict every outcome. Indeed, it is unclear what new insights such an exercise confers. The charge instead is to distill some of the essential features of public policy making, to track the logic that connects them, and then, eventually, to lay out a set of expectations about when presidents will set policy and how Congress and the courts will respond. In the process, we must choose what we will account for and what we will ignore. What is more, this choice is critical, for from it everything falls; the insights of any theory in the end derive from a short set of auxiliary hypotheses.

There are no hard and fast rules about which base assumptions to make, which simplifications to accept, what factors to ignore. It therefore is worthwhile to think broadly about them and identify the resultant gap between the model we build and the reality it seeks to explain. The unilateral politics model reduces a profoundly complex policy process into a sequential, finite game, wherein all of the players know each other's preferences and have just one opportunity to affect where policy settles along a unidimensional continuum. Surely, politics is far more complicated, and far less certain, than this suggests.

The point of reflecting upon the limitations of the unilateral politics model, however, is not to lament its failings. Quite the contrary. By reconsidering the model's assumptions, we can more precisely identify its scope of analysis and the insight it confers about the relative influence presidents wield over public policy in systems of separated powers. This section, as such, reexamines several important factors the unilateral politics model omits and speculates on their likely effect on the president's ability to act unilaterally.

Informational Assumptions

The unilateral politics model assumes complete and perfect information. There is a single status-quo point, of which Congress, the president, and judiciary have a shared understanding; the parameter d and the ideal points of the all players are assumed common knowledge. It is clear, however, that these informational assumptions cannot hold. If they did, Congress would never act to overturn a unilateral directive and the courts would never hear a challenge. As we shall see in chapters 5 and 6, quite the opposite is true.

It certainly is possible to generate a closed form solution under conditions of less than perfect information (by, for instance, introducing uncertainty about the true value of d, or introducing some exogenous shock to the system). What is not clear, however, is the marginal benefit of such a model, other than generating equilibrium strategies where Congress and the judiciary may overturn presidential directives. In the same way that legislative models can account for the presence of presidential vetoes by introducing uncertainty (Cameron 2000), so too will the unilateral politics model allow for congressional and court challenges when informational assumptions are relaxed. Although introducing uncertainty will in some sense better approximate reality, the possibility of generating additional insight into the dynamics of unilateral politics must be weighed against the added complexities introduced.

Transaction Costs

Because it assumes complete and perfect information, the unilateral politics model cannot account for transaction costs. Once again, this reflects an important departure from how policies are actually made. A tremendous amount of time and knowledge is required not only to write a law, but also to discern how other congressional members, the president, and judiciary will respond to it. Coalitions must be forged and sustained through a lengthy legislative process. Interest groups and local constituencies must be consulted. It is precisely because transaction costs are so pervasive that congressional members act strategically when choosing which bills to support, and which to leave to future congresses.

Transaction costs, though, present a difficult problem for game theoretic models. A primary source of transaction costs is uncertainty: uncertainty about the outcomes of a particular bill, about the political future, about member's preferences, even about one's own preferences. If members knew all of these things, then designing a bill and gathering the needed votes to enact it would be virtually costless. But because doubt surrounds all of these things transaction costs find their way into almost every facet of lawmaking.

The dilemma is clear. By design, formal models make strong informational assumptions. While some informational assumptions may be relaxed—about, say, shared information of legislators' preferences, in which case some form of signaling game emerges—it is analytically almost impossible to relax them all without the structure of the model itself unraveling. Indeed, these assumptions in part are what allow us to move from the world of politics, which is replete with nuance and character, to the realm of sequential games, in which complex processes are reduced to a seamless array of decision nodes. If we are to gain intuition about the nature of unilateral politics, this move is essential. But rather than being another parameter for which to account, transaction costs force us to rethink the very analytical structure of these models; and should we decide to account for these costs, the analysis grows increasingly cumbersome.

Political economists have found ways to model various forms of political uncertainty. Important and insightful work has been done on moral hazards and informational asymmetries (Persson and Tabellini 1990), difficulties with making credible commitments (Weingast 1995), uncertainty over policy outcomes (Krehbiel 1992), and instances when individual preferences are not common knowledge (Banks 1991). Unfortunately, though, these efforts do not suggest an obvious way to introduce transaction costs to the unilateral politics model. Indeed, they are almost uniformly intended to explain how different institutions (be they contracts, committees, or constitutions) solve problems associated with political uncertainty. While these models give us a good sense of how different institutional arrangements minimize the incidence of transaction costs, we are left with little understanding of how those transaction costs that remain affect the kinds of policies that legislatures are capable of enacting.

This is not to say that transaction costs cannot find a way into positive theories of lawmaking—some initial strides have already been made (see, for example, Dixit 1996). The job, however, is less than straightforward. Two potential solutions suggest themselves. The first is to assign a fixed cost to each legislator who votes for a bill. This approach has the advantage of being computationally simple, but unfortunately, all of the reasons for assigning this cost go against the model's underlying assumptions that members' ideological preferences can be perfectly represented along a single continuum, that the ideal point of each is common knowledge, and the choice each member will make at any given point in the game can be perfectly anticipated. Alternatively, one might introduce more and more uncertainty to models of lawmaking, and then assign costs to the collection of information actors need to make rational choices. In the long run, this is probably the path to take. But it is unclear exactly how we will progress along it since the relaxation of our information assumptions may mean that there is no closed form solution awaiting us at the end.

We do know, however, that the transaction costs of lawmaking greatly exceed those of acting unilaterally (Moe and Howell 1999a). Whereas Congress must assemble and sustain large enacting coalitions every time it wants to change policy, the president need only decide to act. Thus, as future scholars find ways to introduce transaction costs to formal models of lawmaking, our estimation of the president's power to act unilaterally should only increase.

Finite Game

The unilateral politics model represents policy making as a one-shot game. Each player has one and only one opportunity to affect where the final policy rests—except the president, who can act unilaterally and veto legislation passed by Congress. Surely, this hardly reflects the world in which public policy is actually made. Policies are fashioned and refashioned, tossed about in a continual interplay of court rulings, congressional legislation, bureaucratic initiatives, and presidential directives. The dye is never fixed. The process remains forever dynamic.

The difficulty of transforming the unilateral politics model into an infinite game, however, is that we are then required to identify how

Congress sets the discretionary parameter (d), something that, up until now, we have taken as exogenous. Simply stating some rule is insufficient, for reasons that are intrinsic to the model itself—why, for example, would the veto- or filibuster-pivot accept any value of d that permits the president to shift q further away from their ideal points? In fact, given complete and perfect information, the internal logic of the unilateral politics model suggests that d should always be set at zero. It is only when we allow for uncertainty that we can begin to provide an account of how Congress sets d, and provide a rationale for why it should ever be greater than zero; and it is only then that we can go about constructing something longer than a one-shot game.

Political Parties

Political parties are conspicuously missing from the unilateral politics model. Members distinguish themselves by their policy preferences and nothing more. While Democrats and Republicans may congregate at opposite ends of the ideological continuum, in the model party leaders do not exert any influence over members' voting behaviors.

There is, at present, an ongoing debate about the ability of party leaders to discipline its membership and usher through Congress particularly controversial bills. Gary Cox and Mathew McCubbins argue on behalf of strong parties. Party leaders, they suggest, exert considerable control over committee assignments, the legislative agenda, and coalition building, and as a consequence parties establish a modicum of order that theories based upon "committee government" altogether ignore (1993). Keith Krehbiel, by contrast, insists that individual preferences, rather than party membership, explain most of the variance in members' voting behaviors. As such, "theories of legislative politics with a party component—while perhaps more realistic than their more parsimonious non-partisan counterparts—are not necessarily superior predictors of observable legislative behavior" (1993, 237).

Much of the debate over party strength concerns the composition of enacted legislation; that is, whether policy converges to the median legislator in Congress as a whole or to the median legislator of the majority party. If Cox and McCubbins are correct, then the unilateral politics model may either overstate or understate presidential power depending upon the partisan composition of Congress. On a related matter, however, the existence of strong parties has unambiguous consequences for the president's ability to set policy on his own—in particular, whether parties fortify Congress's general capacity to operate as an effective institution. If parties are able to facilitate the enactment of laws that otherwise would not survive the legislative process, then the unilateral politics model overstates the influence presidents glean from acting unilaterally. On the other hand, if by accounting only for members' preferences the unilateral politics model adequately characterizes Congress's capacity to legislate, then there is little cause to downwardly adjust our assessment of presidential power.

The overarching lesson here is plain, and one that we will return to repeatedly throughout this book. Forces that strengthen Congress—parties or otherwise—crucially mitigate the president's unilateral powers. But where members of Congress stumble—due, perhaps, to prohibitive transaction costs associated with building and sustaining legislative coalitions—presidents discover unique opportunities to strike out on their own.

Discussion

The unilateral politics model turns much of the conventional wisdom of lawmaking on its head. Legislative models of lawmaking generally predict that in equilibrium, status-quo policies are never replaced by more extreme policies, relative to the median legislator; further, super-majoritarian procedures mean that status-quo policies located within the gridlock interval cannot be changed at all (Brady and Volden 1998; Krehbiel 1996, 1998). In the unilateral politics model, however, neither of these predictions holds. It is precisely because of super-majoritarian procedures that Congress has a difficult time constraining the president, and therefore the president may shift policy away from the median player.

The model predicts that presidents use their unilateral powers to influence public policy under two scenarios, depicted by the two shaded regions in Figure 2.3. First, when Congress is poised to enact sweeping policy changes that the president opposes, the president can sometimes preempt the legislative process with more moderate policy shifts. Executive influence, in this instance, is measured by the president's ability to undermine congressional efforts to enact a public policy that he opposed.

Presidents also use their unilateral powers to shift status-quo policies over which Congress remains gridlocked. As Joel Fleishman and Arthur Aufses note, "Congressional inertia, indifference, or quiescence may sometimes, at least as a practical matter, enable, if not invite, measures on independent presidential responsibility" (1976, 24). Here, the mark of presidential influence is not a public policy that is weaker (or stronger) than what Congress prefers—rather, it is the unilateral creation of a policy that otherwise would not exist at all.

The president's power to act unilaterally, however, is only as large as the judiciary and Congress permit. Should the judiciary's decision rule change much at all, presidential powers could rapidly expand or, just as quickly, dissolve. And should congressional members band together, the president's power of unilateral action would amount to little; the median legislator would always set policy at her ideal point, and the president, try as he may, could only stand back and watch.

But it is important to remember that the unilateral politics model presents the president with a particularly difficult set of circumstances. This model depicts a world where there are no transaction costs, where the preferences and moves of all players are common knowledge, and where the policy process is modeled as a one-shot game. Even here, the president is often able to set policy closer to his ideal point than would occur through a strictly legislative process. When we relax these assumptions, as we shall do in future chapters, the president's ability to act unilaterally only expands, allowing presidents to enter into entirely new areas of governance and shift policy in dramatic fashion.

3

Bridge Building

THE unilateral politics model highlights the essential features of unilateral action. The president acts alone at the beginning of the legislative process, and then Congress and the courts have opportunities to respond. At its heart, this is an institutional theory.

In two steps, this chapter facilitates the transition from the unilateral politics model to the real-world politics of direct presidential action. The first section uses the model to interpret the elite-level politics of several examples of presidential policy making: Truman's desegregation of the military, Reagan's imposition of economic sanctions against South Africa, and Clinton's attempt to ban the permanent replacement of striking workers. The second section then derives hypotheses that lay a foundation for more systematic tests of the model than case studies alone can possibly provide. These hypotheses deal with three sets of questions: (1) How does Congress's capacity to enact legislation, and thereby constrain the president, affect the president's ability to act unilaterally? (2) What impact does a presidential election have on the employment of these unilateral powers? and (3) Can the unilateral politics model accommodate the influence of political parties? And if so, how should divided government affect presidential policy making?

Examples of Presidential Policy Making

How do the equilibrium strategies calculated in chapter 2 translate into everyday politics? Do presidents really behave in ways that the unilateral politics model predicts? By considering a handful of case studies, this section makes the first link between theory and reality. While the examples considered below certainly do not serve as a formal test of the unilateral politics model—I reserve that for chapter 4—they do suggest that the model is at least plausible.

Gridlock Politics Scenario

When it is located within the gridlock interval, Congress cannot shift the status quo (q) at all, and thus there are clear advantages to acting

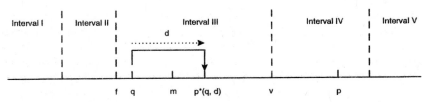

3.1A Gridlock Politics Scenario

unilaterally. Again, if the court was not a constraint, the president could shift q all the way to the veto-pivot's ideal point (v). The best that the president can do, though, is set a unilateral directive $p^*(q, d)$ at ($q + d$). Anything more and the court will overturn the president; anything less and the president does not minimize the distance between the final policy and his ideal point. As future chapters illustrate, this is perhaps the paradigmatic example of unilateral politics: Congress remains gridlocked on an issue and so the president intervenes, wary only of the court's watchful eye.

During the 1940s and 1950s, it was precisely because Congress could not enact civil rights legislation (of either a liberal *or* conservative kind) that presidents were able to step in and define the federal government's role in protecting the rights of black Americans, and later other minorities and women. Consider the events that led up to the desegregation of the armed forces. Demand for blacks' labor, especially within the defense industries, rose to unprecedented levels during World War II. At the same time, vast numbers of blacks moved to the North while liberals initiated voter-registration drives in the South, thereby greatly expanding the number of black voters in the electorate (see, for example, Nathan 1969).

Recognizing the political advantages these developments imparted, black leaders began to demand civil rights legislation. Many of these demands focused on the military. A. Philip Randolph argued publicly that blacks should not join the armed forces or submit to President Truman's newly instituted national draft as long as the military remained segregated. And in 1948, the National Association for the Advancement of Colored People (NAACP) and the Urban League threatened to march on Washington if Congress or the president did not integrate the armed services—just as these groups had successfully done in 1942, compelling Roosevelt to issue Executive Order 8802, which banned discrimination in the military.

Congress heeded the threat.[1] Senator William Langer (R-ND) of the Senate Armed Services Committee introduced seven antisegregation amendments to the 1948 Selective Service Bill (Morgan 1970). But six failed outright. One, which would have eliminated a poll tax imposed on servicemen voting in federal elections, surprisingly passed thirty-seven to thirty-five. Facing staunch opposition from Southern Senators Richard Russell (D-GA) and Burnet Maybank (D-SC), however, the Democratic party leadership subsequently dropped the provision from the Service Bill. Amendments introduced in the House all failed as well.

In the end, Congress looked to executive leadership for "no such [civil rights] law could have passed the Congress of United States" at that time (Powell 1998, 15). In July 1948, Truman responded by issuing Executive Order 9981. This order established a national policy of "equality of treatment and opportunity for all persons in the armed services without regard to race, color, religion or national origin." The president charged the Committee on Equality of Treatment and Opportunity in the Armed Services with enforcing his order.

Just as Congress previously had failed to pass pro-integration legislation, so, too, did congressional attempts to overturn Executive Order 9981 meet defeat. In 1950, when Congress considered extending the 1948 Selective Service Act, Senator Russell introduced a "voluntary segregation" amendment, but it died on the Senate floor. Similar segregationist bills introduced by Representatives Powell and Javits never made it past the House floor. Congressional gridlock earlier had prevented any attempts to shift the status quo to the left on the political spectrum; now, attempts to reverse the president's order met a similar fate.

Preemptive Politics Scenario

Given the direction of the discretionary parameter (d), the president here cannot shift the status quo (q) closer to his ideal point without being overturned by the judiciary. It would seem, then, that the president ought to leave q as is, thus minimizing the distance between $p(q, d) = q$ and president's ideal point (p). Because Congress moves next, however, this strategy will only give the median legislator greater leverage in subsequent rounds to shift $p(q, d)$ closer to the median legislator's ideal point (m), and further from p. In this instance, the median legislator is constrained by the veto-pivot and thus cannot move $p(q, d)$ all the way to m; she can, however, set a bill $c(p)$ as far as $2v - p(q, d)$, which makes the veto-pivot indifferent and a majority of Congress positively happier. From the president's perspective, however, the outcome is much worse, for $c(p)$ is significantly further away from p than is $p(q, d)$.

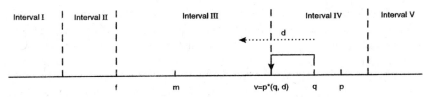

3.1B Preemptive Politics Scenario

Therefore, in equilibrium the president will set a unilateral directive $p^*(q, d)$ at the veto-pivot's ideal point (v). Setting the policy anywhere to the right of v allows the median legislator then to set $c(p)$ equidistant to the left of v, making the veto-pivot indifferent between $c(p)$ and $p(q, d)$, and the president worse off. Setting $p(q, d)$ to the left of v, and into the gridlock interval, ensures that Congress will not be able to act, but makes the president unnecessarily worse off. By setting $p^*(q, d)$ exactly at v, the president can be sure that he will not be overturned by Congress (for no $c(p) \neq p^*(q, d)$ can be introduced that will garner the support of the veto-pivot) or the court (for $p^*(q, d)$ is within the boundaries set by d) and thus the distance between the final policy and p is minimized.

The president's ability to preempt Congress in this way, and hence set policy further away from m than would occur through a strictly legislative process, is not restricted to relatively moderate locations of q. Even when the president cannot shift q all the way to v—due to relatively small values of d, or extreme values of q—he still may be able to constrain Congress's subsequent ability to set $c(p)$ at m. If the president can move q from interval V into interval IV, the final policy $c(p)$ will be closer to p than would occur in a strictly legislative process given the constraint the veto-pivot now plays in subsequent rounds of the game.

Preemptive politics characterized President Reagan's strategy to deal with Congress in the mid-1980s on the issue of South Africa. Spurred by demonstrations at the South African Embassy in Washington, D.C., and by growing violence in South Africa itself, the House and Senate in the summer of 1985 passed bills (H.R. 1460 and S. 995) that would have imposed sweeping sanctions against the apartheid regime. Democrats and Republicans alike overwhelmingly supported the policy shift. Reagan, however, opposed any alteration of the administration's policy of "constructive engagement" with South Africa. Keeping the lines of communication open, Reagan argued, held out the only promise of real reform. Congress disagreed and clearly had the votes to override a presidential veto—H.R. 1460 swept through the House by a 295 to 127 vote, while the Senate version, S. 995, passed eighty to twelve. Left to the traditional legislative process, one of the versions undoubtedly would have become law.

So rather than stand by and watch, in September of 1985 Reagan unilaterally imposed some, but not all, of the sanctions included in the congressional bills. Reagan copied wholesale much of the language of H.R. 1460 and S. 995 into Executive Order 12532, but he also made "major changes that weakened the legislation" (*1985 Congressional Quarterly Almanac*, 84). The executive order included important exemptions in bank loans and nuclear supplies that were not a part of either chamber's bill; the order also reduced the number of requirements South Africa would have to heed if it wanted the sanctions to be either eased or eliminated.

At the September 9 signing ceremony, the media pressed Reagan to explain why, in abandoning his prior position of constructive engagement, he refused to work with Congress to develop an alternative policy. After much hemming and hawing, insisting that he had not really changed his stance at all, Reagan concluded, "I could not sign the [congressional] bill if it came to me containing the economic sanctions which, as we have repeatedly said, would have harmed the very people we're trying to help" (*Public Papers of the President*, 1985, 1057). He continued, "[This executive order] wouldn't have been necessary if I had what a President should have, which is a line-item veto. I could have signed the bill and line-item vetoed out" objectionable sections (1058).

Reagan announced Executive Order 12532 just before Congress had scheduled a compromise version of H.R. 1460 and S. 995 to go to conference. The order hit its mark. It derailed a handful of conservative supporters—supporters who preferred vast sanctions to none, but whose support was lost now that a new, more moderate policy was law. Lacking the votes to override a threatened veto, the congressional bill died before conference members could even consider it.

Again, the preemptive politics scenario captures the logic of Reagan's strategy. We here have a relatively conservative president, a more liberal Congress, and a status-quo policy well outside of the gridlock interval, somewhere in intervals IV or V. Congress was poised to enact new legislation that would have shifted the status quo as far as the median legislator's ideal point. Reagan would have preferred no policy change at all, but managed to contain the damage by introducing a more moderate version of the bill, one that fell on, or near, the veto-pivot's ideal point. The result, then, was to hamstring Congress; while members decried Reagan's "abuse of power," immediate efforts to shift the new policy, Executive Order 12532, all failed.

Deadlock Politics Scenario

Deadlock politics occurs when the median legislator of Congress would like to shift the status quo (q) in one direction, the president would like to shift it in the other, but neither can act because of the institutional constraints placed upon them. The president would like to set $p(q, d)$ to the right of q. And he could do so, without garnering a congressional response, were it not for the judiciary. The median legislator, similarly, would like to shift q to the left. Because q is within the gridlock interval, however, there is no policy proposal that will elude both a filibuster (for which cloture cannot be invoked) and a presidential veto (which cannot be overridden). Consequently, neither the president nor Congress can act on this policy. Deadlock ensues.

This predicament happens all the time. Empirically, though, it is difficult to identify because none of the requisite behaviors are observable. Congress knows it is gridlocked, so no bill is introduced; the president knows the judiciary will overturn him, so no directive is issued. The end product is stasis. The best empirical evidence we can hope to uncover are drafts of bills that Congress meant to introduce, but never did, and the stated intentions of presidents who wanted to act unilaterally, but did not because they feared a reversal by the judiciary.

Actual case studies, therefore, involve off-the-equilibrium-path behavior. Let's consider one such example: the president shifts the status quo away from the median legislator's ideal point, in which case Congress remains incapable of responding, but the courts eventually intervene and overturn the presidential directive. According to the unilateral politics model, this should never occur. In equilibrium, the president will never provoke a reversal by the judiciary. But as we shall see in chapter 6, the courts occasionally do overturn the president. And when they do, the circumstances are almost always the same: Congress remains incapable of changing a public policy, the president unilaterally intervenes, but in doing so he oversteps his statutory authority—exactly the conditions of the deadlock politics scenario.

Consider the federal government's regulation of labor-management relations. In 1935, Congress passed the National Labor Relations Act (NLRA) that, among many other things, formally permitted workers to strike, while companies retained the option to hire replacements during the walkout. It remained unclear, however, whether during these strikes the NLRA allowed companies to hire permanent, or only temporary, replacements. The Supreme Court temporarily resolved this

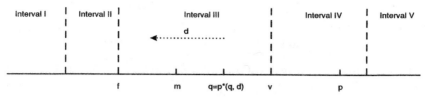

3.1C Deadlock Politics Scenario

issue in *National Labor Relations Board v. Mackay Radio & Telegraph Company* (1938),[2] ruling that employees could be permanently replaced if the cause of their strike was economic (such as low wages), but not if the cause involved unfair labor practices.

During the 1980s, the AFL-CIO devoted vast resources to lobby for legislation that would overrule the Court's 1938 decision. Again and again, however, super-majoritarian procedures stymied their efforts.[3] In July 1991, by a vote of 247 to 182, the House passed legislation that would have made it illegal for companies to permanently replace striking workers, no matter what their cause of action. But there the bill languished, thirty-nine votes short of the two-thirds needed to override President Bush's threatened veto. In 1992, Democrats pushed for identical legislation in the Senate, but there too it expired, three votes short of the sixty required to invoke cloture over a Republican-led filibuster.

As a gesture toward union support during his 1992 presidential campaign, newly elected Bill Clinton vowed to advance their interests. In May 1994 he introduced legislation to Congress that would have overridden *Mackay*. With a Democratic president in office, H.R. 5 easily passed the House. Later that month, the Senate Labor and Human Resources Committee backed a companion bill (S. 55). The president's support, however, quickly proved insufficient and the bill died at the hands of a Senate filibuster. Having already spoken on the issue explicitly, it was clear that the courts would overturn any presidential attempt to unilaterally weaken, or eliminate, the freedom of companies to hire permanent replacement workers.

Clinton, not too wisely, remained undeterred.[4] In 1995, he issued Executive Order 12954, which forbade contractors receiving more than $100,000 in federal funds from hiring permanent replacement workers. Clinton would have preferred to reach all federal contractors, not just those with relatively large federal contracts; doing so, however, would have provoked a congressional response. By accepting a more moderate shift in policy, Clinton ensured that subsequent attempts by Congress to overturn the order would fail to garner the support needed to override a presidential veto. Chair of the Senate Labor and Human Resources Committee Nancy Kassebaum, for example, introduced an amendment to the 1995 Supplemental Defense Appropriations bill (H.R. 889) that would have prohibited the Labor Department from using appropriated moneys to enforce Executive Order 12954. Kassebaum's amendment, however, was two votes shy of the sixty needed to invoke cloture on a Democratic-led filibuster.

Inevitably, though, Clinton's order died in the courts. In 1996, a federal court of appeals ruled that Executive Order 12954 violated the Supreme Court's *Mackay* ruling.[5] The courts, however, did not completely squeeze Clinton out of this policy realm. Substantial ambiguity remained about what exactly constituted economic concerns versus unfair labor practices claims, and this ambiguity provided some discretion to shift policy further along the pro-management direction. Clinton's only opportunity to unilaterally change this policy without being overturned by the courts required a policy move away from his ideal point. There remained little doubt that companies did in fact have a right to permanently replace striking workers, and so the Court ruled out the possibility of any shift in the pro-labor direction.[6]

With the federal court's ruling, policy essentially reverted back to the original status quo, where Congress and the president remained deadlocked. A conservative Congress would have liked to strengthen the pro-management clauses of the NLRA, allowing companies to hire permanent replacements for all striking workers, no matter what the circumstances; it was clear, however, that members could not gather the votes needed to override a presidential veto and/or Democratic filibuster. And when Clinton tried to weaken these same clauses in the 1935 act, making it impossible for companies to ever hire permanent replacements, the courts intervened. In the end, Congress and the president were stuck with a status-quo policy with which neither was particularly pleased.

Presidential Forfeiture Scenario

In this scenario, the status quo (q) is extreme relative to both m and p. If Congress represented the only constraint, the president could shift q as far as the veto-pivot's ideal point (v). But if he is to be upheld by the court, the president can shift q only as far as $q + d$, marked $p(q, d)$. In this scenario, given the extremity of q, both the median player of Congress and the president are made better off when the president does not unilaterally set any new policy. By leaving the status-quo policy alone, Congress can then shift q all the way to m. The median

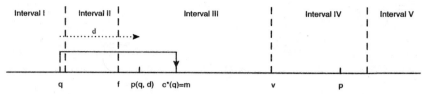

3.1D Presidential Forfeiture Scenario

legislator can move q further than the president simply because Congress is not constrained by the judiciary. Note, however, that as q moves to the right (and into interval II), this advantage must be weighed against the constraint posed by the filibuster-pivot.

Empirically, this story is told over and over in the world of politics. It is the principal reason why Congress and the president together, rather than the president alone, usually act upon relatively extreme status-quo policies—and hence why landmark laws (e.g., Medicare) usually take the form of legislation, while laws of lower-to-intermediate importance fill the ranks of unilateral directives. It is not that the president is incapable of acting on extreme status-quo policies. Rather, it is because both Congress and the president are made better off by this arrangement. The president remains constrained by the judiciary for all values of q; super-majoritarian procedures hamper the median legislator, by contrast, only for relatively moderate values of q. And so, when the median legislator and president agree on the direction of a proposed policy shift, and the status quo is relatively extreme, it is almost always the case that presidents prefer to submit their policy proposals to Congress.

In all of these examples the president's policy preferences are extreme relative to the median legislator's.[7] Such cases present a tough test of the argument that presidents use unilateral powers to shift public policy closer to their ideal points than would occur through a strictly legislative process. Should the ideological orientations of the median legislator and president overlap, then the president will frequently be able to set policies that perfectly match his personal preferences.

Still, in each of these cases the final policy is placed at least as close to the president's ideal point as would occur in a strictly legislative game, one where Congress sets policy and the president wields a veto. In the presidential abdication scenario, the outcome is identical because the president is constrained by the judiciary. In the gridlock politics scenario, rather than being stuck at q, as would occur in a legislative game, the president is able to set $p^*(q, d)$ at $q + d$. In the preemptive politics scenario, rather than having to accept a policy outcome at $2v - q$, the president can unilaterally set $p^*(q, d)$ at v. And should the preferences of the president and median legislator converge, the president's influence over public policy only improves.

Model-generated Hypotheses

The previous case studies highlight the dynamics of unilateral action and provide some basis for believing the unilateral politics model. This section lays the foundation for more rigorous tests of the model. By deriving a set of predictions from the unilateral politics model, we may check whether the case studies examined above are aberrations or whether they indicate broader patterns in presidential policy making. I derive three hypotheses that deal, in turn, with the fragmentation of congressional preferences, presidential elections, and divided government.

I devote a fair amount of attention to these derivations for a reason. Most work on unilateral action, after listing a set of hypotheses that appear plausible, proceeds directly to empirical testing. While some individual findings appear robust, scholars remain at a loss when trying to place them within a larger framework of unilateral decision making. The unilateral politics model establishes this framework. By carefully deriving each hypothesis, even if the calculations appear plodding at times, not only can we be confident about their accuracy, we may also gain some intuition into how they fit within the larger dynamics of unilateral policy making.

The courts are conspicuously absent from this analysis, though they clearly represent an important check on presidential power. Given that most of the comparative statics from the unilateral politics model concern the president and Congress—the judiciary, remember, simply applies a fixed decision rule at the end of the game—I focus here on the relationships between the executive and legislative branches. Chapter 6 examines when the courts rule in favor of the president, when they rule against him, and what impact this has on the president's decision to act unilaterally.

Hypothesis 1: Ceteris paribus, the more fragmented Congress becomes, the more freedom the president has to act unilaterally, and hence, the more significant (i.e., policy-oriented) unilateral directives he issues.

The ability of presidents to act unilaterally depends on other institutions' abilities to stop them. In the extreme, when Congress is incapable of enacting any law whatsoever, the president, conceivably, has only the courts to fear when acting unilaterally. At the other end of the spectrum, when Congress can automatically revise every conceivable policy enactment, the president cannot act unilaterally in any way except that which perfectly reflects the will of Congress.

According to the unilateral politics model, Congress's ability to constrain the president is principally a function of its members' preferences. When preferences are widely dispersed, Congress has a difficult time forming the super-majoritarian coalitions required to pass laws. But when most members share a common ideological orientation, Congress can readily respond to the president.

The notion of the gridlock interval is instructive. As the previous chapter demonstrated, Congress cannot change status-quo policies that fall between the veto– and filibuster-pivots; a majority in Congress may want to, but not the required super-majority, and therefore gridlock persists. Anytime the president shifts policy outside the gridlock interval, though, Congress can shift it back in subsequent rounds of the game, for here a clear super-majority prefers some alternative to the status quo. Accordingly, the longer the interval, the greater the flexibility afforded the president to shift policy. Conversely, as the gridlock interval shrinks, the president's freedom to act unilaterally steadily declines.

But the relationship between the size of the gridlock interval and the probability that the president will act unilaterally is not quite this simple. As we previously witnessed in the preemptive politics scenario, presidents frequently issue executive orders not to shift policy closer to their ideal points, but to undermine Congress's attempts to move them even further away. So as the gridlock interval expands, there are policies that previously fell outside the gridlock interval (to the right of v for $p > m$; to the left of v for $p < m$) that the median legislator could have pulled back in, but now cannot.

Figure 3.2A illustrates this principle. Assume that all status-quo policies are associated with a d that points in the direction of m.[8] There are three time periods, each of which can be interpreted as the alignment of preferences after an election. At T1, the gridlock interval (denoted by the dashed line) is relatively small and, as with all of the examples we have thus far considered, the president is conservative. At T2, the size of the gridlock interval increases noticeably. The filibuster-pivot in T2 shifts to the left of that in T1, opening up new opportunities for the president to act unilaterally. At the same time, however, v_2 shifts to the right of v_1, eliminating a set of policies that

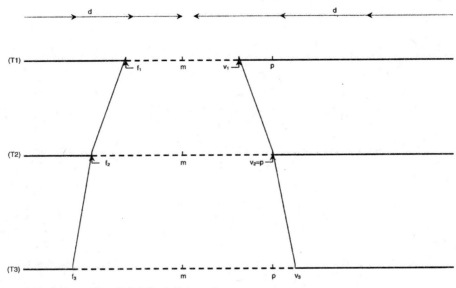

3.2A Expansion of Gridlock Interval

the president at T1 would have acted upon in order to constrain the median legislator, but now needs not. Things are a little different when moving from T2 to T3, for here, as the gridlock interval expands just a little bit wider, p is absorbed within it.

To verify Hypothesis 1, then, we need to calculate the frequency with which the president will act unilaterally in each of these periods. For the sake of simplicity, assume that status-quo policies are distributed standard normal around m. Given this parameterization, we calculate how the expansion of the gridlock interval affects the president's decision to act unilaterally.

Take a look at Figure 3.2B. The thick lines represent the same array of preferences at each time period as shown in Figure 3.2A. Above them are the probabilities that the president will act unilaterally on status-quo policies located within different segments of the continuum. Thus, at T1, the president will act with probability $\alpha_1 < 1$ on status-quo policies to the left of f_1; and for status-quo policies to the right of $2v_1 - m$, the president will act unilaterally with probability $\beta_1 < 1$. At the extremes of the distribution, the president will not act if $c(q) \geq p(q, d)$, and he will if $c(q) < p(q, d)$; α_1 and β_1, then, are just the probabilities that the president will act if one takes a random draw from those status-quo policies that fall either to the left of f_1 or the

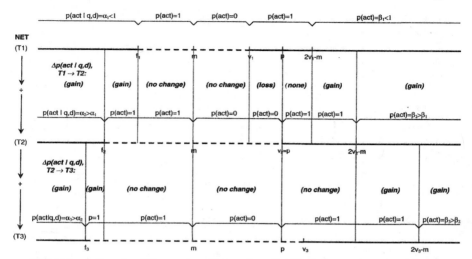

3.2B Calculating the Effects of an Expanding Gridlock Interval on Presidential Policy Making

right of $2v_1 - m$. For policies between f_1 and $2v_1 - m$, the probability that the president will unilaterally change public policy is discrete.

Moving, then, to T2, when the size of the gridlock interval nearly doubles, these probabilities have been recalculated. The dotted lines break up the new array of preferences so that the probabilities at T2 can be compared with those at T1. In parentheses, I have denoted whether each segment's probability increases, decreases, or stays the same. For policies between f_2 and $2v_2 - m$, these comparisons are straightforward. At the ends of the spectrum, however, they require closer attention. The probability that the president will act upon policies to the left of f_2 is greater at time T2 (α_2) than at time T1 (α_1) for the simple reason that f_2 acts as a greater constraint on the median legislator's ability to shift policy than does f_1. Thus, there are a host of policies that at time T1 would fully converge to m but at T2 only partially converge. Remember, for policies within this interval, the president will act unilaterally when $p(q, d) \geq c(q)$; thus, as $c(q)$ decreases, the probability that $p(q, d)$ is greater than $c(q)$ increases. Consequently, $\alpha_2 > \alpha_1$.[9] The exact same logic applies to status-quo policies to the right of $2v_2 - m$.

After glancing at Figure 3.2B, it is easy to see that on the whole, the probability that the president will act at T2 is greater than at T1. The losses between v_1 and v_2 are offset by gains between f_2 and f_3.[10] The expected gain in probability, then, is as follows:

$$E_{T2}(\text{Act}) - E_{T1}(\text{Act}) = \left[(\alpha_2 - \alpha_1)\int_{-\infty}^{f_2} f(q)\right] + \left[(1 - \beta_2)\int_{2v_2 - m}^{2v_1 - m} f(q)\right]$$

$$+ \left[(\beta_2 - \beta_1)\int_{2v_2 - m}^{\infty} f(q)\right]$$

Given $\beta_2 > \beta_1$, $\alpha_2 > \alpha_1$, and $\beta_2 < 1$, this expression is clearly positive.

Much the same story is told when comparing the probabilities at T2 to those at T3. The differences now, however, are not relegated to the tails of the distribution. As p moves into the gridlock interval, a new set of policies (those between p and v_3) that the president will act upon opens up within it. Whereas moving from T1 to T2 shut down a set of policies for the president (given that d is unidirectional), no such losses are incurred when moving from T2 to T3. The differences, then, are as follows:

$$E_{T3}(\text{Act}) - E_{T2}(\text{Act}) = \left[(\alpha_3 - \alpha_2)\int_{-\infty}^{f_3} f(q)\right] + \left[(1 - \alpha_2)\int_{f_3}^{f_2} f(q)\right]$$

$$+ \left[(1 - \beta_2)\int_{2v_2 - m}^{2v_3 - m} f(q)\right] + \left[(\beta_3 - \beta_2)\int_{2v_3 - m}^{\infty} f(q)\right]$$

Every term in this expression is positive. What is more, this expected gain is larger than the one calculated when moving from T1 to T2, even though the relative increase in the size of the gridlock interval is smaller, suggesting that the effect of an expanding gridlock interval on presidential policy making may be nonlinear.[11]

Hypothesis 1 speaks to the distinctiveness of unilateral powers. These powers are defined not by constitutional mandate, but by the ability of Congress to respond to presidential actions after they have already occurred. The degree of fragmentation within Congress, denoted by the expanding gridlock interval, should be an important predictor of presidential policy making.

Hypothesis 2: Ceteris paribus, incoming presidents who are of the opposite party as the previous administration issue more unilateral directives than do either incoming presidents of the same party as their predecessor or second-term presidents.

What happens when a liberal president replaces a conservative president? Within the unilateral politics model, the president's ideal point flips from one side of the median legislator's to the other. In addition, though, the number of status-quo policies that the new president will want to unilaterally shift greatly expands. By transposing p, and holding constant d, f, and v, a whole host of policies that the previous president chose not to act upon will attract the new president's attention, and others that the previous president shifted to the right, the new president will shift back to the left.

When the location of p swings from one side of the gridlock interval to the other, the new president will want to act upon a greater number of status-quo policies than if p shifts slightly to the right or left of the previous president's ideal point. Incoming presidents who are of the opposite party as the previous administration should issue more significant executive orders in their first term than they should in their second term, or than first-term presidents of the same party as their predecessor.

This hypothesis suggests that presidential elections do not have a uniform effect on unilateral politics. Their impact varies according to the preferences of incumbent and newly elected presidents, and how much each differs from the other.

Hypothesis 3: While the exact relationship depends upon the distribution of status-quo policies, presidents usually issue more significant unilateral directives during periods of unified government, ceteris paribus, than during periods of divided government.

Much of the existing literature on executive agreements suggests that presidents act unilaterally in order to bypass a hostile Congress. Nathan and Oliver (1994, 99) go so far as to argue that "presidents . . . have developed and employed the executive agreement to circumvent Senate involvement in international agreements almost altogether." If true, presidents should act unilaterally precisely when they cannot get their legislative initiatives through Congress. When presidents enjoy a strong measure of support within Congress, they need not act at all, for, more often than not, its members will take up their initiatives. Lisa Martin (1999) has appropriately labeled this perspective the "evasion hypothesis."

If the evasion hypothesis is true, presidents should exercise their powers of unilateral action more often when at least one chamber of Congress is governed by the opposite party. During periods of unified government, meanwhile, presidents should have a much easier time working with Congress, and thus should submit most proposals to the legislative process. In this sense, unilateral action is seen as a viable alternative to the traditional legislative process, and the extent to which presidents will want to use it depends critically on the divergence of congressional and presidential preferences.

While this claim seems reasonable, it ignores the constraining effect of Congress. Though presidents may want to exercise their unilateral powers more often during periods of divided government, they should have a harder time doing so. When Congress is controlled by the opposite party, legislative restrictions on presidential powers are greatest. Presidents, ironically, enjoy the broadest discretion to act unilaterally precisely when they have the weakest incentives to take advantage of it—during periods of unified government. It is possible, then, that the heightened incentives to act unilaterally are cancelled out by the losses in discretion to do so, nullifying any effect divided government might have on presidential policy making.

What insight can the unilateral politics model shed on this issue? This is less than straightforward, for the model is entirely preference-driven. Parties, to the extent that they play any role whatsoever, can only be considered proxies for members' ideal points. A strict interpretation of the model would suggest that divided government should not affect presidential policy making at all. Having controlled for the types of preferential arrangements laid out in Hypotheses 1 and 2, divided government should have no additional impact.

The underlying assumption here, of course, is that party leaders regularly defer to their members and exert little or no additional influence on policy outcomes. As governing bodies, parties serve only as convenient voting cues for poorly informed citizens. This supposition is certainly suspect (Cox and McCubbins 1993). While there is little evidence that parties force individual members to vote against their own preferences, much suggests that parties can, and do, manipulate the legislative agenda: "Through their control of committee assignments, the appointment of committees and committee chairs, and the use of the legislative calendar, the majority party is able to control the use of plenary time, that is, it controls which bills do and do not get on the House agenda, and thus, ultimately, which bills get passed and which do not. In this way they control the legislative agenda" (Cox and McCubbins 1999, 4). If true, divided government ought to have some substantive impact on not only legislative productivity, with which Cox and McCubbins are principally concerned, but also presidential policy making.

While parties are not explicitly represented in the unilateral politics model, it is possible to incorporate their influence into the model's framework. To do this, we need only replace the median legislator of Congress with the median legislator of the majority party—which is exactly what Cox and McCubbins do in their "cartel agenda" model (1999). Extreme status-quo policies (in intervals I and V) thus will converge fully to the majority party's median legislator; more moderate status-quo policies (in intervals II and IV) will partially converge; and as before, status-quo policies within the gridlock interval will not move at all.

This simple adjustment captures the influence of parties' "negative agenda power." By controlling the agenda, the majority party can ensure that only those amendments that shift policy closer to its ideal point (represented by its median legislator) are introduced. Much of the time, this will have no substantive effect on the legislation Congress enacts, for the interests of the median legislator of the majority party often will coincide with those of the median legislator of Congress as a whole. But occasionally their interests will conflict. For extreme status-quo policies, for example, a majority in Congress would normally enact legislation that perfectly reflects the interests of the chamber's median legislator, but because the majority party sets the agenda, these members can only shift policy as far as the median legislator of the majority party. Again, this does not require that any member of Congress vote contrary to her own preferences—the majority party need only control the agenda.

Figure 3.3 depicts the effect divided government has on presidential policy making. Assume that the Democrats are the majority party of Congress, and thus policies will converge to m_{dem}.[12] Divided and unified government, then, are a function of whether the presidency is housed by a Republican or Democrat. Assuming that the discretionary parameter (d) points in the direction of m_{dem}, how often will the president act unilaterally?[13]

Consider first the unified government case. For values of q to the left of $m_{dem} - f$, the president will act with some probability $\alpha_1 < 1$. For status-quo policies between $m_{dem} - f$ and f, the president will always act. He will never act on status-quo policies between f and m_{dem}, for doing so only needlessly shifts policy further away from his ideal point. Continuing across the spectrum, the president will always act upon all status-quo policies between m_{dem} and v. For status-quo policies between v and $2v - m_{dem}$, the president will act with some other probability $\lambda_1 < 1$; and for status-quo policies to the right of $2v - m_{dem}$, the president will act with a third probability $\beta_1 < 1$.

Things change significantly under the divided government scenario. Three differences are worth highlighting. First, for status-quo policies to the left of $m_{dem} - f$, the president now will act with some probability $\alpha_2 < \alpha_1 < 1$. The probability α_2 is less than α_1 for the following reason: whereas under the unified government the president would act anytime he could shift a status-quo policy from interval I into interval II, and thus constrain Congress's ability to set $c(p)$ even further away from his ideal point, under the divided government the

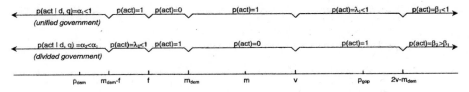

3.3 Impact of Divided and Unified Government on Presidential Policy Making

president will only act when $p(q)$ is greater than $c(q)$. As a moment's notice makes clear, the probability that a Republican president will want to preempt congressional action on an extreme status-quo policy is less than the probability that a Democratic president will want to unilaterally undermine Congress's subsequent efforts to legislate.

The second difference involves the probability the president will act upon status-quo policies within the gridlock interval. Under the unified government case, the president will act with probability zero whenever the status quo falls between f and m_{dem}, and probability one for status-quo policies between m_{dem} and v. The reverse, of course, holds true for the divided government case. The difference, though, is that the area within the gridlock interval where the president will act is significantly greater under periods of unified government than divided government.

The third important difference involves status-quo policies to the right of $2v - m_{\text{dem}}$. The logic for why α_1 is greater than α_2 applies in reverse when comparing β_1 and β_2. Whereas the Democratic president will act only on extreme status-quo policies when he can set $p(q)$ closer to his ideal point than $c(q)$, the Republican president will act whenever he can shift a status-quo policy from interval V into interval IV. And thus, clearly, β_2 is greater than β_1.

We now are in a position to calculate the expected values of unilateral action under divided and unified government. Again, assume that status-quo policies are distributed standard normal around the mean (m). The expected values of unilateral action under unified and divided government are as follows:

$$E(\text{act} \mid \text{uni.government}) = \alpha_1 \int_{-\infty}^{m_{\text{dem}}-f} f(q) + \int_{m_{\text{dem}}-f}^{f} f(q)$$

$$+ \int_{m_{\text{dem}}}^{v} f(q) + \lambda_1 \int_{v}^{2v-m_{\text{dem}}} f(q) + \beta_2 \int_{2v-m_{\text{dem}}}^{\infty} f(q)$$

$$E(\text{act} \mid \text{div.government}) = \alpha_2 \int_{-\infty}^{m_{\text{dem}}-f} f(q) + \lambda_1 \int_{m_{\text{dem}}-f}^{f} f(q)$$

$$+ \int_{f}^{m_{\text{dem}}} f(q) + \int_{v}^{2v-m_{\text{dem}}} f(q) + \beta_2 \int_{2v-m_{\text{dem}}}^{\infty} f(q)$$

Or, in terms of the difference between the two,

$E(\text{act} \mid \text{uni.government}) - E(\text{act} \mid \text{div.government}) =$

$$\left[(\alpha_1 - \alpha_2) \int_{-\infty}^{m_{\text{dem}}-f} f(q) \right] + \left[(1-\lambda_2) \int_{m_{\text{dem}}-f}^{f} f(q) \right]$$

$$+ \left[(0-1) \int_{f}^{m_{\text{dem}}} f(q) \right] + \left[(1-0) \int_{m_{\text{dem}}}^{v} f(q) \right]$$

$$+ \left[(\lambda_1 - 1) \int_{v}^{2v-m_{\text{dem}}} f(q) \right]$$

$$+ \left[(\beta_1 - \beta_2) \int_{2v-m_{\text{dem}}}^{\infty} f(q) \right]$$

The first, second, and fourth terms of this expression are positive, while the third, fifth, and sixth are negative, leaving us with a conditional expectation. Rather than divided government having a fixed effect on presidential policy making, its impact critically depends upon the distribution of status-quo policies, $f(q)$. As the variance of the distribution decreases, more policies ought to be concentrated within the gridlock interval, and hence unilateral activity should be greater under unified government. But as the tails of the distribution thicken, the relative size of the fifth and sixth terms in the above expression will increase, indicating that presidents should act unilaterally with greater frequency during periods of divided government.

Unfortunately, we simply do not have enough data points to test the various predictions associated with every possible distribution $f(q)$. By and large, however, it seems fair to assume that status-quo policies will be concentrated within the gridlock interval. Legislative studies, at least, generally concede as much (Krehbiel 1998). What is more, over the past fifty years the ideological orientations of the median Democratic legislator and median Republican legislator have steadily diverged, further increasing the weight of the fourth term in the above expression (Poole and Rosenthal 1997). Consequently, we should expect that the expression as a whole will be greater than zero, indicating that more significant executive orders are issued during periods of unified rather than divided government—exactly opposite the prediction of the evasion hypothesis.

This is the only prediction that depends upon a particular conception of the judiciary's decision rule. Expectations about the size of the gridlock interval and a switch in presidential administrations are not at all sensitive to any particular operationalization of the discretionary parameter (d). As long as d points in the direction of the median legislator, we should expect presidents to act unilaterally more frequently during periods of unified government than during periods of divided. But if we allow d to point in both directions away from the status-quo policy, then this prediction disappears—divided government should not impact presidential policy making at all. If this prediction bears out in the data, then, the cause may depend upon the judiciary's influence on presidential power, rather than simply being a function of legislative-executive relations.

The underlying intuition here is simple, though it has largely eluded scholars who study the effects of divided government. During periods of unified government, the president is especially likely to shift status-quo policies located within the gridlock region in the direction of the ideal point of the majority party's median member. The courts, then, whose job it is to interpret the "will of Congress," should be more likely to uphold the president's action. As long as the judiciary imposes a strictly procedural decision rule that interprets the will of the enacting coalition—and this will is defined by the interests of the median member of the majority party and *not* the median member of the chamber as a whole—then presidents will generally enjoy greater freedom to act unilaterally during periods of unified government than during periods of divided government. Take away either assumption and the prediction is nullified. But if empirically they hold, then it is the additional constraining effect of the courts, rather than of Congress, that generates the prediction about divided government's impact on presidential policy making.

A full presentation of the courts, and their effect on presidential policy making, must wait until chapter 6. Nonetheless, we may draw upon some preliminary findings that support the notion that the courts play an important part in constraining presidential powers during periods of divided government. Of the fifteen instances in which the federal courts overturned an executive order issued by the president between 1942 and 1996, fully twelve occurred during periods of divided government. While certainly not definitive, these data suggest that the judiciary, at a minimum, may fruitfully be included in predictions regarding the effects of divided government on unilateral policy making.

Dynamics of Presidential Policy Making

While the unilateral politics model certainly assumes away a great deal about everyday politics, it nonetheless provides a solid framework for understanding the strategic calculations presidents must make at the head of the legislative process. At its heart, the choice is quite simple. What can Congress and the president produce together, via the legislative process? And what can the president accomplish alone, knowing that Congress and the judiciary may overturn him? Depending on which yields the greatest benefits, presidents will either propose legislation to Congress or strike out on their own.

In each of the case studies examined in this chapter, we witnessed presidents of very different ideological and personal dispositions making exactly this calculation. It was precisely because Congress could not enact any substantive civil rights policy during the 1940s that Truman decided to unilaterally desegregate the military; Reagan unilaterally established sanctions against South Africa, not because they were part of his foreign policy agenda, but rather because doing so stalled Congress's efforts to enact even more sweeping reforms; and as Clinton's efforts to ban the permanent replacement of striking workers makes clear, there are some policies that cannot be changed legislatively or unilaterally—gridlock remains even in a world where presidents can act on their own.

Even the best case studies, however, are only illustrative. They may elucidate certain aspects of presidential policy making, but they cannot always distinguish anecdotes from larger patterns in American politics. To test the predictive capacity of the unilateral politics model, therefore, we must take a more systematic approach. Largely because of the strong informational assumptions made, it is possible to extract a set of formal expectations about when presidents will exercise their powers of unilateral action. Some simple math generates hypotheses about how ideological divisions within Congress, presidential elections, and divided government affect presidents' decisions about when to act unilaterally.

These hypotheses lay a foundation for empirical analyses to come. Using new data on significant executive orders issued between 1945 and 1998, the next chapter finds consistent, albeit not uniform, support for each of the three theoretical expectations established here.

4

Theory Testing

Too often, the value we attribute to game theoretic models hangs on their intuitive appeal alone. Frequently, this is no fault of the modelers themselves: the equilibria they identify are simply too nuanced, too contingent to invite real empirical corroboration. Additionally, these theories, especially those having to do with lawmaking, often lack a dependent variable, making it virtually impossible to test them. Case illustrations therefore replace systematic analyses, and scholars are left at a loss when trying to determine how or when a theoretical insight might reveal larger trends in American politics.

As the field of positive political theory has matured, however, an increasing number of studies have attempted to connect theory with data. Recently, scholars have found innovative ways to test models of lawmaking and delegation (Cameron 2000; Epstein and O'Halloran 1999; Krehbiel 1998). This body of work represents one of the most promising developments in the literature on American political institutions.

Having laid out the central theoretical propositions of the unilateral politics model, I now test them. I proceed in two steps. First, I build a measure of presidential activism in the realm of unilateral policy making. This measure consists of the number of significant executive orders issued during the twentieth century; conceptual and measurement issues will be discussed in full. In the second section I then use this measure to test each of the propositions derived in chapter 3. These tests support the unilateral politics model and the central intuition that the president's unilateral powers are defined in the negative: they are as large or small as Congress is weak or strong.

The Construction of a Dependent Variable

To test the unilateral politics model, I examine the president's authority to issue executive orders. Although executive orders have not been studied extensively by students of the American presidency, there are presently three modest literatures on the subject; one is situated in legal studies, another in public administration, and the last within political science. None, unfortunately, has given a good deal of attention to the political context in which the president's powers of unilateral action are actually exercised.

The work of legal scholars is rooted in normative concerns about the law—and although they discuss examples of actual executive orders, they are primarily interested in whether powers of unilateral action in some sense can be considered constitutional (Cash 1965; Chemerinsky 1983, 1987; Fleishman and Aufses 1976; Hebe 1972; Neighbors 1964; Rodgers 2001). While this work has amassed an impressive array of arguments for why judges should try to constrain the president, it has failed to shed much light on the political circumstances under which presidents make unilateral policy decisions. In fact, this literature mostly laments that presidents do at all, and scolds the courts for having failed to "use a consistent approach in dealing with the issue of inherent executive power" (Chemerinsky 1983, 863). According to David Adler, presidents' seizure of vast unilateral powers in the modern era, most especially in foreign affairs, "represents a fundamental alteration of the Constitution that is both imprudent and dangerous" (Adler 1998, 25). If we are to "deter the abuse of power, misguided policies, irrational action, and unaccountable behavior," and if we are to secure the benefits of "joint policymaking [that] permits the airing of sundry political, social, and economic values and concerns," then the president's unilateral powers, Adler argues, must be curbed (23–24).

Within public administration, Phillip Cooper has written quite extensively on the unilateral powers of the presidency (2002). Cooper's work does an excellent job of cataloguing the mechanisms presidents have at their disposal to exercise their unilateral powers. Further, Cooper traces the ways in which unilateral directives are formulated and implemented, regularly highlighting the policy implications of presidential actions. Still, like the legal literature, there is a strong normative dimension to Cooper's writing. Cooper repeatedly raises concerns about how presidents can (and do) abuse their unilateral powers, and beckons Congress, the courts, and the public to protect the Constitution and ensure a more equitable balance of powers. Ultimately, and perhaps appropriately, this work calls upon the president himself to proceed with caution and exercise restraint: "It is true that chief executives must have discretion in the performance of their duties and must retain flexible instruments for policy development. In general, however, it would be better law and better administration to administer through public service than by decree" (1986, 256).

Recently, political scientists have cast their attention toward the powers of unilateral action. There is a growing body of quantitative work that is taking pioneering steps toward a more rigorous treatment of the subject (Cohen and Krause 1997; Cooper 1986, 1997, 2002; Deering and Maltzman 1998; Gomez and Shull 1995; Krause and Cohen 1997, 2000; Mayer 1999; Wigton 1991). This work introduces a degree of empirical sophistication and analytical rigor heretofore missing from the study of direct presidential action. Rather than surveying the history of executive orders or focusing on single case studies, as much of the legal literature does, political scientists have used a range of econometric modeling techniques to systematically study how changes in political institutions co-vary with the president's exercise of his unilateral powers.

Nonetheless, two basic problems continue to afflict this research. First, little attention is paid to theory. While a number of these papers do test theoretical propositions, it is unclear exactly where these propositions come from or how they fit together into a logic of policy change. There is no larger framework to guide our thinking about unilateral politics, and from which we might distill a set of testable and interrelated hypotheses.

This same problem has plagued legislative studies as well. For years, political scientists offered up a batch of independent variables that were meant to explain when Congress would enact significant legislation (Brady 1988; Key 1964; Mayhew 1991; Wilson 1961). Strong parties, unified government, and electoral realignments all played prominent roles. It has only been recently, however, that political scientists have begun to build actual theories of lawmaking (Ferejohn and Shipan 1990; Krehbiel 1998).

So it is with presidential policy making. While political scientists have suggested a host of predictors for when presidents will act unilaterally, until now we have proceeded without the guide of a general theory of unilateral action. The unilateral politics model stands to serve this need. Rather than stringing together rationales for why some factors should matter more than others, it attempts to clearly specify a set of joint conditions under which presidents will forgo the legislative route and exercise their unilateral powers instead.

The second problem with the political science literature on executive orders is methodological. Almost without exception, this research uses as a dependent variable the total number of executive orders issued by presidents. Its professed job, then, is to explain patterns in the time-series.

This approach, unfortunately, fails to distinguish significant from insignificant orders. This is of crucial importance, for the vast majority of executive orders, like laws, concern rather mundane affairs: renaming agencies, amending the retirement status of personnel, transferring small tracts of land from one government department to another. To the extent that we are interested in explaining when presidents set policy, however, and not when they issue administrative directives, we must find some method of separating those orders that are significant from those that are not. For if these two time-series noticeably differ from one another—and, as we shall soon see, they do—then whatever claims that political scientists have made about the institutional factors that affect the issuance of executive orders remain provisional. The following section redresses exactly this problem.

"Significant" Executive Orders

Policy significance is an inherently subjective concept and any attempt to measure it is vulnerable to obvious criticisms. Problems of source bias, censored data, and intertemporal inconsistencies abound (Epstein and Segal 2000; Howell et al. 2000). But if we are to understand how presidents have used their unilateral powers to change policy, rather than tend to their administrative duties, then we must work through these issues and find a meaningful way of distinguishing important orders from trivial orders. There clearly are many pathways to policy significance; large budgets, policy innovation, and political controversy all offer footing. The challenge is to develop objective criteria that account for these plainly subjective features of significance.

One approach is to differentiate executive orders by policy content. On the whole, civil service orders are unlikely to have much substantive policy content; orders that involve defense matters, by contrast, more often than not will. While certainly an improvement over the use of raw count data, however, this approach remains insufficiently discriminating. Many defense orders (as with orders in all categories) involve fairly unimportant matters. All that may distinguish them from administrative orders is that they are generally directed at the armed services (or some other administration or agency), and not the civil service. Conversely, while the vast majority of the civil service orders issued this past century were almost completely devoid of policy content, a few were of monumental importance; Reagan's Executive Order 12291, for example, required administrative agencies to submit impact statements when proposing new reforms, and thereby greatly enhanced his ability to oversee the federal bureaucracy.

Rather than sort the executive orders based upon their content, we might instead allow contemporary political observers (e.g., print journalists) to identify which are important. Alternatively, we might scour the existing literature on the presidency and allow historians and policy experts to spot the more significant orders. Both of these approaches were employed by David Mayhew, whose "Sweep One" of laws enacted between 1947 and 1991 focused on contemporary notions of legislative significance, while "Sweep Two" relied upon the retrospective judgments of policy experts (1991).

Unfortunately, when examining executive orders, rather than laws, each of these approaches also presents difficulties. The problem with the Sweep One methodology is that prior to 1969 there are no electronic databanks (as of this writing) that permit searches of major newspapers for mentions of executive orders; and unlike the *New York Times*'s and *Washington Post*'s coverage of laws, no newspaper includes a summary listing of important executive orders at the end of each year. While in principle the Sweep Two methodology provides a plausible alternative, there simply is not a large enough literature on executive orders upon which to conduct a systematic survey.

To overcome these assorted problems, I constructed an altogether different measure, one based upon political sources that are easily referenced and cover the entire twentieth century. I deem significant any executive order that is mentioned in either the appendix of the *Congressional Record* or in the federal court opinions of at least two different cases. To be placed on the list, neither Congress nor the courts need have taken action on an executive order; all that is required is that they cite it. Presumably, congressional representatives and judges will only mention an executive order if, by some measure, they consider it important. The order that excused Maggie Thompson of the Environmental Protection Agency from having to retire on her sixtieth birthday, for example, is unlikely to make the grade; Reagan's order that helped launch the war on drugs by establishing mandatory drug testing policies for federal employees, by contrast, assuredly will.

This approach incorporates both the contemporary and retrospective judgments of political actors. Executive orders that are deemed immediately significant should be mentioned at their time of issuance. Orders that may not have been considered important at birth, but which over time climbed the ranks of significance, should be cited by later congresses and courts.

A basic problem remains, however. An executive order issued in 1930 will have had upwards of seventy years to make it into either the *Congressional Record* or a judge's opinion, whereas an order issued in 1990 will have had only ten years. The further back we go, the less of a problem this presents. If an order has not been mentioned after thirty or forty years, chances are it never will be. But for executive orders of more recent vintage this problem is quite serious. There is often a lag between the time an order is issued and the time judges and congressional representatives find cause to cite it. The longer the lag, the greater the possible source bias.

I settled on a fifteen-year cut-off date. The vast majority of orders, if mentioned at all, make it into the *Congressional Record* or a court opinion within this time period; only a handful are cited for the first time after more than fifteen years. Given that these data were collected in 2000, therefore, the Congress/court citations provide a meaningful indicator of which executive orders are significant up until 1985.

To bring the time series up to the present, therefore, we require additional source materials. I rely upon the *New York Times*, which is easily referenced back until 1969. I documented every executive order mentioned anywhere in the *New York Times* within one year of the order's issuance—in total, the *New York Times* mentioned 284 orders between 1969 and 1998, or on average 9.8 annually. Because these mentions strictly involve the contemporary judgments of policy experts, this second time-series does not suffer from the bias associated with the first. The only shortcoming here is that we cannot collect these data as far back as we otherwise might like.

These two time-series are not mutually exclusive. The *New York Times*, Congress, and courts generally cite a common lot of orders. Since the *New York Times* covers these political institutions, it ought to share a similar conception of which presidential actions are significant, and hence worthy of attention, and which are purely administrative, and hence not.

Table 4.1 tests this hypothesis between 1969 and 1985, when both time-series are consistent and reliable. It shows the number of orders that are mentioned only in the *New York Times* (column 1), the number in both the *New York Times* and the *Congressional Record* or a court opinion (column 2), and the number just in the *Congressional Record* or court opinion (column 3). If journalistic and political bodies have a common notion of policy and political significance, then most orders should load into column 2. If, on the other hand, the sources have very different ideas of which orders are important, and which not, then the orders should load almost exclusively into columns 1 and 3.

While the overlap between the two categories is not perfect, it is considerable. Column 4 shows the probability that the *New York Times* and Congress/court sources would randomly cite at least as many of the same orders as they do, assuming random draws without replacement. The smaller the probability, the less likely it is that the *New York Times* and Congress/court mentions represent independent draws. For the vast majority of years, this probability is quite small, suggesting that the *New York Times* and Congress/court sources generally agree on which executive orders are significant.

TABLE 4.1
Source Validation

	New York Times Only (1)	Cited in New York Times and Congress/Courts (2)	Congress/ Courts Only (3)	Probability of Occurrence by Chance (4)
Year				
1969	10	4	4	0.07
1970	9	6	10	0.07
1971	8	6	8	0.05
1972	7	3	6	0.21
1973	5	1	14	0.81
1974	4	5	11	0.03
1975	8	1	7	0.71
1976	1	3	7	0.02
1977	3	6	9	0.00
1978	12	5	11	0.24
1979	6	5	13	0.07
1980	8	3	9	0.26
1981	7	19	4	0.00
1982	4	7	3	0.00
1983	3	4	4	0.01
1984	1	4	4	0.00
1985	3	4	3	0.01

"*New York Times* Only" refers to the number of executive orders that were mentioned only in the *New York Times*. "Cited in *New York Times* and Congress/Court" refers to the number of executive orders that were mentioned in both the *New York Times* and either the *Congressional Record* or two separate federal court cases. "Congress/Court Only" refers to the number of executive orders that were mentioned in either the *Congressional Record* or two separate federal court cases, but not the *New York Times*. Probabilities were calculated assuming nonordered draws without replacement from a tagged subset (*New York Times* articles) of the overall population of executive orders.

We now are in a position to use the *New York Times* mentions to extend our original list of important executive orders up until the present. Using basic regression analysis and testing various functional forms, I verified the structural relationship between the *New York Times* and Congress/court time-series. Table 4.2 reports the results of a simple bivariate regression. Because the Congress/court time-series represents both contemporary and retrospective assessments of which orders are significant—plus the fact that these institutions do not face space limitations in their publications—we would expect that they mention more executive orders than does the *New York Times*. As the size of the constant makes clear, the prediction holds. In addition, the

TABLE 4.2
Relationship between Source Materials, 1969–1985

	Congress/Court Mentions
New York Times Mentions	0.57***
	(0.16)
Constant	6.33***
	(1.98)
Adjusted R^2	.41
(*N*)	17

Ordinary least squares regression conducted. *** significant at .01 level, one-tailed test. Standard errors reported in parentheses.

relationship between the *New York Times* mentions and Congress/ court mentions is statistically significant, and in the expected direction. For every additional executive order mentioned in the *New York Times*, the model predicts that 0.6 additional executive orders are cited in Congress or the courts.

Using the number of *New York Times* mentions for each year after 1985, this model generates predicted values for the Congress/court time-series.[1] By combining these two segments, the first of Congress/ court mentions, the second of predicted values, we have a consistent time-series for the entire twentieth century. The data are presented in Figure 4.1. The top panel displays the raw number of executive orders issued between 1900 and 1998; the bottom panel shows the number of significant orders during the same time period.

A couple of important differences between the two series stand out. First, the raw number of significant orders issued each year is but a small fraction of the total number of orders. On average, "nonsignificant" orders outnumbered "significant" orders more than twenty to one.[2] Second, whereas the raw number of orders has steadily declined over the past century, the number of significant orders has increased. Between 1900 and 1945, significant orders constituted less than 2 percent of the total number of orders issued (2.7 significant orders on average annually); since 1945, however, significant orders have made up fully 15 percent of the total number of orders issued (9.8 significant orders on average annually). There is no reason to believe that this is an artifact of the source materials consulted. If anything, because older orders have a greater chance of making it into the time-series than do more recent orders, these figures probably underestimate the upsurge of unilateral activity in the latter half of the twentieth century.

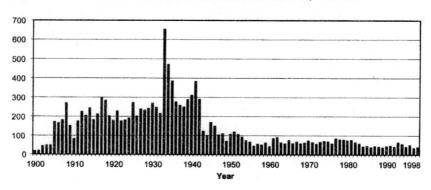

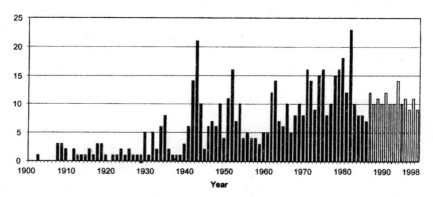

4.1 Executive Order Time-Series. Columns after 1985 in Panel B are not colored because they represent predicted values.

The rise of significant executive orders reflects the general growth of presidential power in the modern era (Cronin and Genovese 1998). Unilateral powers appear to be just another component of the steady expansion of executive authority since FDR. But while scholars long have had the sense that presidents are using unilateral powers to greater and greater effect, this is one of the first pieces of systematic evidence to document the fact.[3]

The two time-series, however, are not altogether different from one another. Both reveal a striking periodicity. Each peaks at the New Deal, World War II, the Korean War, the early stages of the Vietnam War, and the Iran Hostage Crisis.[4] In addition, both time-series exhibit considerable short-term fluctuations. While the overall trend for the raw number of executive orders is down and for significant orders it is up, there remains much variance in both to be explained.

This is the central objective of this chapter. By testing the hypotheses drawn from the unilateral politics model in chapter 3, we may better understand when presidents act unilaterally and when they look to Congress to change public policy. We now can do so, for we have our dependent variable in hand.

Testing the Unilateral Politics Model

Recall the following hypotheses:

Hypothesis 1: Ceteris paribus, the more fragmented Congress becomes, the more freedom the president has to act unilaterally, and hence, the more significant executive orders he issues.

Hypothesis 2: Ceteris paribus, incoming presidents who are of the opposite party as the previous administration issue more executive orders than either incoming presidents of the same party as their predecessor or second-term presidents.

Hypothesis 3: While the exact relationship depends upon the distribution of status-quo policies, presidents generally issue more significant executive orders during periods of unified government than during periods of divided government.

To test Hypothesis 1, I employ two party-based measures. In each, party membership is used only as a proxy for members' underlying policy preferences. The first measure consists of the average size of the majority parties in the House and Senate.[5] Presumably, as majorities increase, divisions within Congress should attenuate, and the gridlock interval should shrink. Conversely, as majorities in the two chambers decline, the gridlock interval should expand. The null hypothesis is that *Majority Size* will have an effect on the number of significant executive orders issued each congressional term that is greater than or equal to zero.

Southern Democrats present obvious problems for partisanship-based measures of preferential heterogeneity. While Democrats enjoyed large majorities in the House and Senate in the 1960s, they also faced strong divisions within their ranks. To address this shortcoming, Joseph Cooper, David Brady, and Patricia Hurley constructed "legislative potential for policy change" (LPPC) scores (1977). They base LPPC scores on four factors: (1) the size of the majority party; (2)

the majority party's internal cohesiveness; (3) the size of the minority party; and (4) its cohesiveness.[6] When the majority party is relatively large, unified, and faces minimal opposition from the minority party, the gridlock interval should be relatively small, and Congress should enjoy more opportunities to enact new legislation. Conversely, when the majority party is relatively small and divided, and the minority party is larger and more unified, gridlock should prevail. To subject Hypothesis 1 to further tests, I take the average of the *LPPC Scores* for House and Senate. The null hypothesis is that the coefficient on *LPPC Scores* is greater than or equal to zero.[7]

To test Hypothesis 2, I used an indicator variable (*Change Party*) that is coded one if a newly elected president is of the opposite party of his predecessor, and zero if an incumbent president is in his second term or if a newly elected president is of the same party as his predecessor. The null hypothesis is that the coefficient for *Change Party* is less than or equal to zero.

Finally, to test Hypothesis 3, I included an indicator variable (*Divided Government*) for periods of divided government. Divided government is defined as any instance when either the majority party of the House or Senate (or both) differs from that of the president. Because the majority party of the House and Senate are the same for the vast majority of the post–World War II era congresses, it makes no substantive difference whether we define divided government as instances when one or both chambers are of the opposite party as the president. The null hypothesis here is that *Divided Government*'s estimated effect on presidential policy making is less than or equal to zero.

Table 4.3 provides summary statistics for all dependent and independent variables.

Diagnostics

Problems of nonstationarity often plague time-series data. If a series is stationary, then the mean, variance, and autocorrelations are time-invariant, and standard regression techniques are then appropriate. But when a time-series is not stationary, associated t and F-tests may be seriously misleading. Before we can test the hypotheses drawn from the unilateral politics model, we must first carefully examine the structure of our dependent variable.

Figure 4.2 displays two versions of the dependent variable. The first relies upon Congress/court mentions to determine which executive orders are significant; the data points between the 79th and 105th

TABLE 4.3
Summary Statistics

	(N)	Mean	S.D.	Minimum	Maximum
Signif. E.O.s—Congress/ Court mentions (79th–105th Congress)	27	19.67	6.83	7	33
Significant E.O.s—*New York Times* mentions (91st–105th Congress)	15	18.93	7.35	12	37
Total E.O.s (79th–105th Congress)	27	133.82	52.98	76	316
E.O.s Overturning Prior Orders	27	59.07	21.36	23	117
"Nontrivial" Laws (79th–105th Congress)	27	88.33	31.35	47	183
Standardized LPPC Scores	27	0.43	.26	0	1
Average Percentage of Seats Held by Majority Party in House, Senate	27	57.77	4.51	50.4	67.9
Divided Government	27	.59	.50	0	1
Change Party	27	.44	.51	0	1
War	27	.37	.49	0	1
Unemployment	27	5.55	1.52	2.9	8.65

Congresses (1945–1998) are labeled "CC." (The data are aggregated by congressional term because virtually all of variation in the key independent variables occurs across two-year time spans).[8] The second version begins in the 92nd Congress and relies upon the *New York Times* to determine which executive orders are significant. Data points for this time-series are labeled "NYT." The solid and dotted lines represent robust, nonlinear smoothers that reveal underlying patterns in the Congress/court and *New York Times* time-series. As the diagnostics in section 1 would indicate, the two series track one another almost perfectly.

Eyeballing the figure, neither series appears to follow a clear deterministic trend. By the 85th Congress, presidential policy making as measured by the Congress/court time-series steadily declined from its World War II-peak, then increased through the 97th Congress, and then dropped again slightly before leveling off through the 105th Congress. Similarly, the *New York Times* mentions showed considerable variation from the 92nd to the 99th Congress but stabilize at the tail end of the time period.[9]

Because I am using event-count data, I estimate a series of Poisson

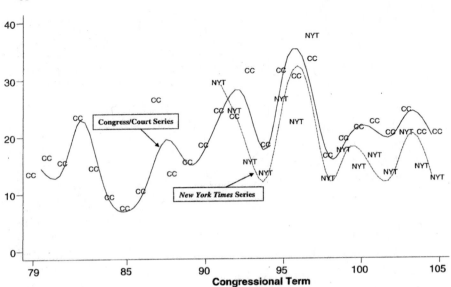

4.2 Number of Significant Executive Orders Issued in Post-War Era. These figures show the number of significant executive orders issued each Congress, as determined by either Congress and the courts or the *New York Times*. The solid and dashed lines represent robust, nonlinear smoothers that reveal underlying trends in the data.

regressions with robust standard errors to correct for heteroskedasticity. Poissons are a special case of negative binomial regressions where the mean and variance are assumed equivalent. If this condition holds, then the ancillary parameter (or dispersion parameter), α, should equal zero. Likelihood ratio tests of nested models show that we cannot reject the null hypothesis that α equals zero, making Poissons appropriate.[10] Further, autocorrelation function plots do not reveal any dynamics in the significant executive order time-series, obviating the need to estimate more complex time-series event-count models (Brandt and Williams 2001; Brandt, Williams, Fordham, and Pollins 2000).[11]

The event-count models presented below control for fixed presidential effects. Even when the powers of unilateral action are equally available to all presidents, some presidents may take advantage of them more often than others, possibly because of the public's mood (Stimson 1999), their ability to rally public opinion (Kernell 1986), their "place in history" (Skowronek 1993), or their leadership styles (Barber 1972). The estimated coefficients of each of the explanatory variables cited above, then, should be the same for all presidents, though the baseline from which each operates may vary according to any number of factors that lie outside the bounds of the unilateral politics model.[12] By including indicator variables for each president, we appropriately allow the intercept to fluctuate while assuming that the effects of each institutional variable remain constant.[13]

Regression Results

We first test the three hypotheses independently, using as key explanatory variables measures of congressional strength, an indicator for shifts in presidential administrations, and another for divided government. The dependent variable consists of the raw number of significant orders—as determined by Congress/court mentions—issued each congressional term between the 79th and 105th congresses (1945 and 1998, respectively). All models control for fixed presidential effects. Table 4.4 presents the results.

We find strong initial support for Hypothesis 1. The estimated coefficients for both *Majority Party* and *LPPC Scores* are significant and in the expected direction. As majority parties grow and become increasingly unified, indicating contractions of the gridlock interval, presidents issue fewer significant executive orders. As majorities decline, presidents issue more significant executive orders.[14] Holding all of the presidential fixed effects at their means, a standard deviation increase in these two variables translates into a decline, on average, of roughly two significant executive orders issued each congressional term—or an 11 percent drop in unilateral activity.[15]

These initial models do not support Hypothesis 2. While the estimated coefficient is positive, it does not even approach standard thresholds of statistical significance. Newly elected presidents of the opposite party as their predecessors do not appear to exercise their unilateral powers any more often than either second-term presidents or newly elected presidents of the same party as their predecessors. Just as Hypothesis 3 stipulated, however, *Divided Government* has a statistically significant and negative impact on the number of significant executive orders issued. When different parties govern the legislative and executive branches, presidents issue on average four fewer significant executive orders each Congress, which constitutes a 22 percent decline in unilateral activity.

The estimated effects of the indicator variables generally reinforce the impressions of presidency scholars about the personal differences between presidents in the modern era. Eisenhower, who came into

TABLE 4.4
Testing the Three Hypotheses Independently, 1945–1998

	Number of Significant Executive Orders Issued			
	Model 1A (1)	Model 1B (2)	Model 2 (3)	Model 3 (4)
Hypothesis 1:				
Size of Majority Party	− .03** (.02)	—	—	—
LPPC Scores	—	− .40* (.26)	—	—
Hypothesis 2:				
Administration Change	—	—	.06 (.13)	—
Hypothesis 3:				
Divided Government	—	—	—	− .22** (.08)
President Fixed Effects:				
Eisenhower	− .54*** (.17)	− .52*** (.17)	− .55*** (.18)	− .41** (.14)
Kennedy	.34* (.26)	.34* (.26)	.09 (.30)	.10 (.27)
Johnson	.22* (.14)	.18* (.13)	− .02 (.13)	− .06 (.14)
Nixon	.46*** (.11)	.46*** (.12)	.40** (.19)	.61*** (.13)
Ford	.30** (.14)	.29** (.14)	.07 (.11)	.24** (.11)
Carter	.79*** (.13)	.75*** (.11)	.54*** (.17)	.55*** (.13)
Reagan	.30** (.16)	.34** (.17)	.25** (.16)	.45** (.18)
Bush	.29*** (.09)	.33*** (.10)	.23** (.12)	.39*** (.11)
Clinton	.22** (.13)	.28** (.11)	.20* (.15)	.33*** (.11)
Constant	4.34*** (.93)	2.92*** (.13)	2.81*** (.11)	2.87*** (.13)
Pseudo R^2	.24	.24	.23	.24
Log likelihood	− 72.97	− 73.19	− 73.92	− 73.23
(N)	27	27	27	27

The dependent variable is the number of significant orders issued during each congressional term. Poisson regressions estimated. * signifies coefficient is significant at .10 level, one-tailed test conducted; ** significant at .05 level; *** significant at .01 level. Robust standard errors reported in parentheses.

office without any domestic agenda and who shied away from most outward displays of force, registers significantly below the baseline (represented by Truman), while every president since Nixon comes in well above it. Still, there are some curiosities worth noting. Kennedy and Johnson appear to have been less willing to issue significant executive orders, even though they clearly had active legislative agendas; while Ford and Bush, hardly standouts in any scholar's preferred list of strong presidents, appear to have been noticeably eager to do so. When trying to equate the frequency with which individual presidents issue significant orders and presidential strength, though, caution is warranted. It could be that a large and positive coefficient attached to these indicator variables signals that the president had an aggressive legislative agenda, or simply that he was more willing than most to exercise this power. This is true for any analysis that focuses on a single presidential power. The fact that Ford issued more vetoes per year than any other modern president is not in itself evidence that he was particularly strong (or weak for that matter), but rather indicates only that Ford was more willing, and perhaps had greater cause, to utilize this particular power.

Table 4.5 presents the estimated effects when the three hypotheses are tested simultaneously.[16] Little changes. Both of the congressional strength variables continue to have statistically significant and negative impacts on the number of important executive orders issued each congressional term; changes in presidential administrations continue to register null findings; and presidents exercise their unilateral powers less frequently during periods of divided government. In both models, Wald tests show that the three regime variables are jointly significant at $p < .05$.

When running the model with only the presidential indicators, the pseudo R-squared value drops to just .17, suggesting that the three regime variables account for a sizeable chunk of the variance explained. While idiosyncratic qualities (personal dispositions, leadership styles, or reputations) do affect the number of orders presidents issued each congressional term, so, too, does the larger institutional environment. In this sense, the personal and institutional presidencies *both* appear to play prominent roles in the politics of direct presidential action.

Clearly, there are a host of factors for which the unilateral politics model does not account; factors that nonetheless affect presidents' willingness to exercise their unilateral powers. By including the fixed presidential effects, we have implicitly controlled for the personal qualities of each president. In addition, though, when the country is at war or the economy is performing badly, presidents may respond

TABLE 4.5
Testing the Three Hypotheses Jointly, 1945–1998

	The Number of Significant Executive Orders Issued			
	Model 1A (1)	Model 1B (2)	Model 2A (3)	Model 2B (4)
Hypothesis 1:				
Size of Majority Party	− 0.03**	—	− 0.04**	—
	(0.02)		(0.02)	
LPPC Scores	—	− 0.42**	—	− 0.47*
		(0.25)		(0.29)
Hypothesis 2:				
Administration Change	− 0.01	− 0.01	− 0.05	− 0.04
	(0.12)	(0.12)	(0.10)	(0.11)
Hypothesis 3:				
Divided Government	− 0.25**	− 0.23**	− 0.24***	− 0.22**
	(0.09)	(0.10)	(0.11)	(0.11)
Controls:				
War	—	—	0.01	0.01
			(0.10)	(0.10)
Unemployment Rate	—	—	0.05	0.04
			(0.05)	(0.05)
Constant	5.11***	3.45***	5.00***	3.15***
	(1.17)	(.25)	(1.29)	(0.43)
Pseudo R^2	.25	.25	.25	.25
Log likelihood	− 71.92	− 72.34	− 71.57	− 72.13
(N)	27	27	27	27

The dependent variable is the number of significant orders issued during each congressional term. Poisson regressions estimated. Each model includes president-specific intercepts (not reported here). * signifies coefficient is significant at .10 level, one-tailed test conducted; ** significant at .05 level; *** significant at .01 level. Robust standard errors reported in parentheses.

by issuing more executive orders.[17] In columns 3 and 4 of Table 4.5, accordingly, I control for years when the United States was at war (an indicator variable) and the national, civilian unemployment rate (a continuous variable).[18]

The findings appear robust. *Majority Parties* and *LPPC Scores* continue to have statistically significant and negative impacts on the number of important executive orders presidents issue each congressional term. Changes in presidential administrations still have negligible impacts on outcomes. Presidents continue to issue fewer significant executive orders during periods of *Divided Government*. Finally, while presidents issue more orders during periods of war and high unemployment, neither effect is statistically significant.

The results presented up until now provide strong support for Hypotheses 1 and 3, and very little support for Hypothesis 2. One ought to be concerned, though, if these findings ride on the inclusion of the post-1985 predicted values in our dependent variable. While these predicted values enable us to extend the dependent variable until 1998, they remain somewhat suspect—their validity hinges upon the overlap between mentions in the *New York Times* on the one hand and the *Congressional Record* and court cases on the other. As Table 4.1 makes clear, while this overlap is considerable, it is far from perfect. If the strength of these findings diminishes substantially when we exclude the predicted values, then considerable doubt may be cast upon them.

Table 4.6 presents the regression results from models of two separate time-series: one based upon mentions in the *Congressional Record* and court cases between 1945 and 1985 (79th–98th congresses); the other based upon coverage in the *New York Times* between 1969 and 1998 (91st–105th congresses). As before, we include controls for war and unemployment. Given that we are truncating what is already a very short time-series, it is important to pay as much attention to the consistency of the findings as the significance of any one.

Far from weakening the size or significance of our estimated coefficients, most are strengthened when we exclude the predicted values. In both time-series, *Majority Parties* and *LPPC Scores* continue to have statistically significant and negative impacts on the number of significant orders issued. For the *New York Times* time-series, presidents issue fewer numbers of significant orders during periods of *Divided Government*; though negative, the effect of *Divided Government* in the Congress/court time-series is no longer statistically significant. While changes in presidential administrations continue to register null effects on the Congress/court time-series, they appear to have a positive and significant effect on the number of *New York Times* orders.[19] In addition, according to both models, presidents issued greater numbers of significant executive orders during periods of war. The effects of unemployment rates are rather sporadic, and only once do they appear statistically significant.[20]

When reviewing the existing empirical literature on unilateral powers, I highlighted the importance of differentiating substantively important executive orders from orders that are purely administrative in nature. The results in Table 4.7 indicate why. When reestimating the effect of all of the regime variables, controls, and presidential

TABLE 4.6
The Impact of Regime Variables on Two Independently Constructed
Significant Executive Order Time-Series

	Congress/Court Mentions (1945–1984)		New York Times Mentions (1969–1998)	
	Model 1A (1)	Model 1B (2)	Model 2A (3)	Model 2B (4)
Hypothesis 1:				
Size of Majority Party	− 0.04**	—	− 0.13*	—
	(0.02)		(0.10)	
LPPC Scores	—	− 0.48*	—	− 2.81***
		(0.33)		(1.08)
Hypothesis 2:				
Administration Change	− 0.14	− 0.14	0.52***	0.44***
	(0.13)	(0.15)	(0.13)	(0.07)
Hypothesis 3:				
Divided Government	0.05	0.03	− 0.95**	− 1.14**
	(0.24)	(0.26)	(0.57)	(0.37)
Controls:				
War	0.38**	0.34	0.09	0.24
	(0.29)	(0.29)	(0.25)	(0.19)
Unemployment Rate	0.12	0.10	− 0.08	− 0.17**
	(0.11)	(0.11)	(0.09)	(0.08)
Constant	3.88***	2.07*	12.23**	5.63***
	(1.74)	(1.34)	(6.98)	(1.17)
Pseudo R^2	.32	.31	.24	.28
Log likelihood	− 53.40	− 54.04	− 40.87	− 38.80
(N)	20	20	15	15

The dependent variable in columns 1 and 2 is the number of orders mentioned by
Congress or the judiciary during each congressional term. The dependent variable in
columns 3 and 4 is the number of orders mentioned in the *New York Times*. Poisson
regressions estimated. Each model includes president-specific intercepts (not reported
here). * signifies coefficient is significant at .10 level, one-tailed test conducted; ** significant at .05 level; *** significant at .01 level. Robust standard errors reported in
parentheses.

fixed effects on the total number of executive orders issued from 1945
to 1998, a very different pattern of results emerges. In none of the
models do the coefficients for *Majority Parties, LPPC Scores,* or *Divided
Government* come close to rejecting their respective null hypotheses.
Whereas strong and unified governing coalitions in Congress discour-

TABLE 4.7
The Impact of Regime Variables on Total Number of Executive Orders
Issued, 1945–1998

	Total Number of Executive Orders Issued			
	Model 1A (1)	Model 1B (2)	Model 2A (3)	Model 2B (4)
Hypothesis 1:				
Size of Majority Party	0.01 (0.01)	0.01 (0.01)	—	—
LPPC Scores	—	—	0.08 (0.14)	0.05 (0.12)
Hypothesis 2:				
Administration Change	0.19*** (0.08)	0.09 (0.07)	0.18*** (0.07)	0.07 (0.06)
Admin. Change * First 2 Years	—	0.23*** (0.06)	—	0.23*** (0.05)
Hypothesis 3:				
Divided Government	0.00 (0.11)	0.10 (0.11)	−0.01 (0.11)	0.09 (0.08)
Controls:				
War	0.33*** (0.12)	0.33*** (0.11)	0.33*** (0.12)	0.33*** (0.12)
Unemployment Rate	−0.00 (0.04)	0.00 (0.04)	0.01 (0.04)	0.01 (0.03)
Constant	3.89*** (0.58)	3.84** (0.59)	4.38*** (0.38)	4.31*** (0.33)
Pseudo R^2	.65	.67	.64	.67
Log likelihood	−116.38	−107.57	−117.12	−108.27
(N)	27	27	27	27

The dependent variable is the total number of executive orders issued each congressional term. Poisson regressions estimated. Each model includes president-specific intercepts (not reported here). * signifies coefficient is significant at .10 level, one-tailed test conducted; ** significant at .05 level; *** significant at .01 level. Robust standard errors reported in parentheses.

age presidents from issuing substantively important executive orders, they appear to have no impact on the total number of executive orders presidents issue each congressional term.

Changes in presidential administrations, by contrast, now appears to be highly statistically significant.[21] On average, a change in presidential administrations corresponds with an average increase of between twenty-one and twenty-four executive orders. Many of these orders overturn and amend orders issued by their predecessors, and consequently, presidents are likely to issue them early in their terms. In columns 2 and 4, therefore, I interact *Administration Change* with an indicator variable that is coded one for the first two years of a president's term. Doing so, the main effect quickly shrinks to zero, while the interaction term is quite large and statistically significant.[22] As elections usher in new presidential administrations, spikes in the total number of executive orders are observed during the first two years.

At various intervals, we found positive support for all three hypotheses. When focusing on substantively important executive orders, *Majority Party* and *Divided Government* have consistently significant impacts on outcomes. We find support for the second hypotheses when looking at those executive orders that the *New York Times* covered between 1969 and 1998 (91st–105th congresses), and the total number of executive orders issued between 1945 and 1998 (79th–105th congresses). These models estimate effects for somewhere between eleven and fifteen parameters with just twenty-seven observations, making these findings quite remarkable. Given the consistent performance of different models that use different data sets, the findings probably are not due to "overfitting," a statistical problem that arises when too much is demanded of too little data. Quite the contrary, with such short time-series coefficients generally are biased to zero, making the observed support for the unilateral politics model especially noteworthy.

LEGISLATIVE VERSUS EXECUTIVE ACTION

Presidents have a choice about how to implement their policy agendas. They can either submit legislation to Congress, or they can proceed on their own. Up until now, our empirical tests have examined the frequency with which modern presidents exercised the latter option. But in all of these models, the counterfactual to a policy issued unilaterally was a policy created by legislation, or no policy at all. Unfortunately, nothing in the event-count models allows us to distinguish between these latter two possibilities.

To address this censoring problem, I simultaneously estimate models of policy making by legislation and by executive action. I estimate two seemingly unrelated Poisson regressions where the dependent variable in one equation is the number of significant executive orders; and in the other the annual number of "nontrivial" policies (as determined by their coverage in the *New York Times*, the *Washington Post*, and *Congressional Quarterly*) created by legislation (King 1989).

Nontrivial laws are the sum of the number of "landmark," "important," and "ordinary" laws enacted each Congress. Landmark enactments consist of the Sweep One laws identified in David Mayhew's *Divided We Govern* (1991). By measuring the amount of coverage laws received in the *New York Times*, the *Washington Post*, and the annual *Congressional Quarterly* almanacs, Howell et al. categorized all of the remaining laws as important, ordinary, or trivial (2000). Between 1945 and 1998, 17,906 total laws were enacted, 1.3 percent of which were deemed landmark, 1.7 percent important, 10.0 percent ordinary, and 87.0 percent trivial.[23] The models of legislative productivity presented in this chapter focus on the 13 percent of laws enacted during the modern era that surpass the lowest threshold of policy significance.

To keep things as simple as possible, I estimate effects for only the three regime variables and the fixed presidential effects. The results, which are reported in Table 4.8, highlight one of the most important aspects of the politics of direct presidential action: the very forces that enhance Congress's capacity to legislate restrict the president's discretion to strike out on his own. While *Majority Parties* and *LPPC Scores* have large, positive, and statistically significant impacts on the number of nontrivial laws that Congress enacts each session, they have large and negative effects on the number of significant executive orders that presidents issue. As preferences within Congress diverge, possibilities for legislating diminish, and concomitantly, opportunities and incentives for presidents to exercise their unilateral powers flourish. The estimated coefficients for the measures of congressional strength across equations are statistically significantly different from one another at $p < .01$. Holding all other variables at their means, a two-standard increase in either measure of congressional strength leads, on average, to a decline of approximately six significant executive orders issued each term, and an increase of eight nontrivial laws being enacted.

In his analysis of legislative activity in the post–World War II era, Mayhew found that equal numbers of landmark laws were produced during periods of unified and divided government (1991). The findings in Table 4.8, however, suggest something altogether different. When simultaneously estimating the production of significant executive orders and a broader range of important legislative enactments, *Divided Government* has a uniformly negative impact on public policy making. For each two-year interval that different parties govern the presidency and Congress, fully twenty-four fewer nontrivial laws are enacted and five fewer significant executive orders are issued— amounting to an overall 27 percent decline in congressional and presidential policy making.

TABLE 4.8
The Impact of Regime Variables on Significant Legislation and Executive
Orders, 1945–1998

	Significant Executive Orders		"Non-Trivial" Legislation	
	Model 1 (1)	Model 2 (2)	Model 1 (3)	Model 2 (4)
Hypothesis 1:				
Size of Majority Party	−0.03**	—	0.03***	—
	(0.02)		(0.01)	
LPPC Scores	—	−0.42**	—	0.42***
		(0.25)		(0.11)
Hypotheses 2:				
Administration Change	−0.01	−0.01	−0.24***	−0.23***
	(0.12)	(0.12)	(0.10)	(0.09)
Hypothesis 3:				
Divided Government	−0.25***	−0.23**	−0.28***	−0.28***
	(0.09)	(0.10)	(0.07)	(0.09)
Constant	4.58***	2.97***	3.05***	4.37***
	(0.99)	(0.13)	(0.37)	(0.05)
(N)	27	27	27	27

The dependent variable in columns 1 and 2 is the number of significant executive
orders issued each congressional term. The dependent variable in columns 3 and 4 is
the number of "nontrivial" laws enacted during each congressional term. Seemingly
Unrelated Poisson regressions estimated (columns 1 and 3 and columns 2 and 4 estimated simultaneously). Each model includes president-specific intercepts (not reported
here). * signifies coefficient is significant at .10 level, one-tailed test conducted; ** significant at .05 level; *** significant at .01 level. Robust standard errors reported in
parentheses.

As before, changes in presidential administrations do not appear
to affect the number of significant executive orders issued. Such
changes, however, appear to correlate negatively with the number of
nontrivial enactments. Upon reflection, it is not at all clear why this
should be so. I suspect that this isolated finding reflects the perils of
working with such a short time-series, and not something substantive
about the underlying data generating process.

Discussion

These findings highlight two important lessons about the president's
power of unilateral action. First, the boundaries of unilateral powers

are fundamentally institutional in nature. Both Congress and the courts (which will receive the greater measure of attention they deserve in chapter 6) define what the president can accomplish on his own. Not all presidents will choose to take advantage of all the discretion granted them, but Congress's ability and the courts' willingness to overturn them remain the final arbitrators of what presidents can accomplish should they decide to act unilaterally.

This insight is not limited to the United States. Countries with fractured legislatures and ineffectual court systems, no matter what their government's formal structure, are likely to have strong executives who rely heavily upon their "executive decree authority" (Carey and Shugart 1998). The executives of Russia, Italy, Peru, and Brazil all rely upon their unilateral powers precisely because of their legislatures' inability to act decisively. In England, by contrast, the prime minister cannot act unilaterally except in ways that clearly reflect the interests of the majority party in parliament specifically because of the country's strong party system. To predict the size of the unilateral powers enjoyed by an executive in any country, one need only look at the strength of those political bodies that can overturn him.

This leads to a second lesson. Congress's (or any legislature's) ability to overturn the president is not constant over time. When members' preferences are widely dispersed, it is relatively difficult for legislative coalitions to form, and presidents can seize upon new opportunities to exercise their unilateral powers. By contrast, when members' preferences line up tightly around one another, it is relatively easy to enact legislation, and the president's freedom to act unilaterally declines. With each election Congress is made weaker or stronger depending upon the composition of members within it and the strength of the parties that organize them. In our system of divided powers, with branches of government continually pressing for distinct advantage, a gain for Congress automatically signals a loss for the president, and vice versa.

These two points help to explain what presidents *can* do. But what of the president's incentives to act in the first place? Much of the existing literature on the presidency focuses on the personal qualities of each passing president. Barber's "active, positive" president will exercise these powers whenever possible, while the "passive, negative" president may use them only intermittently (1972). These presidential types, and the qualities they embody, may play some part in an explanation of presidential policy making; the relative strength of the fixed effects examined in this chapter's models testifies to that fact. Even here, however, there is an institutional component that has been largely ignored. Newly elected presidents of the opposite party as their predecessor have a greater incentive to exercise their powers of unilateral action than do second-term presidents and new presidents of the same party as their predecessor, *no matter what personal qualities either brings to the office.* Without knowing anything about their personal biographies, we can safely bet that after twelve years of Republican rule Clinton had more reason to act unilaterally than did either the elder George Bush, who replaced a president who spent two terms shifting policy to reflect their joint interests, or Reagan in his second term.

There is a clear institutional logic that explains both when presidents *will be able* to act unilaterally, and when they *will want* to act unilaterally. These two dynamics need not operate in concert. Indeed, there may be occasions when a president has strong incentives to act unilaterally, but he cannot given the relative strength of Congress (for instance, Clinton after the 1994 election). Similarly, there may be other occasions when the president enjoys considerable discretion to strike out on his own, but he has little incentive to exercise it given the current distribution of status-quo policies (as with Truman after World War II). But when these forces converge, we can expect to witness the low and high points of presidential policy making.

Thus far, we have managed to specify the logic of direct presidential action and show that it matches reasonably well with the broad patterns of presidential policy making. To do this, we have focused intently on the unilateral politics model. In the next couple of chapters, we take a step back and examine in greater detail the respective abilities of Congress and the courts to constrain the president. To do so, we shift focus somewhat. Rather than examining the conditions under which presidents issue significant executive orders, we explore how, and whether, Congress and the courts subsequently respond to the president's actions.

5

Congressional Constraints on Presidential Power

THE unilateral politics model identifies the basic, and sometimes counterintuitive, dynamics of presidential policy making. The model explains why presidents unilaterally set policies that a majority within Congress may oppose. It specifies how changes within Congress (caused generally, though not exclusively, by elections) translate into either an expansion or contraction of executive discretion to act unilaterally. And it clarifies how these powers enable the president not only to set policies that Congress on its own accord would not pass, but also to undermine congressional efforts to enact laws that the president opposes.

We repeatedly return to a basic theme about systems of governance defined by their separated powers: executive power is inversely proportional to legislative strength. Presidential power expands at exactly the same times when, and precisely the same places that, congressional power weakens. The occurrence is hardly coincidental. Indeed, the forces operate in tandem, for it is the check each places on the other that defines the overall division of power.

In absolute terms, though, the unilateral politics model probably overestimates Congress's ability to constrain the president, and consequently underestimates presidential power. This chapter surveys some of the reasons why this is so, focusing on several aspects of the policy-making process that deserve a fuller measure of attention than they have received up until now.

The first concerns informational advantages. The president often knows more about policy matters than do members of Congress, and he uses this fact to his advantage when deciding to act unilaterally. Members of Congress frequently depend upon the president to learn about goings-on in the executive branch: how agencies are performing, moneys are spent, and laws are enforced. Should the president decide to move in a particularly controversial direction, he may release information selectively, or simply not inform Congress at all. Either way, the president etches out a margin of discretion completely ignored by the unilateral politics model.

The second feature of lawmaking that the unilateral politics model overlooks concerns transaction costs. Congress often cannot overturn policies unilaterally set by the president, even when a super-majority may prefer some alternative. Because Congress is a collective decision-making body, transaction costs pervade the legislative process, making it extremely difficult for members to coordinate an effective and timely response to the president. An account of congressional behavior based solely on members' preferences identifies a lower bound of what presidents can accomplish unilaterally. The location of the ceiling remains uncertain.

To assess how informational asymmetries and transaction costs impact Congress's ability to contain presidential power, this chapter also presents new findings on congressional responses to executive orders issued in the modern era. Sometimes Congress responds legislatively, overturning an executive order, turning an existing order into law, or something in between. Other times Congress deliberates on whether to appropriate funding for a presidential program or agency. Both occasions provide opportunities to check presidential power. But as we shall soon see, while the budget affords members of Congress additional control over the president's use of his unilateral powers, legislative attempts to constrain presidential actions that have already occurred are most distinctive for their consistent, albeit not uniform, failures.

The Institutional Makeup of Congress

For years, formal theories of lawmaking and bureaucratic oversight regularly treated Congress as a unitary actor, and doing so, they glossed over the considerable problems facing a collective decision-making body and overestimated the institution's ability to reign over other branches of government.[1] By explicitly incorporating the filibuster and veto-override pivots, the unilateral politics model renders a more realistic depiction of Congress, defining a range of status-quo policies that even a majority of its members are unable to change. Nonetheless, the model expressly omits other important aspects of the institution's design, aspects that critically affect legislators' capacity to constrain the president's unilateral powers.

Who Is in the Know and What Does It Matter?

By virtue of the broad powers delegated to them in the modern era and the additional advantages associated with being an executive (Moe and Howell 1999a, 1999b), presidents, on the whole, have access to more information about public policy and its implementation than any other branch of government. An enormous bureaucracy exists, in large part, to advise the president on policy matters. Nowhere, perhaps, is this more apparent than in the realm of foreign affairs, where a massive network of national security advisors, an entire intelligence community, and diplomats and ambassadors stationed all over the globe report more or less directly to the president.

In most areas of foreign policy, information is collected and assembled first within the executive branch, and then disseminated to other branches of government. Because of this arrangement, presidents can tailor their presentation of facts in ways that strengthen their position. While members of Congress may rightly distrust them, they often can do little to protest, if only because they lack comparable information. Should the president decide that it is in the nation's interest to unilaterally send troops into Grenada, Lebanon, Haiti, or Somalia, he can simply do so, for generally Congress lacks the information required to offer any substantive objection—at least in the early stages of a conflict.

Take the example of national security directives, which are kept confidential, making it virtually impossible for members of Congress to regulate them. Presidents have used national security directives to escalate the war in Vietnam, to initiate support for the Nicaraguan Contras in the 1980s, to direct the war on drugs, to develop a national policy on telecommunications security, to monitor affairs within Iraq prior to Desert Shield/Desert Storm—and these directives, which recently have been declassified, represent but a fraction of the total (Cooper 1997).

At a 1988 congressional hearing on presidential directives, Representative Lee Hamilton (D-IN), chair of the committee overseeing the Iran/Contra investigation, vented his frustration over Congress's inability to monitor the president's use of national security directives:

> I think all of us have had the experience of listening to testimony by executive branch officials who are articulating policy of the Federal Government, and have had those officials refer to an NSDD [National Security Decision Directive] as the basis of that policy. We don't know what that NSDD is and we cannot evaluate the official's comments without reference to it, but it is not available to us.

Not knowing, neither Hamilton nor any of his colleagues could do much about them, leaving the president virtually unopposed in the legislative arena. As Representative Jack Brooks (D-TX), the chair of the hearing, lamented, the inability to check the president "undermines democracy, leaving Congress and the Nation in the dark as to just how our Government is being run. The mobilization of resources and formulation of policy affected through these directives without congressional oversight amounts to nothing more than the imposition of secret law."[2]

The vast number of ways by which presidents can unilaterally set policy—executive orders, executive agreements, national security directives, memos, memoranda, proclamations—makes it extremely difficult for Congress to keep up. And so twice during the 1970s, Congress enacted legislation designed specifically to address these informational problems and thereby curb a perceived expansion of presidential power. The first was the 1972 Case Act that required presidents to report every "international agreement, other than a treaty" to Congress within sixty days. In 1977, and then again in 1979, Congress passed additional legislation that reduced the reporting period to twenty days and expanded the scope of the act to include international agreements brokered by executive agencies and departments.[3]

The intent of the Case Act and its subsequent amendments was clear: to give Congress an opportunity to assess the terms of agreements settled between the executive branch and foreign nations. The Act, however, never lived up to its promise. Because presidents have a tremendous amount of flexibility when deciding how to issue an international agreement, the Case Act hardly limits what presidents can accomplish unilaterally. If the president has good reason to believe that Congress will overturn an executive agreement, he may simply repackage the same agreement in another form, and thereby dodge the Act entirely.[4] Presidents Nixon, Ford and Carter all did so by relabeling as "arrangements" or "accords" a batch of international agreements concerning South Vietnam, Sinai, and nuclear disarmament (Hall 1996, 267). Because it remains quite unclear what differentiates orders from agreements from arrangements from accords, and because presidents can refashion and rename these directives much as they please, presidents can avoid many of the reporting requirements Congress tries to impose.

The second and more celebrated example of congressional resurgence was the 1973 War Powers Resolution. This law requires that "in every possible instance" presidents consult with Congress before introducing military forces into foreign hostilities. Should Congress not authorize the action within ninety days, the president then must withdraw the troops.[5] According to its authors, the resolution promised an end to the president's ability to freely decide when, and for how long, to send troops abroad. By having to obtain congressional authorization, it was supposed, presidents would have to supply members of Congress with information about the scope, potential costs, and objectives of a military engagement. And should members disagree with the president's decision to enter into the conflict, they could then force him to withdraw.

During the 1970s, congressional scholars heralded the War Powers Resolution as the paradigmatic example of their institution's ability to rein in an imperial presidency (Franck and Weisband 1979; Frye 1975; Zeidenstein 1978). No longer would Congress be excluded from the collection and assessment of information relevant to the nation's security and foreign interests, as it had been in Vietnam, Cambodia, and Laos. At last, it seemed, Congress's place in foreign policy making was secure.

Two decades hence, however, conventional wisdom on the matter has shifted dramatically. There is little if any evidence that subsequent presidents have become more attuned to congressional interests than their predecessors when contemplating military action. During the 1980s and 1990s, presidents directed military initiatives in Europe, Africa, Central America, the Caribbean, and the Middle East without congressional authorization ever being secured. Presidents have conducted, and continue to conduct, international wars on drugs and terrorism without tripping over the resolution. Indeed, the War Powers Resolution, if it has accomplished anything at all, probably has expanded the president's freedom to act unilaterally. This resolution deals presidents a three-month grace period during which they can pursue any military objective they like; and once this period expires, Congress is poorly situated to force a withdrawal.

> The War Powers Resolution, by giving a green light to presidential wars during the 60–90 day period, concedes a measure of authority to the president that would have astonished the framers. The authors of the Resolution claimed that they had restricted presidential power; in fact, they widened it. There are good reasons for concluding that the resolution, seriously compromised from the start and weakened over time, should be repealed. (Fisher 1998, 201–2)

Despite the best efforts of Congress, presidents still do not regularly consult with members about military affairs, and their informational advantages remain quite undiminished.

This fact is not lost on presidential scholars. There is general consensus, for example, that presidents are better able to rally public support for foreign policy initiatives than for domestic initiatives precisely because they have more information, relative to Congress, in one sphere than the other (Page and Shapiro 1992). What has been less appreciated, however, is that Congress often does not even know what policy directives the president has issued, and consequently can do little about them. The unilateral politics model aside, in the real world of policy making Congress is often left quite in the dark, forced to play catch up, piecing together bits of information about what policies the president has issued and what effect, if any, they might have on their constituencies.

In the final assessment, then, the unilateral politics model's assumption of complete information appears distant from the everyday realities of presidential policy making, especially within foreign affairs and when considering the full range of unilateral directives available to the president. Congress almost never overturns national security directives, if only because these directives remain strictly confidential; and because the president can package unilateral directives in any number of forms, the job of monitoring every executive act is extremely cumbersome. The two most prominent attempts by Congress to deal with these problems, the Case Act and the War Powers Resolution, are, in retrospect, failures. Rather than restricting what presidents can accomplish unilaterally, in some instances, these laws actually strengthened the president's statutory authority to set policy on his own.

The picture we are left with, then, looks quite a bit different from the unilateral politics model. Rather than overseeing every action taken by the president, and freely deciding whether or not to amend it, Congress regularly is left scrambling for details—as is currently the case, what with Congress desperately trying to keep pace with Bush's antiterrorism campaign. Obviously, presidents cannot conceal all of their unilateral actions all of the time; in the many areas of domestic governance, especially where Congress's role is well established, presidents must be forthcoming about their unilateral activities. But in selected policy arenas, such as those that involve foreign affairs, presidents can choose which unilateral actions to reveal, and then may decide to release only selective information about them.

Assessing Congressional Activism

In the case of executive orders, especially those involving domestic policy, the unilateral politics model's informational assumptions are less problematic. Congress is better informed about the content of executive orders, and, at least in principle, is free to accept, overturn, or amend them. Nonetheless, even here Congress is significantly weaker than supposed heretofore.

The unilateral politics model stipulates that Congress will act on every status-quo policy that lies outside of the gridlock interval, the segment along a policy continuum where no alternative to the status quo enjoys sufficient support to invoke cloture *and* override a presidential veto. Never, the model predicts, can the president set policy outside of this interval without provoking a congressional response. But in the everyday contest of public policy making, the president often does just this, while members of Congress deliberate and posture, but ultimately fail to enact corrective legislation. Three factors explain why.

TRANSACTION COSTS

Transaction costs run rampant in Congress. Members often do not know what the outcomes of a particular policy will be (Gilligan and Krehbiel 1987, 1990). To the extent that public opinion changes over time, legislators' support for any given policy remains provisional; and while a few institutions attenuate the problems associated with enforcing vote-trades between legislators (such as committees), coordination problems and possibilities for miscommunication still interfere with enacting coalitions ever forming in the first place (Weingast and Marshall 1988). To limit these uncertainties and address the difficulties they present, members expend vast resources, in terms of both time and staff allocations, to design policy, build and sustain coalitions, and monitor a proposal's progress through the legislative process. In the end, the number of laws Congress is capable of enacting in any given session is substantially limited.

Such uncertainties generally do not encumber the president. While the relationship between a policy and its outcome may remain unclear, the information the president requires to satisfactorily address this issue is far simpler than the information 535 representatives, from 485 districts, provinces and states, demand. Rather than coordinating and negotiating with literally hundreds of other members, each with their own constituencies, interests, and schedules, the president sits alone atop his governing structure and is free to set policy on his own (Moe 1989; Moe and Wilson 1994). While he may choose to consult with advisors, and he may worry about whether subordinates will comply with his orders, the president does not face a lengthy and burdensome policy-making process comparable to that of Congress. And because of this disparity, the president has an important edge over Congress.

The immediate effect of transaction costs on the unilateral politics model is to expand the length of the gridlock interval, and thereby increase the discretion afforded the president to act unilaterally. Whereas for $p > v$ the model predicts that Congress will shift a status-quo policy located at $v + \epsilon$ to $v - \epsilon$, in reality, given the high transaction costs associated with designing and pushing through any legislative proposal, chances are Congress will leave be the president's action. Building on this logic, the higher the transaction costs, the further the president can set policy outside of the gridlock interval without having to worry about Congress overturning him.

Policy making is not a seamless process. Substantial costs are incurred. These costs, however, are not equally distributed across the branches of government. For Congress, they are frequently prohibitive, making involvement in a whole host of policy matters virtually impossible. For the president, meanwhile, these costs are relatively quite small, and rarely, if ever, do they force him to choose between competing policy initiatives—a decision Congress faces everyday. Because of this asymmetry, the president has an important advantage in the politics of unilateral action.

ALL POLICIES ARE NOT CREATED EQUAL

Members have a short time, two or six years, to prove that they can effectively represent and serve their constituencies. They must allot their time and resources wisely, and focus principally on those matters that maximize their chances of staying in office (Mayhew 1974). Some of the time this involves providing constituent services—holding town hall meetings and responding to the requests of individual voters. Other times, though, members must engage the policy-making process itself, and whenever possible, direct its benefits home—something not easily done, for reasons that are quite familiar by now.

But given limited resources, members of Congress can draft and rally support for just a few major legislative proposals in any given session. When deciding whether or not to confront the president on a particular issue, members of Congress must always weigh the attendant electoral costs and benefits. The results of this calculation have clear implications for presidential power.

Richard Hall's distinction between "revealed preferences" and "revealed intensities" is instructive (1996). While members may have formulated preferences about a whole range of policy issues, they can focus their attention on just a few. While the unilateral politics model certainly accounts for the distribution of these preferences, like all models of policy making it patently omits the intensities with which members hold them. Rather than reduce congressional members' utility functions to a simple quadratic equation, equally summed over all policies, a finer representation of political reality would weight each policy based upon its saliency to a member's district. While a representative coming out of rural Kansas might care a great deal about agriculture subsidies and federal loan programs to farmers, she is probably less concerned with other policies having to do with international trade or military appropriations, even when she, along with many others, ostensibly prefers some alternative to the status quo.

On the whole, members take on those issues that most affect their reelection prospects, and pay considerably less attention to the rest. This fact has direct consequences for presidential power. Presidents must be especially careful when changing policies that directly affect members' constituencies. But on those issues that attract little interest within Congress, the president is afforded a residuum of discretion above and beyond that predicted by the unilateral politics model.

Again, it is useful to distinguish between foreign and domestic policy. Given that the costs of monitoring foreign affairs are great and the electoral rewards are (usually) small, members have strong incentives to delegate broad powers to the president in foreign policy (Canes-Wrone, Howell, and Lewis 1999). This then frees up members to focus on, and claim credit for, those policies that matter most to their constituents. More often than not these policies are domestic in nature, for the average citizen surely pays closer attention to the quality of life in her own neighborhood than she does international tariff rates or disaster relief efforts conducted abroad.

While presidents are highly sensitive to the composition of Congress when they write domestic policy, they often unilaterally set foreign policy without worrying too much about retaining the support of key committee members or a chamber majority. For while members may object to presidential directives in foreign affairs, they are unlikely to do much about them given the high transaction costs and low electoral benefits: a press conference, hearing, or speech on the floor of the House condemning the unilateral action often is all that the president need fear.

There are many other ways to estimate the likelihood that Congress will act upon different categories of public policies. James Q. Wilson's distinction between interest group, majoritarian, entrepreneurial, and client politics provides another alternative (1989). According to this typology, when deciding whether to change a public policy members estimate the distribution of costs and benefits it places on the public. When costs and benefits are either widely distributed or highly concentrated (majoritarian and interest group politics, respectively), Wilson argues that intervention is uncertain—much depends upon the sway of public opinion and the composition of Congress. But in two situations, the probabilities of congressional intervention are quite clear. When the costs of regulatory activity are highly concentrated and the benefits are widely distributed (entrepreneurial politics), congressional intervention is unlikely, as members have much to lose from antagonizing organized interests and little to gain from placating the general public. On the other hand, when costs are disbursed but benefits are concentrated (client politics), intervention is quite likely, as members can respond to key interest groups without having to pay any immediate electoral costs. Given that presidential activism is the complement of congressional activism, presidents ought to enjoy the most freedom in client politics, and the least in entrepreneurial politics.

We can taxonomize public policies in any number of ways. But which scheme one finds most compelling is less important than a more basic realization about the relationship between congressional activism and presidential power. Because lawmaking is costly, members of Congress carefully and conscientiously decide which policies to change, and which to leave alone. The unilateral politics model identifies the full range of policies upon which Congress can act. But as soon as we think critically about Congress as an institution and what motivates its members, it becomes quite clear that what Congress in a costless world *will* do, and what, in a world of transaction costs, it *can* do, are very different. Given that it is the latter and not the former that defines the boundaries of unilateral power, the president, at least in some policy spheres, appears even more powerful than we had previously supposed.

PROTECTING INSTITUTIONAL INTERESTS

Members of Congress, surely, are cognizant of the handicaps they face when squaring off against a president who can set public policy without its consent. Interestingly, though, these same members also possess the ability to strip the chief executive of these powers and the advantages they grant. Unlike the president's power to veto legislation or appoint bureaucrats and judges, powers that are clearly enumerated in the Constitution, the ability to act unilaterally is subject at least partially to the tacit approval of Congress. Should Congress choose to do away with the president's capacity for direct action or restrict it in any fundamental sense, unilateral powers may be substantially reduced.

As the Case Act and War Powers Resolution make clear, Congress has tried to address the informational advantages enjoyed by the president. Congress, however, has never successfully stripped the president of his express power to issue executive orders, or any other unilateral directive for that matter.[6] Upon reflection, this appears strange. Why would members of Congress agree to a policy-making process whereby its institution is burdened with collective action problems and high transaction costs, while the president can act unilaterally without either, *given that legislators themselves possess the power to construct a more level playing field*?

The short answer is that members' incentives to act and their ability to effectively do so are not usually in alignment. Any deliberate attempt to limit the president's power is sure to confront, at a minimum, a presidential veto, and more often than not members lack the votes to override. But the one occasion in recent history when the majority party had veto-proof margins in both chambers (the 89th Congress), Congress and the president were both Democratic and neither had much reason to undermine the other's power. When different parties govern the legislative and executive branches, the fight over presidential power should be most intense; but without exception, during these periods the majority party in Congress has lacked the votes to override a presidential veto, greatly reducing its ability to circumscribe the president's unilateral powers.

Outside of what Congress can do, there is also good reason to believe that Congress will not expend the resources required to abolish the president's power to act unilaterally, no matter his party identification or policy stances. The reason, once again, traces back to institutional motivations. Presidents serve national constituencies and have only two terms (at most) to establish their place in history. As a consequence, presidents have strong incentives to continually expand their influence and to constantly protect their base of power. Congressional representatives, meanwhile, face reelection every two or six years, serve localized interests, and hence pay comparatively less attention to the power of their institution as a whole. The job of attending to constituent interests rarely overlaps with that of protecting Congress's institutional integrity. While members may regularly lament the abuses of an imperial presidency, only occasionally will they try to shore up their own institution and stem the steady shift of power to the executive branch.

Terry Moe has written extensively on this subject, and is worth quoting at length:

> On issues affecting the institutional balance of power, presidents care intensely about securing changes that promote their institutional power, while legislators typically do not. They are unlikely to oppose incremental increases in the relative power of presidents unless the issue in question directly harms the special interests of their constituents—which, if presidents play their cards right, can often be avoided. On the other hand, legislators are generally unwilling to do what is necessary to develop Con-

only when about their Constituents

gress's own capacity for strong institutional action. Not only does it often require that they put constituency concerns aside for the common good, which they have strong incentives not to do, but it also tends to call for more centralized control by party leaders and less member autonomy, which they find distinctly unattractive. (1999, 448)

When are members of Congress likely to object to an expansion of presidential power? Whenever the president does something that clearly affects their constituents. What are these members likely to do about it? Fight like hell on this particular issue, while, at various intervals along the legislative path, abandoning efforts to address the larger imbalance of power.

If members of Congress took active steps to prevent executive encroachments into the legislative arena, their institution might profit. David Mayhew highlights the importance of "institutional maintainers" whose job it is to "work toward keeping the institution [of Congress] in good repair" (1974, 146). Unfortunately, though, nowhere in Mayhew's own argument can a convincing rationale be found for why a member should serve this function.[7] While rewards by the party leadership might provide some ostensible benefits (what Mayhew calls the "internal currency of Congress"), it remains extremely doubtful that enough members—given their underlying incentives— will serve their institution, to the neglect of their constituents, in order to mount a forceful and sustained fight against the president over the proper balance of power. What is more likely, and what historically has taken place, is that the institutional power of Congress steadily wanes, while that of the president, with each unilateral action taken, expands further and further.

How Congress Has Responded to Unilateral Actions

In equilibrium, the unilateral politics model predicts that the presidents anticipate how Congress will respond to every directive they issue. If the model as specified perfectly characterizes unilateral politics, Congress should never overturn the president, not because Congress does not constrain presidential power, but because the president is fully informed about what he can and cannot get away with and behaves accordingly.[8]

The real world, obviously, is much more complicated than the unilateral politics model supposes. Uncertainties abound, and presidents frequently set policies without any assurance of congressional acquiescence. It is worth considering, then, how presidents fare on those occasions when Congress does respond to a presidential directive. Do presidents tend to win most of the time? Or does Congress consistently crack the legislative whip, effectively enervating imperialistic presidents?

Our theoretical expectations are relatively clear. Because the president has access to more (and better) information about goings-on in the executive branch, members of Congress will try to change only a small fraction of all status-quo policies in any legislative session, and we should anticipate that members will leave alone the majority of unilateral directives that the president issues. While the president may occasionally overreach on a particularly salient issue, provoking a congressional response, in most instances Congress either will do nothing at all or will endorse the president's actions.

To test this supposition, I inventoried congressional responses to executive orders issued by modern presidents. I did not consider speeches made on the House or Senate floor condemning or praising particular orders, or hearings held on the president's power to issue executive orders generally. To make it into the database, a bill that sought to amend, extend, overturn, or codify in law a particular executive order must have been introduced to a committee and assigned a bill number. Congress, however, need not have enacted the bill into law. Indeed, the very reason for collecting these data is to evaluate Congress's ability to use its statutory powers to circumscribe the president's freedom to act unilaterally. If Congress represents a potent force, then we should find at least a handful of laws that overturn the president, standing as a continuing reminder of the limits of presidential power.

Unfortunately, there is no single source that offers a comprehensive listing of bills that address executive orders issued by the president. Rather than identifying the universe of such bills, then, we can only hope to assemble a subsample. Via three surveys of different primary sources, I examined congressional activity between 1945 and 1998. Appendix 3 explains the data-collection procedures in fuller detail.

Table 5.1 tracks the legislative histories of those bills that Congress explicitly designed to either overturn or substantially amend a particular executive order. Each column notes whether a bill made it to a particular phase in the legislative process. Bills that were enacted into law, therefore, typically have check marks in every column. Several features of the data stand out. First, Congress rarely tries to change an executive order. During the post–World War II era, I identified a total of forty-six bills that Congress introduced to overturn or amend a standing executive order. Limiting the analysis to the post-1972 years, when the data are most complete, less than 3 percent of the executive orders issued by presidents received any measure of critical attention

TABLE 5.1
Bills Introduced to Amend or Overturn Executive Orders*

Bill #	House Comm	Senate Comm	House Floor	Senate Floor	Pass House	Pass Senate	Sent to Pres.	Public Law
1 H.R. 4318 (1998)	✓							
2 H.R. 4422 (1998)	✓							
3 H.R. 4861 (1998)	✓							
4 H.R. 2807 (1998)	✓	✓	✓	✓	✓	✓	✓	105-312
5 H.R. 3465 (1998)	✓	✓						
6 S. 891 (1997)		✓						
7 H.R. 1378 (1997)	✓	✓						
8 H.R. 596 (1997)	✓							
9 H.R. 94 (1997)	✓							
10 S. 1295 (1995)	✓	✓						
11 S. 989 (1995)	✓	✓	✓	✓				
12 H.R. 1159 (1995)	✓							
13 S. 603 (1995)	✓	✓						
14 H.R. 1176 (1995)	✓	✓	✓					
15 H.R. 1868 (1995)	✓	✓	✓	✓	✓	✓	✓	104-107
16 H.R. 2127 (1995)	✓	✓	✓	✓	✓			
17 H.R. 2058 (1989)	✓							
18 H.R. 1633 (1989)	✓							
19 H.J.Res 738 (1986)[1]	✓							
20 H.R. 4590 (1984)	✓							
21 H.R. 1204 (1983)[2]	✓							
22 S. 1080 (1981)	✓	✓		✓				
23 S. 2319 (1980)		✓				✓		
24 H.R. 2068 (1980)	✓							

Bill		Public Law
25 H.R. 6272 (1980)	✓	
26 H.R. 4499 (1979)	✓	
27 H.R. 4389 (1979)	✓	
28 S.Up.A. 205 (1979)	✓	
29 S. 996 (1979)	✓	
30 H.R. 2625 (1979)	✓	
31 S. 519 (1979)	✓	
32 S. 3290 (1978)	✓	
33 S.Up.A. 1368 (1978)	✓	
34 S.Up.A. 1202 (1978)	✓	
35 H.R. 9804 (1977)	✓	
36 H.R. 8231 (1975)[3]	✓	
37 H.R. 1531 (1975)	✓	
38 H.R. 1331 (1975)[4]	✓	
39 H.C.R. 166 (1973)	✓	
40 H.R. 15067 (1973)	✓	93-549
41 H.R. 1419 (1972)	✓	
42 S. 2466 (1971)	✓	
43 S. 2770 (1971)[5]	✓	92-500
44 H.R. 15067 (1962)	✓	
45 S. 1459 (1947)	✓	

* An earlier version of this table was presented in Moe and Howell 1999.

[1] The Appropriations Committee attempted to raise grazing fees (which were established via E.O. 12548). The bill eventually passed (99–591), but not before the committee's proposal was dropped.

[2] This bill would have eliminated the president's power to issue executive orders generally.

[3] This bill would have required the president to submit all executive orders to Congress for review.

[4] This bill would have required the president to submit copies of every executive order no later than two days after issuance.

[5] Nixon issued E.O. 11574, which directed the Army Corps of Engineers and the EPA to work together to devise a water pollution permit program. S. 2770 ordered the EPA to develop strict guidelines for the discharge of water pollutants. Nixon vetoed the bill, but was overridden by Congress.

by Congress. Because Congress chose not to do anything about the rest, by default they retained the force of law.

The second prominent feature of the data is the consistency with which these bills died en route to enactment. Congress enacted only four, all of which involved relatively unimportant matters. Public law 105-32 overturned executive orders issued in 1934 and 1941 that had assigned jurisdiction of the "Killcohook Coordination Area" (roughly 1,500 acres of land in New Jersey and Delaware) to the Fish and Wildlife Service of the two states; public law 104-107 repealed an executive order issued by Clinton that permitted funding of international agencies that either sponsored or administered abortions; 93-549 fixed federal employees' salaries in response to a Nixon order that indexed government salaries to "industry standards"; and, finally, 92-500 ordered the Environmental Protection Agency (EPA) to develop strict guidelines for the discharge of water pollutants, nullifying an order that previously directed the Army Corps of Engineers and the EPA to work together to devise a water pollution permit program. During a time when presidents were unilaterally defining affirmative action policies, redesigning much of the bureaucracy, negotiating trade agreements with foreign countries, and implementing all sorts of new social policies, Congress chose these four issues to do something about, and left the rest be. In context, this hardly seems a major affront to presidential power.[9]

The remaining forty-one bills all died somewhere along the legislative track. Two managed to get through a chamber, one (H.R. 15067 [1962]) was even sent to the president, but died when the president vetoed it. Fully 74 percent of bills introduced to amend or overturn an executive order never even made it out of committee. If these bills served any purpose whatsoever, they simply provided members of Congress with an official mechanism by which to express their disapproval of a president's actions.

Among those bills that died, several (H.R. 1204 [1983]; H.R. 8231 [1975]; H.R. 1331 [1975]) meant to limit the president's ability to issue executive orders generally. Some tried to do this by requiring that presidents submit all executive orders to Congress for review, others by designing strict reporting guidelines, others by altogether doing away with the president's power to issue orders. None of these bills, however, ever so much as made it out of committee.

Congressional resolutions provide another alternative means by which Congress may respond to the president, and one that members often turn to given the inherent difficulties of enacting legislation. Because the president does not sign resolutions, they do not have the legal standing of legislation. Nonetheless, resolutions do provide

TABLE 5.2

House and Senate Resolutions Recommending That the President Issue or Revoke an Executive Order*

Bill #	House Comm	Senate Comm	House Floor	Senate Floor	Pass House	Pass Senate	Sent to Pres.	Resolution
1 H.C.R. 236 (1998)	✓							
2 H.R. 1378 (1997)	✓							
3 H.R. 596 (1997)	✓							
4 S. 1295 (1995)		✓						
5 S. 989 (1995)		✓						
6 S.Res. 264 (1994)[1]		✓		✓		✓		Res.
7 H.Res. 16 (1993)	✓							
8 S.Res. 324 (1992)[2]		✓		✓		✓		Res.
9 H.C.R. 39 (1991)	✓							
10 S.Res. 318 (1990)		✓		✓		✓		Res.
11 S.Res. 516 (1982)		✓						
12 H.Res. 1060 (1978)	✓							
13 H.C.R. 658 (1978)	✓							
14 S.Res. 40 (1977)[3]		✓						
15 S.Res. 219 (1975)		✓						
16 H.Res. 1179 (1974)		✓						
17 S.Res. 213 (1973)		✓						
18 H.Res. 1067 (1972)	✓							
19 H.Res. 772 (1972)	✓							
20 S.Res. 299 (1972)		✓		✓		✓		Res.
21 S.Res. 98 (1945)[4]		✓		✓		✓		Res.

* An earlier version of this table was presented in Moe and Howell 1999.

[1] This resolution, passed by the House and Senate, encouraged the President to issue an executive order that would expand federal assistance to Indian institutions of higher learning.

[2] This resolution calls on the president to issue an executive order requiring that all executive departments and agencies declassify materials relating to POWs and MIAs.

[3] This bill opposed any general presidential pardon of Vietnam draft dodgers by executive order.

[4] This resolution commissioned a study of the constitutionality of executive orders.

Congress with easy opportunities to present facts, principles, opinions, and requests on various policy matters.[10] All of the resolutions listed in Table 5.2 either expressed condemnation for an executive order that a president had already issued or requested that the president issue a unilateral directive on some specific policy matter.[11] The actual impact of congressional resolutions on presidential power, though, is probably marginal at best.

Congress rarely uses the legislative process to overturn the president, and when Congress does, it almost always fails. But when deciding how to respond to the president, Congress can do more than offer up a set of amendments. Congress often introduces legislation in support of an executive order, either by appropriating funds for a unilaterally created agency or commission, extending the timeline of its mandate, or simply codifying the order in law. Not surprisingly, when doing so Congress appears significantly more active and successful.

Table 5.3 traces the legislative histories of bills introduced to Congress that in one way or another supported a particular order issued by the president. The three surveys identified fifty-eight such bills. Considering the legislative histories of these bills, Congress appears nothing short of eager to back up the president when he exercises his unilateral powers. Often times Congress simply turns an executive order into a law. H.R. 1420 (1997), for example, literally copied the text of a Clinton order on wildlife refuges and made it law; H.R. 5431 (1990) attempted to write into law key portions of an order the elder George Bush issued to block Iraqi access to its financial assets in the United States. In other instances, Congress takes positives steps to strengthen an order issued by the president. S. 1 (1993), for example, declared that no official within the executive branch could prohibit research of fetal tissue, and thereby expanded the breadth of an order issued by Clinton earlier the same month; H.J.Res. 1298 (1968) granted new subpoena powers to the Commission on the Causes and Prevention of Violence established by Johnson earlier that year. Other times, Congress simply appropriates funds to commissions and agencies set up by the president, such as the Equal Employment Opportunity Commission, which was initially funded by H.R. 17522 (1965), or the Peace Corps by H.R. 7500 (1961).

When it decides to support an executive order, Congress has a significantly higher chance of succeeding than when it tries to amend or overturn an executive order. Sixty-three percent of the bills cited in Table 5.3 eventually became law, almost as many as the total number of bills in Table 5.1. Whereas the vast majority of the bills that were designed to amend or overturn an executive order died in committee, only 28 percent (sixteen in total) do here.

These data are more illustrative than conclusive. Much of the haggling over the content of executive orders that occurs between Congress and the president is never recorded in a discrete set of bills that members introduce. Presidents often back away from orders that are particularly controversial so as not to jeopardize the support they need for other aspects of their legislative agenda.[12] Clinton's grandstanding and subsequent backtracking on gays in the military in 1992 is an obvious example. Within the first couple of weeks of his administration, Clinton gave Congress an ultimatum: either lift the ban on gays in the military statutorily by July 1, or face an executive order that does the same. In response, Sam Nunn (D-GA) and Robert Dole (R-KS) threatened to kill the Family and Medical Leave Act, which

TABLE 5.3
Bills Introduced to Extend or Codify Executive Orders*

Bill #	House Comm	Senate Comm	House Floor	Senate Floor	Pass House	Pass Senate	Sent to Pres.	Public Law
1 S. 2455 (1998)		✓						
2 H.R. 1420 (1997)	✓		✓	✓	✓	✓	✓	105-57
3 H.R. 411 (1997)	✓							
4 H.A. 249 (1995)	✓							
5 S. 1 (1995)	✓	✓	✓	✓	✓	✓	✓	104-4
6 H.R. 2333 (1994)[1]	✓	✓	✓	✓	✓	✓	✓	103-236
7 H.R. 2873 (1993)	✓		✓					
8 H.R. 1395 (1993)	✓							
9 H.R. 667 (1993)[2]	✓							
10 H.R. 901 (1993)	✓							
11 S. 255 (1993)		✓						
12 S. 1 (1993)	✓	✓	✓	✓	✓	✓	✓	103-43
13 S. 1216 (1992)	✓	✓	✓	✓	✓	✓	✓	102-404
14 S. 50 (1991)								
15 H.R. 5431 (1990)	✓		✓		✓			
16 H.R. 4739 (1990)	✓	✓	✓	✓	✓	✓	✓	101-510
17 S. 358 (1990)	✓	✓	✓	✓	✓	✓	✓	101-649
18 H.C.R. 126 (1989)	✓							
19 H.R. 2235 (1989)	✓							
20 H.R. 1769 (1989)	✓							
21 H.R. 4903 (1988)	✓							
22 H.R. 1827 (1987)	✓	✓	✓	✓	✓	✓	✓	100-71
23 H.A. 568 (1984)	✓		✓					
24 H.C.R. 419 (1982)	✓							
25 S. 643 (1980)	✓	✓	✓	✓	✓	✓	✓	96-212
26 S. 1545 (1979)		✓						
27 S. 210 (1979)	✓	✓	✓	✓	✓	✓	✓	96-88
28 H.R. 61 (1979)	✓							
29 H.R. 8638 (1978)	✓	✓	✓	✓	✓	✓	✓	95-242
30 S. 3853 (1977)		✓						
31 H.R. 1746 (1977)	✓	✓	✓	✓	✓	✓	✓	95-12
32 H.C.R. 762 (1976)	✓							
33 S. 1439 (1976)	✓	✓		✓				
34 H.R. 12169 (1976)	✓	✓	✓	✓	✓	✓	✓	94-385
35 H.R. 15067 (1974)	✓	✓	✓	✓	✓	✓	✓	93-549
36 H.R. 11793 (1973)	✓	✓	✓	✓	✓	✓	✓	93-275
37 S. 1435 (1973)	✓	✓	✓	✓	✓	✓	✓	93-198
38 H.R. 11139 (1973)	✓							
39 H.R. 10751 (1972)	✓	✓	✓	✓	✓	✓	✓	92-578
40 H.R. 4383 (1972)	✓	✓	✓	✓	✓	✓	✓	92-463
41 H.R. 14989 (1972)	✓	✓	✓	✓	✓	✓	✓	92-544
42 S. 3117 (1972)		✓						
43 H.R. 9272 (1971)	✓	✓	✓	✓	✓	✓	✓	92-77
44 S.J.Res. 55 (1971)	✓	✓	✓	✓	✓	✓	✓	92-8
45 H.R. 10947 (1971)	✓	✓	✓	✓	✓	✓	✓	92-178
46 S. 2891 (1971)	✓	✓	✓	✓	✓	✓	✓	92-210
47 H.R. 4148 (1970)	✓	✓	✓	✓	✓	✓	✓	91-224

TABLE 5.3
(*continued*)

Bill #	House Comm	Senate Comm	House Floor	Senate Floor	Pass House	Pass Senate	Sent to Pres.	Public Law
48 S. 1075 (1969)	✓	✓	✓	✓	✓	✓	✓	91-90
49 H.J.Res. 1298 (1968)	✓	✓	✓	✓	✓	✓	✓	90-338
50 H.R. 17522 (1968)	✓	✓	✓	✓	✓	✓	✓	90-470
51 H.R. 9207 (1967)	✓							
52 H.J.Res. 976 (1964)	✓	✓	✓	✓	✓	✓	✓	88-296
53 S. 2772 (1964)	✓	✓	✓	✓	✓	✓	✓	88-311
54 H.R. 4801 (1964)	✓	✓	✓	✓	✓	✓	✓	88-265
55 H.R. 7500 (1961)	✓	✓	✓	✓	✓	✓		87-293
56 H.R. 8603 (1961)	✓	✓	✓		✓			
57 S. 279 (1961)	✓	✓	✓	✓	✓	✓	✓	87-274
58 H.R. 12200 (1960)	✓	✓	✓	✓	✓	✓	✓	86-633
59 H.R. 5752 (1959)	✓	✓	✓	✓	✓	✓	✓	86-362

* An earlier version of this table was presented in Moe and Howell 1999.

[1] Clinton objected to various aspects of this law (principally those which strengthened conditions on the importation of foreign goods) and signed it only reluctantly. The law, however, did codify aspects of E.O. 12850.

[2] This bill would have required that all executive orders regarding gays in the military that were in effect as of January 1993 remain in effect unless changed by law. The bill was introduced in response to an executive order Clinton threatened to pass that would have permitted gays in the military. As such, this bill does not represent congressional support for the current president's policy.

was a hallmark of Clinton's 1992 presidential campaign. If he hoped to enact the Family and Medical Leave Act, Clinton needed to win the support of a super-majority within Congress. In the end Clinton chose not to unilaterally overturn the ban on gays in the military so as to conserve the support he needed for his preferred Family and Medical Leave Act. Later that same year Congress passed the Act and, not coincidentally, included within it the compromise "don't ask, don't tell" policy on gays in the military.

Exchanges of support across issues may occur from time to time, but they are not easily captured by the simple bill counts presented in Tables 5.1–5.3. Nonetheless, these data illustrate that when the president and Congress go head to head over a single unilateral directive, the president almost always wins. Indeed, far from posing as a potential threat to unilateral power, Congress often appears to be a great promoter.

When Congressional Appropriations Are Involved

Up until now, our formulation of unilateral action has been straightforward enough. The president issues a directive, and absent a congressional or judicial response, the directive assumes law-like status. Rather than count on Congress legislating, the president acts in the hope that Congress will do nothing at all. Nonaction on the part of legislators often is functionally equivalent to support, for an executive order retains the weight of law until and unless someone else over-turns it. Should the president establish new environmental regula-tions, revamp the reporting procedures of federal agencies, raise or lower import and export tariffs, require that industries receiving fed-eral contracts comply with certain government hiring and firing prac-tices, he does not depend upon Congress for legislative endorsement. As James Lindsay and Wayne Steger note, "If Congress ignores the president's proposal to cut the capital gains tax, the proposal dies, but if Congress fails to act on the president's decision to terminate a treaty with Taiwan, or to sign an executive agreement with Israel, or to dispatch troops to Saudi Arabia, the president's proposal prevails" (1993, 105).

Things are slightly different, however, when the president uni-laterally establishes a new federal commission, agency, or program, for here he needs funding. Oftentimes, presidents can stir up discre-tionary moneys to fund a controversial program or commission for a year or two (more on this later). Over the long haul, however, impor-tant social programs and government agencies require some form of congressional appropriation. Without it, eventually they will die. And here members have a unique opportunity to influence the kinds of unilateral actions presidents can take. Members can attach any num-ber of stipulations on how the president spends the appropriated moneys, limiting what the program, agency, or commission does, whom it serves, what it reports, and how effectively it operates.

This suggests an important distinction. The president's powers of unilateral action are greatest when they do not require Congress to take any subsequent action, something not easily done given the vast transaction costs and collective action problems that plague the insti-tution. But where funding is involved, and nonaction on the part of Congress spells the demise of an agency or program, the president's powers of unilateral action diminish significantly.

Consider, by way of example, Reagan's efforts to promote a "drug-free federal workplace" during his second term as president. As part of the nationwide war on drugs, in September of 1986 Reagan issued Executive Order 12564. The order required every federal agency to begin mandatory, random drug testing of its employees, and if em-ployees tested positive, agencies had to either fire them or refer them for counseling.

Reagan's order drew swift criticism from the National Treasury

Employees Union and the American Civil Liberties Union, who jointly brought suit in the federal district court claiming that the order violated the Fourteenth Amendment's protections against "unreasonable searches and seizures."[13] In November 1986, a New Orleans federal district judge ruled that random drug testing was indeed unconstitutional. Later that month, the Attorney General appealed the ruling to the Supreme Court.

In the meantime, the president turned his attention to Congress and introduced the "Drug Free America Act of 1986." The administration's proposal allocated funding for numerous drug and alcohol abuse prevention programs, treatment and rehabilitation programs for federal employees, stricter penalties for drug violations, and measures to combat international drug trafficking. The "most controversial part of the administration's proposal," however, involved funding for the mandatory drug testing of federal employees (Havemann 1986). In addition to concerns about employees' privacy and civil liberties, members of Congress expressed serious reservations about the financial cost of constructing a full-scale drug-testing program. Most members believed that if they approved funding for mandatory drug tests, Congress "would be lucky not to bump its head on the deficit ceiling imposed by the Balanced Budget Act [of 1985]" (Morrison 1986).

Given this controversy and the fact that the courts had temporarily ruled the executive order unconstitutional, Senators Robert Dole (R-KS) and Robert Byrd (D-WV) dropped the funding required to implement the order's drug-testing program. The bill then passed both chambers with overwhelming support. On October 27, 1986, Reagan signed it into law.

It wasn't until the next year that Congress returned to Reagan's order. Given overwhelming public support for the order, as part of the Supplemental Appropriations Act of 1987 (H.R. 1827) Congress finally appropriated the funding needed to begin drug testing. The act, however, added strict guidelines on how the order would be implemented. It required the executive branch to provide Congress with regular cost estimates, develop a uniform program for testing workers in different agencies, and certify that safety, quality control, and employee-rights guidelines be followed. In addition, Congress temporarily exempted the Transportation and Energy departments from testing; testing of these departments did not begin until the fall of 1987.

Two years later, the Supreme Court upheld the government-mandated drug tests in *Skinner v. Railway Executives' Association*[14] and *National Treasury Employees v. Von Raab*.[15] In both cases the Court found that the government had a "compelling interest" in promoting the health and safety of its citizens, and that randomized drug testing effectively served this objective.

In the end, then, the president had his way. Reagan secured the funding he needed to implement his order, and then he won in the courts. As we shall soon see, this case is quite typical. Executive orders that require congressional appropriations usually are funded and when challenged in the courts, the president usually wins. But another lesson is also apparent. When funding programs that are set up by executive order, Congress need not issue a blank check, appropriating whatever sum of money the president requested. Restrictions and amendments are commonplace, and they can come in any number of forms: line-item appropriations, earmarking of funds, or strict reporting requirements. In this instance, Congress dictated who could be randomly tested, what penalties employees might receive and when they could receive them. Precisely because Congress set the terms by which funds would be appropriated, Reagan needed more than just his unilateral powers to establish an effective drug-testing program. Having to bargain with Congress, Reagan then had to summon all the resources Richard Neustadt (1991, [1960]) highlights as the foundation of presidential power: his reputation, public support, and powers of persuasion.

Scholars have long recognized the ways in which Congress carefully crafts budgets to amplify its control over the president (Fenno 1966; Kirst 1969). Going back to W. F. Willoughby, an assistant director of the Bureau of the Census and a key member of the 1910 Taft Commission on government reorganization, political observers have insisted that specifying appropriations to "the greatest practical detail . . . is the only practicable way that [Congress] has discovered by which it can exercise its function, which all must agree is its, of supervising and controlling the manner in which the executive performs its duties" (Willoughby 1913, 80). Willoughby and other members of the Taft Commission, especially Chairman Frederick Cleveland, argued vehemently over the proper scope of Congress's influence. No one doubted, however, the facts of the matter: as long as Congress retained the power to decide which agencies would receive funding and the terms under which agencies could spend it, Congress held a key strategic advantage over the president (Arnold 1998).

But let us not overstate the case. The federal government looks very different today than it did in 1912, when the Taft Commission issued its final report. The government's size alone has increased dramatically, and with it the length and complexity of the federal budget. It no longer is practical for Congress to specify how every dollar in every budgetary account is spent. Among the thousands of programs and agencies that are funded by the federal government, Congress can carefully monitor the spending habits of only a relative handful (Fisher 1975). As a function of total expenditures, therefore, the number of appropriation items in the budget has steadily declined over the past six decades, lending modern presidents and agency heads considerable freedom to enforce orders and design programs that Congress on its own might not support (Arnold 1998; Fisher 2000; Howell and Lewis 2002; Lewis 2002).

The president, as a result, is not completely hamstrung when his unilateral actions require congressional appropriations. Presidents may request moneys for popular initiatives and then, once secured, siphon off considerable portions to controversial programs and agencies that they have unilaterally created. Presidents can reprogram funds within certain budgetary accounts or, when Congress assents, they may even transfer funds between accounts. Either way, "the opportunity for mischief is substantial" (Fisher 1975, 88).

Within the Pentagon and intelligence communities, for example, executive officials enjoy a considerable amount of freedom to transfer funds between accounts. Many of the military projects Congress funds are highly classified, making it extremely difficult for members to keep track of how administrators actually spend their appropriations. Consider a 1999 House Appropriations Committee report that detailed recent examples of military expenditures on programs that Congress had previously cut. According to the report, the Air Force illegally started and financed a highly classified project known as the "black program" in 1998; that same year it purchased an $800 million military communications satellite without congressional authorization; it diverted funds from an unspecified program to update the C-5 transport plane; and it maintained the "Star Wars" missile defense program that Congress had previously cancelled (Weiner 1999). Nor is this the first time the Pentagon has received such criticism. In 1986, the General Accounting Office issued a similar report on the Pentagon's consistent flouting of congressional stipulations attached to military appropriations.[16] Despite its best efforts, Congress's attempts to stipulate military appropriations do not always dissuade Pentagon officials from continuing to fund favored projects.

In addition to transferring funds between accounts, presidents can also dig up the funding they need in contingency accounts (Morrow 1968). These contingency accounts typically set aside moneys for unforeseen disasters. But because there are no hard and fast criteria for when these funds can be spent, presidents often use them not to direct emergency relief programs, but instead to support projects, foreign and domestic, that Congress itself opposes. Kennedy, for example, funded the Peace Corps for the first year of its operation using contingency funds; just as Johnson kept the President's Commission on Civil Disorders in business during its first year, despite considerable criticism from Republicans within Congress.

Electorally, it usually does not make sense for members of Congress to cut these accounts altogether. All it takes is one major disaster—an American serviceman killed or an embassy bombed—for members to lose their seats. Rather than punishing those who abuse contingency accounts, members usually publicly criticize presidents for individual transgressions, all the while keeping the coffers full.

Though these contingency funds generally enable a president to fund a program or agency for only a short interim, often this is sufficient to generate the momentum needed over the long haul. When the president finally does seek legislative appropriations for such projects, Congress frequently has little choice but to continue their funding. Again, in no place is this truer than in foreign affairs. As long as the president can gather the funds needed to launch a military engagement abroad, he usually can rest assured that Congress will not strike it down prematurely. The District of Columbia Court of Appeals made exactly this observation in a 1973 decision on the War Powers Resolution:

> In voting to appropriate money or to draft men a Congressman is not necessarily approving of the continuation of a war no matter how specifically the appropriation or draft act refers to that war. A Congressman wholly opposed to the war's commencement and continuation might vote for the military appropriations and for the draft measures because he was unwilling to abandon without support men already fighting.[17]

If every military engagement required a congressional appropriation from the start, many would never get off the ground. Operations in Bosnia, Haiti, and Somalia are just recent examples. But because the president can strike first, directing funds for the initial deployment, Congress often has little choice but to follow, dispensing huge sums of money for actions it may have originally opposed.

While the point is clearest with regard to military operations overseas, it applies to all sorts of bureaucratic agencies and programs, as well. If the president can assemble the funds needed to jump-start a controversial project, he quickly puts Congress on the defensive. Rather than debating whether or not to create an agency from scratch, Congress now is placed in the uncomfortable position of having to either continue funding projects it may oppose, or eliminate personnel who have already been hired and facilities that have already been purchased. In this context, recall Kennedy's use of contingency accounts to fund the Peace Corps in its first year. As we have already noted, Republicans in Congress were not exactly thrilled with the idea of expending millions on a "juvenile experiment" whose principal purpose was to "help volunteers escape the draft" (Whitnah 1983). But when Congress finally got around to considering whether or not to finance an already operational Peace Corps in 1962, the political landscape had changed dramatically—the program had 362 Washington employees and 600 volunteers at work in eight countries. Not surprisingly, Congress stepped up and appropriated the funds Kennedy requested.

A Survey of Agencies Created in the Post–World War II Era

Though presidents generally rely upon Congress to create the largest and most important federal agencies, they often get away with unilaterally establishing lower-tier agencies that Congress on its own would not support. Even where appropriations are involved, presidents manage to carve out an important measure of discretion over the design of the federal bureaucracy.

Here I draw upon an impressive dataset assembled by David Lewis on federal agencies created between 1946 and 1996 (Lewis 2003; Howell and Lewis 2002). Lewis tracks 427 agencies, 178 of which were created by legislation, 29 through government reorganization plans, 43 via executive orders, and another 177 via secretarial orders.[18] These agencies served a wide range of functions, from monitoring foreign affairs to establishing social policy to regulating the domestic economy.

As one might expect, agencies created by the president alone (or by those acting on his behalf) are usually smaller, and slightly less important, than agencies that Congress and the president build together. As Table 5.4 shows, roughly 48 percent of agencies established unilaterally have their own line in the budget, as compared to 70 percent of agencies created legislatively. While *Congress and the Nation* included 27.6 percent of federal agencies created by legislation in its index, suggesting some baseline of significance, it only cited 20.9 percent of agencies created by executive order, and 6.9 percent created by departmental order.[19]

Agencies created by administrative action are generally smaller than agencies created through legislation. In 1992 dollars, the average budget for an executive-created agency at its inception is $2 billion—the high is $99.5 billion for the Office of Revenue Sharing. The average budget for a legislatively created agency is $4.13 billion, or about

TABLE 5.4
Agency Creation, 1946–1997

	Agencies Created by . . .			
	Legislation (1)	Executive Order (2)	Department Order (3)	Reorganiza-tion Plan (4)
Number of agencies created:	182	43	177	30
Indicators of agency importance:				
Percent with line in budget:	70.6%	41.9%	48.6%	86.7%
Of those with line, mean budget request:	$4.13 billion	$174 million	$2.50 billion	$2.14 billion
Percent mentioned in Congress & Nation	59.7%	41.9%	22.0%	63.3%
Average number of years agencies lasted:	17.3	8.3	11.6	—
Percent politically contro-versial:	27.6%	20.9%	6.9%	26.7%
Function of agency:				
Foreign Affairs	20.3%	37.2%	20.3%	20.2%
Social Policy	17.0	7.0	16.4	20.2
Regulation of Economy	4.4	18.6	10.7	0.0
Other	61.0	37.2	53.7	59.6
Total	100.0%	100.0%	100.0%	100.0%
Proximity of agency to president:				
Located in E.O.P.	9.9%	48.8%	0.0%	16.7%
In Cabinet	46.2	18.6	84.2	30.0
Independent Agencies	13.2	25.6	13.0	43.3
Independent Commissions	18.7	7.0	2.8	10.0
Government Corporations	12.1	0.0	0.0	0.0
Total	100.0%	100.0%	100.0%	100.0%
Restrictions on agency appointments:				
Fixed term appointments:	30.9%	0.0%	0.0%	10.0%
Agency headed by board or commission:	44.2%	41.9%	5.2%	20.0%

TABLE 5.4
(*continued*)

	Agencies Created by . . .			
	Legislation (1)	Executive Order (2)	Department Order (3)	Reorganization Plan (4)
Limitations placed on qualifications of potential applicants to agencies:	40.9%	25.6%	2.3%	13.3%
Party balancing requirements:	11.5%	0.0%	0.0%	6.7%

Source: Lewis 2003.

Data on agency duration do not account for the censoring problem associated with agencies that continued to operate after 1997. Ninety-four agencies created by legislation are censored, as were six agencies created by executive order and sixty-three by secretarial order. The values presented here, therefore, do not represent the absolute number of years these agencies survived. They do, however, provide a limited basis for comparison.

twice that of executively created agencies. In addition to the greater resources devoted to them, agencies created by legislation also tended to have significantly longer life spans than those created by executive or departmental order. The average duration of legislative agencies is 17.3 years; for agencies created by executive orders, just 8.3 years; and for agencies established by departmental order, 11.6 years.

The fact that unilaterally created agencies are less important, however, does not mean that they are unimportant. The dataset from which these cases are drawn excludes advisory agencies, educational and research institutions (e.g., West Point or the National Eye Institute), and multilateral international agencies. There are literally hundreds of unilaterally established commissions and agencies that are omitted from these data. The unilaterally created agencies that are included, therefore, should not be dismissed as trivial. These agencies employ thousands of people, operate sizeable budgets, and are important enough to be in the *United States Government Manual*.

Using their unilateral powers, presidents have created some of the most important agencies of the modern era. Among those agencies created by executive order, the National Security Agency, the Occupational Safety and Health Administration (OSHA), and the Bureau of Tobacco, Alcohol, and Firearms are obvious standouts.

Frequently, rather than issuing a unilateral directive himself, a president will allow his appointees (usually secretaries) to create agencies on his behalf. While less directly attributable to presidential action, these agencies nonetheless are created within the purview and control of the White House and are designed by executive actors who usually share the president's concern for centralization, hierarchy, and political control. Since 1946, departmental orders are responsible for creating fully 41 percent of all new agencies listed in the *United States Government Manual*. Highlights include the Welfare Administration, the National Marine Fisheries Service, and the Defense Intelligence Agency.

Until 1983, when Congress struck down the legislative veto, Congress frequently gave presidents and their subordinates reorganization authority (Fisher 1998).[20] Typically, presidents submitted reorganization proposals to Congress, and unless Congress took positive steps to alter or negate the plans, they automatically assumed the weight of law after a specified period of time; the length of time necessary to expire before a plan became effectual varied from policy to policy. While certainly a weaker form of unilateral action—rather than having to enact new legislation to overturn a reorganization plan, Congress needed only to pass a one-house veto, a two-house veto, or a joint resolution—reorganization plans nonetheless granted presidents important discretion over the design of administrative agencies. These plans created the Department of Health, Education, and Welfare, the Drug Enforcement Agency, and the Federal Emergency Management Agency.

As might be expected given the importance of some of these agencies, presidents use their unilateral powers to design agencies in such a way that maximizes their influence over them. Not surprisingly, these agencies are much less likely to be insulated from presidential control. It is no accident that fully 67 percent of agencies created by executive order and 84 percent of agencies created by departmental order are placed either within the Executive Office of the President or the cabinet, as compared to only 57 percent of agencies created legislatively.

Presidents are also less likely to create agencies that are governed by independent boards or commissions. Rather, agencies created through executive action almost always report directly to the president. Independent boards or commissions, which dilute presidential control, govern only 13 percent of all agencies created unilaterally, as compared to 44 percent of agencies created through legislation.[21]

By creating agencies unilaterally, presidents also increase their control over the kinds of appointments they can make. Forty percent of agencies created through legislation have some form of qualifying restrictions for political appointees, as compared to only 8 percent of

executively created agencies. In addition, presidents have never imposed party-balancing limitations on a commission they have created
on their own.

Presidents also enjoy significantly more discretion to fire appointees
to unilaterally created agencies than agencies established through legislation. Not a single federal agency created by executive order or
department order during the 1946–1997 period has fixed terms for
political appointees. Political appointees serving for fixed terms govern only three agencies created through reorganization plans, including the Federal Maritime Commission and Federal Labor Relations
Authority. By contrast, over one-third of all agencies designed through
legislation have fixed-term appointments.

To show that presidents enjoy greater influence over agencies created unilaterally than those created legislatively, however, does not
establish that Congress's influence is reduced to nothing. In the final
analysis, one might argue, Congress holds the purse strings and
therefore has absolute say over any agency that the president might
want to unilaterally create. But things are not quite so simple. First, as
the previous section illustrated, Congress's control over the budget
process is imperfect at best—presidents often transfer moneys between accounts, and find cover under the larger budget process, in
order to fund particularly controversial agencies. And second, given
the massive growth of the bureaucracy in the modern era, it does not
make practical sense for Congress to insist that every agency have its
own line in the budget. If it reexamined every line, and challenged
the president on every spending item, Congress could not possibly
complete the budget every year. Consequently, many agencies, even
those opposed by a majority in Congress, are funded year in and year
out through the momentum and cover provided by larger budget battles (Kaufman 1976). At the point where the president must explicitly
ask Congress for appropriations, Congress rarely refuses the request.

Presidential powers of unilateral action do not yield much influence when applied to the handful of agencies Congress cares most
about. But beyond, presidents can basically do what they want, secure in the knowledge that Congress will pay little attention and that
funding for their projects can be found (if necessary) by juggling
around other budgetary accounts.

Congress Strikes Back: The Russell Amendment

The history of agency-creation in the post–World War II era illustrates
an important point: presidents can unilaterally establish and secure

funding for new agencies and programs that members of Congress oppose. Presidents have found novel ways of financing these projects, and often once initiated, Congress has little choice but to continue to support them. But this is not to detract from the underlying point. Executive powers of unilateral action *are* seriously constrained when presidents require congressional appropriations, for should presidents continually disregard the appropriations process, Congress can retaliate.

The history of the Fair Employment Practices Commission (FEPC) and its subsequent incarnations in the 1940s and 1950s highlight the ways in which Congress uses appropriations, and not legislation, to check the president. As America was preparing to enter World War II, demand for African Americans' labor, especially within the defense industries, was rising. The National Association for the Advancement of Colored People and the Urban League, recognizing the political advantages this demand imparted, threatened to organize a march on Washington if Congress or the president failed to enact civil rights legislation. They scheduled the mass demonstration for July 1, 1941, and expected 100,000 people to attend.

Civil rights initiatives did not figure prominently on either the president's or Congress's legislative agenda. Nonetheless, both wanted to avoid the distraction of a major civil rights protest while they negotiated a war oversees.[22] It was clear that Congress would not (and most likely could not) act in time (Morgan 1970). Five days before the scheduled demonstration, therefore, Roosevelt established the FEPC with Executive Order 8802. Aware of congressional opposition to any civil rights initiatives, Roosevelt then bypassed the formal appropriations process and used discretionary moneys to fund the agency (Nathan 1969, 88).

Its mandate required the FEPC to ensure that defense industries administered training and vocational programs "without discrimination because of race, creed, color, or national origin." Executive Order 8802, however, did not establish standards of discrimination and failed to allocate direct enforcement powers. While the FEPC was to "receive and investigate complaints of discrimination in violation of the provision of this order," Roosevelt did not give it any formal powers to prosecute. Consequently, the order's importance largely derived from its symbolic value.

The following year Congress considered several bills that attempted to deal with these deficiencies. Representative Vito Marcantonio (D-NY) introduced legislation (H.R. 7412) to make the FEPC a statutory agency, with the added power to issue cease and desist orders. These orders were subject to judicial review and would thereby lend critical enforcement powers to the FEPC. Marcantonio's bill, however, never even made it out of committee.

Frustrated, civil rights leaders in 1943 once again threatened to demonstrate. And once again, the president took the initiative required to avoid a confrontation. Roosevelt issued Executive Order 9346 in May 1943.[23] In several important respects, this order built upon the foundation laid by Executive Order 8802. Executive Order 9346 placed the FEPC within the Office for Emergency Management (the precursor for the Federal Emergency Management Agency, or FEMA) and thereby made the agency directly beholden to the president; the order required that all government contracts (not just defense contracts) include a nondiscrimination clause; and the order increased the number of FEPC committee members and their salaries. Subsequently, between 1943 and 1946, over 14,000 complaints were filed with the FEPC, and over 5,000 were successfully resolved (Weiss 1997, 38).

Senator Richard B. Russell (D-GA), a member of the Senate Committee on Appropriations, vehemently objected to the president's unilateral dealings with civil rights groups. Aware that Congress could not pass legislation either supporting or overturning the president's actions, Russell instead focused on the president's failure to ever request an appropriation from Congress for the FEPC (Nathan 1969, 87–88). In order to combat what he perceived to be a usurpation of congressional power by the executive, in 1944 Russell introduced an amendment to the 1940 Independent Offices Appropriation Act. The Russell Amendment required congressional approval of all funds for agencies established by executive order and operational for more than one year. Congress passed the amendment (as a rider to H.R. 4070, Public Law 79-358) in late June of 1944 and the president signed it the next month.

It is unclear why Roosevelt did not veto the appropriation. The Russell Amendment represented a clear challenge to presidential power, and Congress most likely could not have gathered the votes needed to override a presidential veto. Because Roosevelt reversed his usual practice of funding the FEPC using discretionary funds (he requested a congressional appropriation for the FEPC in early 1944, before the Russell Amendment had even passed), it is plausible that Roosevelt willingly conceded this issue given the larger challenges facing the nation abroad (Ruchames 1953, 87–99). Again, civil rights did not figure largely in Roosevelt's legislative agenda.

Though FEPC bills continued to circulate in Congress, the Russell Amendment proved to be a major setback for civil rights.[24] Congressional members on the House Committee on Un-American Activities complained about the "Communist influence" within the FEPC. Southern Democrats staunchly opposed civil rights legislation in any form. Subject to the formal appropriations process, the FEPC now had little chance of survival. While Executive Order 9664 extended the life of the FEPC for one last year, the War Appropriation's Act of 1946, passed in December of 1945, allocated $250,000 to "liquidate the committee's affairs" (*Congressional Quarterly Almanac 1945*, 453).[25]

The Russell Amendment temporarily incapacitated the president, and so civil rights groups redirected their lobbying efforts toward Congress (Moreno 1996, 428–30). Once again, efforts to enact a permanent FEPC law constituted "a story of frustration and defeat" (Ruchames 1953, 199). Between 1946 and 1948, members introduced fifteen FEPC bills to the House Education and Labor Committee alone. All died in committee (Morgan 1970, 34). In 1948, Irving Ives proposed a bill (S. 984, which bore the signatures of eight additional prominent senators) to a subcommittee of the Labor and Public Welfare Committee. The committee reported the bill in February 1948, but Republican leaders, "pessimistic about its chances and afraid that any attempt to bring the bill to the floor would result in a Southern filibuster, never called it up" (Morgan 1970, 34). Finally, in 1949, an FEPC bill (H.R. 4453; S. 1728) made it out of House and Senate committees. When southern Democrats threatened a filibuster, the authors of the bill submitted a compromised version, which actually passed in the House. The Senate, however, never took action.[26]

Eventually, after several years of congressional floundering, presidents found ways to reenter the fray. Taking advantage of a clause in the 1946 Independent Offices Appropriation Act which allowed interdepartmental committees "engaged in authorized activities of common interest" to be financed by executive departments, presidents found the justification they needed to bypass the Russell Amendment and once again unilaterally establish and fund civil rights commissions.[27] Truman, Eisenhower, Kennedy, and then Johnson all relied upon this act to justify the continued funding of civil rights commissions. Still, because of the Russell Amendment and the restrictions it placed on agencies created by executive order, all of these presidents had to pay closer attention to Congress when acting unilaterally than had Roosevelt in 1941.

The Russell Amendment focused on the appropriations process for a simple reason: whenever Congress challenged (or supported) the president legislatively, its efforts flopped. By requiring that agencies created by executive order either receive a congressional appropriation or close up shop, however, Congress could meaningfully influence the kinds of civil rights agencies subsequent presidents unilaterally established.

While powerful, though, the appropriations process does not stop presidents dead in their tracks. By relying upon other kinds of unilateral directives, establishing lower-level agencies for short periods of time and then simply reassigning their duties before the one-year deadline expires, and by shuffling around various budgetary accounts, presidents have discovered ways to work around the Russell Amendment and use their unilateral powers to create agencies that Congress may well oppose. Presidential powers of unilateral action do diminish substantially when appropriations are involved—but they do not disappear entirely.

Discussion

When we stand back and think broadly about its institutional capacities, Congress hardly appears the force it did in the unilateral politics model. Multiple veto-points scattered all along the legislative route inhibit its ability to overturn the president; transaction costs further reduce the chances that members will design legislative amendments to presidential directives, and then build and sustain the coalitions needed to enact them; and because they lack reliable information about the full range of unilateral directives presidents issue, members often cannot respond to the president quickly and effectively. The notion that a watchful Congress will rise up and snub any president who dares challenge it could hardly be further from the truth. For reasons built into the design of their respective institutions, the president can set all kinds of public policies on his own, confident that Congress will not subsequently overturn him.

This assessment, however, changes somewhat where congressional appropriations are involved. When their actions require funding, presidents must pay special attention to Congress, for here they must rally the support of its members. By attaching stipulations on how moneys can be spent, members of Congress can strip presidents of much of the influence that unilateral powers usually afford. While presidents may eventually get their agency or program, by the time it has made it through the appropriations process, chances are it looks quite a bit different from what they originally envisioned.

But we should not overstate the case. Even when presidents do require appropriations, they frequently can borrow funding from other budgetary accounts to jump-start their initiatives. And when presidents finally submit their projects to the formal appropriations process, Congress frequently has little choice but to offer support. Rather than deciding whether to create an agency de novo, here members must make the difficult decision of either firing existing personnel and facing the interests that have grown up around them, or simply tolerating the existing program. Congressional opposition, then, does not automatically signal the demise of a controversial program or agency. Presidents, by acting first, can often manipulate the set of choices members of Congress face and thereby win support for programs that under different circumstances would never pass.

One last point deserves particular emphasis. While the range of possible agencies and programs that presidents can unilaterally establish may be relatively limited, presidents can build these agencies in ways that maximize their influence over them. It is no accident that unilaterally created agencies generally are placed in closer proximity to the president, and have far fewer restrictions on the kinds of appointments the president can make to them, than agencies established via legislation. Presidents design them this way in order to augment their control over them. What presidents lose over the scope or power of a particular agency, they often gain back in the control they can exert over it.

When squaring off against Congress, presidents seem to do quite well. While they must remain attentive to the interests of its members, and careful not to provoke their constituents, presidents still can claim a measure of influence over public policy that the unilateral politics model largely ignores. But the constraints Congress places upon the president are only half of our institutional story. The courts remain a viable threat to the president, and one that is not afflicted by the sorts of collective action problems and transaction costs that weaken Congress. The next chapter turns to the federal judiciary and estimates its capacity to limit presidential power.

6

The Institutional Foundations
of Judicial Deference

WHEN the president takes independent executive action, what are the chances that the courts will overturn him? When deciding whether to issue an executive order, executive agreement, proclamation, or memorandum, need the president fear judicial interference? These questions go to the heart of our system of separated powers, for each president's influence over public policy is critically affected by the checks that the judiciary places upon him.

According to most legal scholars, everything depends upon the relevant facts of the case, prior court rulings, and whether Congress or the Constitution delegated the requisite authority for executive action. Should a congressional statute expressly forbid the president's action, or should the action overextend the legal authority delegated by Congress, judges faithfully and predictably strike down the president. Judges, by this account, act as impartial referees in a separation-of-powers game, setting well-defined bounds on executive authority and ensuring that presidents remain within them (Mikva and Lane 1997; Shane and Bruff 1988). This account is remarkably consistent with the unilateral politics model's depiction of the courts as procedural bodies that measure the discretionary authority granted the president against the actions that he takes.

Two literatures within political science, meanwhile, offer a very different view of judicial decision making. The "attitudinal" and "strategic" models both suggest that judges (and especially Supreme Court justices) decide cases based upon their own policy preferences; they differ only over whether their decisions reflect judges' sincere preferences or strategic calculations.[1] Judges, according to this view, support the president when they approve of his policy choices, and they overturn him when they disapprove. By this view, the canons of law (e.g., statutory interpretation, the "plain meaning" doctrine) are simply a ruse to justify judicial policy making. This second account of judicial decision making complies with the version of the unilateral politics model that represents judicial preferences along the same policy dimension as those of Congress and the president.

While both legal precedent and policy preferences may generally inform judges' rulings, there is an institutional component to judicial decision making that is particularly relevant in cases involving presidential power, but that cannot easily be incorporated into spatial models of lawmaking. To understand how judges confront challenges to presidential actions, and the constraints they place on presidential power, we need a richer institutional theory of executive-judicial relations. This chapter presents just such a theory. Rather than isolating individual enumerated powers that help presidents to influence court rulings—for example, the right to appoint like-minded judges—this chapter presents and tests a theory of executive-judicial relations that focuses explicitly upon the design of our system of separated powers. It begins by recognizing that the judiciary can render judgments but cannot implement them alone. For enforcement, judges look to the executive branch.

In most cases, the fact that judicial power depends upon executive backing is immaterial. Judges can count on the president, and those within his administration, to faithfully execute their decisions. When asked to curb presidential powers, however, judges confront a serious quandary, for here they face the very individual charged with implementing rulings that they cannot enforce themselves. As Edward Corwin noted more than forty years ago, "presidential exercises of power will generally have produced some change in the external world beyond ordinary judicial competence to efface" (1957, 16). In cases involving presidential power, an appreciation for their institution's limitations may influence judges' rulings just as much as legal doctrine or policy preferences.

Judicial Constraints on Executive Power

The theoretical argument laid out here can be situated at the intersection of three scholarly literatures: "legal pragmatism" that examines when judges withdraw from conflicts in order to protect the integrity and perceived legitimacy of their institution (Bickel 1962; Scharpf 1966; Strum 1974); the "new institutionalism" that highlights the various institutional constraints (both exogenous and endogenous) that shape judges' rulings (Clayton and Gillman 1999); and assessments of the institutional capacity of the courts to resolve different kinds of civil and political disputes and act as agents of social change (Cavanaugh and Sarat 1979; Rosenberg 1991).

We begin by noting a peculiar aspect of the design of our system of separated powers. Judges can render decisions, but alone they cannot ensure that their decisions are heeded. As Alexander Hamilton recognized in *Federalist No. 78*, the courts "have neither FORCE nor WILL but merely judgment; and must ultimately depend upon the aid of the executive arm even for the efficacy of its judgments" (1999 [1788], 433). In an important sense, for judges to exercise power, they require the cooperation of the president and those within his administration.

The second foundation of this institutional argument concerns the basis of judicial power. Without any formal and independent means of enforcement, the weight of judicial opinion derives from the institution's public standing. The pomp and circumstance of court proceedings, the formal titles bestowed upon judges and justices, the continual homage paid to canons of law (precedent, rules of procedure, the notion of equality before the law), the "abiding sense of judicial integrity that comes with the robe" all mean to generate the same effect: to reinforce the impression that judges transcend the everyday thicket of politics, that they stand to defend the central principles upon which the Republic was founded, that they remain the most "detached, dispassionate, and trustworthy custodians that our system affords," and for these reasons alone, their opinions must be heeded (Abraham 1996, 82; the latter quote is Justice Robert H. Jackson's epitaph). It is no accident that judges, more than anyone else in government, fastidiously promote the dignity and honor of their institution. They do so because their reputation is all they have.

The third axiom of this argument relates the first two: the reputation of the judiciary is imperiled when its rulings go unheeded. The institution's reputation and prestige derive from, as much as they contribute to, the willingness of other political actors to heed court rulings.

> The Court, of course, has no police officials of its own, and its independence is therefore of a limited kind. This might not be too significant in an individual case, but the Court's publication of worthless decisions has a cumulative effect. If one decree is ignored the Court loses some of its immense prestige, and each unenforced decision increases the possibility that the next will also go unheeded. Proportionately to the ineffectiveness of its rulings, the operational validity of the Court disappears, and it can eventually cease to exist as a body performing a valuable function. (Strum 1974, 3–4)

Court rulings retain authority by virtue of their legal enforceability. When enforcement is wanting, however, in a fundamental sense the ruling is compromised. And with the compromise of the ruling comes the compromise of the institution that delivered it.

In most cases, judges can rely upon the backing of the executive branch and render decisions according to legal dicta, their own personal policy preferences, or any other criteria. But in those select cases when opposition is mobilized against the judiciary, and executive enforcement is uncertain, judges may temporarily relinquish their power to rule.[2] Indeed, "it is an axiom of constitutional justice that any decision which the Court thinks will not be enforced will probably not be made" (Strum 1974, 3–4).

Surely, judges rarely admit as much. To the contrary, Supreme Court justices insist, "though we may not compel the President to comply, it is not within the contemplation of the law that he would fail to comply."[3] This claim is perfectly understandable. The Court's mandate is to uphold the Constitution. This mandate, further, is not formally subject to compromise. To openly recognize the issue of enforcement is to "destroy its image as a neutral, objective, eternal body" (Strum 1974, 143). Judges dismiss the relevance of politics not because they render decisions in a hermetic environment, but because they have a stake in maintaining their reputation as the sole branch of government that rises above the latest partisan trends. The "cult of the robe," and the perceptions of authority it fosters, requires that judges insist, against all facts to the contrary, that they remain independent and impartial interpreters of the Constitution (Brigham 1987).

In cases involving presidential power, however, judges have a problem. When the potential source of resistance is the president himself (rather than an interest group, firm, or even some other branch of government at the state or federal level) the courts are most vulnerable. For here, the very person whose actions are under dispute has ultimate authority over the enforcement of the court's ruling.

Need judges always fear that the president will summarily dismiss every ruling against him? Certainly not. When ignoring the courts is likely to evoke a strong political backlash from Congress, interest groups, or the public, presidents may have little choice but to comply. Just as having its decisions go unheeded may damage the judiciary's legitimacy, so, too, may defying a court ruling exact considerable political costs from the president. When these latter costs are high enough, executive compliance is likely and judges can feel free to rule against the president. On the other hand, when the costs of disregarding the courts are low, the issue of enforcement asserts itself most forcefully. Rather than risk issuing a decision that the president may ignore entirely, or implement only selectively, we can expect judges to usually uphold the president, even when legal principles and policy preferences demand otherwise.

A Plausible Argument?

For the most part, judicial scholars have cast only passing attention to the issue of executive enforcement. While scholars generally concede that legal considerations and judges' personal policy preferences influence court rulings, few have considered the prospect that judges retreat from certain rulings for fear that presidents will ignore their orders. This section briefly sketches two occasions when presidents did exactly such. The first involves conflicts between federal courts and state governments over school desegregation in the mid–twentieth century; the second concerns the standoff between Chief Justice Roger Brooke Taney and President Abraham Lincoln in the latter nineteenth. The details of these episodes take us far afield from the central purpose of this chapter, that being to specify the conditions under which courts overturn executive orders. Still, the events underscore a critical and heretofore underappreciated aspect of the politics of unilateral action: when judges rule, and especially when they rule on presidential policies, executive enforcement is not always forthcoming.

School Desegregation

Judicial power depends upon executive enforcement. Without it, court rulings become catalogues of beliefs about what is and is not constitutional. This fact was made abundantly clear in the political fallout of *Brown v. Board of Education*, the original focal point of prudentialist theories of jurisprudence.[4] In the years following the 1954 decision, southern politicians publicly pledged their allegiance with segregationists, and little headway was made in addressing the problems identified by the Court. After years of skirting the issue, the U.S. Court of Appeals for the Eighth Circuit finally demanded in 1957 that the school board of Little Rock, Arkansas, take active and immediate steps to integrate its schools; the Supreme Court later upheld the appellate court ruling.[5]

Arkansas Governor Orval Faubus opposed any efforts to integrate Arkansas' public schools. And he certainly was not willing to let a federal court decide how local schools in his state would educate their children. To demonstrate his opposition, Faubus deployed the Arkansas National Guard to ensure that no black students entered the all-white Central High School in Little Rock, the top-performing high school in the state and the first slated to be integrated under *Brown II*. The governor, backed by military power, quite openly derided the Court's ruling.

The federal judiciary confronted a mounting crisis. Without any standing army of their own, federal judges could not possibly overcome armed resistance to their rulings. The law enforcement agencies capable of forcing the hand of Governor Faubus rested within the executive branch of the federal government.

Unfortunately for the courts, during the summer of 1957 President Eisenhower refused to commit the federal troops required to enforce the Court's ruling. At a press conference on July 17, Eisenhower went so far as to claim, "I can't imagine any set of circumstances that would ever induce me to send federal troops . . . into any area in order to enforce the orders of a federal court" (Perret 1999, 550). For four months, not a single black student was permitted to enroll at Central High. The new school year approached and tensions in Little Rock mounted. On September 4, the first day of classes, the Arkansas National Guard blocked nine black children who attempted to enroll, and a mob formed around the school.

In mid-September Eisenhower finally intervened, resurrecting, quite consciously, the integrity of the courts. "Mob rule cannot be allowed to override the decisions of our courts," he declared. He issued a proclamation ordering the mob to disperse, and an executive order that directed the 101st Airborne Division to maintain the peace and ensure the safety of any black students who wished to enter Central High. The appellate and Supreme Court rulings were finally given the executive backing they required. Governor Faubus succumbed, and integration efforts were able to proceed. Without Eisenhower's military support, however, it is quite clear that the Court's rulings would have gone unheeded.

After Little Rock, modest efforts to desegregate school districts proceeded throughout the South, but resistance to federal court rulings remained widespread and deeply entrenched. While basically no southern black students attended majority-white public schools in 1954, a decade later only 2.3 percent did so, and by 1967 only 14 percent did so.[6] Frustrated with the slow pace of change, in the late 1960s the Supreme Court once again issued a series of rulings meant to rally the cooperation of the federal executive branch, as well as state and local governments.

In *Alexander v. Holmes County Board of Education* (1969), the Court articulated its strongest rebuke of southern strategies to undermine desegregation efforts.[7] On July 3, 1969, the United States Court of Appeals for the Fifth Circuit ordered the submission of new plans to accelerate desegregation of the thirty-three school districts in Mississippi. The vast majority of these districts had employed "open school choice schemes" that continued to funnel white and black students and faculty into different schools. That summer, nonetheless, the Department of Justice and the Secretary of Health, Education and Welfare, under Nixon's orders, recommended that the date for submitting desegregation plans be delayed. The court of appeals obliged. On August 28, on motion from the Department of Justice, that court suspended the July order and postponed the date for submission of new plans to December 1, 1969.

On October 29, however, the Supreme Court intervened. The justices unanimously remanded the case back to the circuit court of appeals, ordering that the Mississippi districts (and every other "dual school system based upon race or color") end desegregation "at once." The Court's ruling outwardly repudiated efforts at delay. As the majority opinion noted, "With regard to a case involving plans for desegregation of public schools, a United States Court of Appeals should deny all motions for additional time, where the fundamental rights of thousands of schoolchildren who are presently attending state schools under segregated conditions are involved." The Court ruling replaced the Warren Court's insistence that local school districts desegregate "with all deliberate speed," which, according to Justice Hugo Black, "has turned out to be only a soft euphemism for delay." The issue of enforcement, and its timing, again was put front and center.

Publicly, the Nixon administration expressed its intention to faithfully abide by the Court's ruling. Press Secretary Ron Ziegler announced that, "the administration will carry out the mandate of the Court." Privately, however, Nixon ruminated to the contrary. As Richard Reeves notes in his biography of Nixon, "When Haldeman told him of the [Court] decision, Nixon smiled and said, 'Now let's see how they enforce it'" (2001, 142).

At first, Nixon appeared compliant. In a January 1970 meeting with his speechwriters, Nixon noted that, "somewhere down the road I may have to carry out this law. I can't throw down the gauntlet to the Court" (Reeves 2001, 158). That year, the administration brought forty-three lawsuits against recalcitrant school districts, and joined in on another dozen cases brought by private parties. The Justice Department brought statewide school desegregation suits against both Texas and Mississippi. And in August, the Internal Revenue Service revoked the tax exemption status of eleven all-white private schools in Mississippi (Wilhoit 1973, 275–76).

The Nixon administration's willingness to actively enforce the Court's desegregation orders, however, quickly dissipated. In 1968 and 1969, the Department of Health, Education, and Welfare (HEW) had conducted respectively twenty-eight and sixteen reviews of school districts to make sure they were complying with court orders. In 1970, the number dropped to fifteen and steadily declined to zero by 1974. Further, when an HEW review recommended that a district lose funding, the department's Office of the General Counsel delayed acting on the matter for years. In a September 1974 report, the Center for National Policy Review concluded that, "there is little question that the Nixon Administration's negative policy declarations have impaired enforcement action and demoralized the HEW civil rights staff." The next year, historian Richard Kluger noted: "In school desegregation, the administration's policy was more than Fabian; it became downright obstructionist, and those in the Justice Department who disagreed with it either left or were purged" (1975, 764).

In the years following *Alexander*, unable to solicit the active support and cooperation of the Nixon administration, the Supreme Court steadily backtracked. In *Swann v. Charlotte-Mecklenburg Board of Education* (1971), the Supreme Court affirmed a district court's powers to order local authorities to prepare a more effective desegregation plan.[8] At the same time, however, the Court suggested that "the constitutional command to desegregate schools does not mean that every school in every community must always reflect the racial composition of the school system as a whole." While not immediately relevant to the case at hand, this language provided the Court with some distance from its earlier decisions demanding immediate and uncompromising desegregation.

When attention shifted to northern public schools, the Court backtracked even further. In *Milliken v. Bradley* (1974) the Supreme Court distinguished the de facto segregation of the North from southern de jure segregation. The Court found that suburban school districts in the North had never practiced the legalized racial segregation of the South. The segregation that had occurred was simply the result of families' private choices about whether to live in cities or suburbs—the Constitution did not require integration across district lines.[9] After this decision, further integration of northern schools stumbled to a halt.[10]

Nixon's unwillingness to actively support the Court's desegregation orders in the late 1960s and early 1970s was not the only cause of the Court's turnaround. Nixon appointed several conservative justices to the bench, including Chief Justice Warren Burger, who were less sympathetic toward judicial meddling in local school affairs. Still, the open hostility that the Court faced from state and local governments, and the tepid support from the federal executive branch, surely played some part in the Court's decision to pull back. Rather than continuing to issue rulings that realized few substantive changes, justices began to adopt a more measured approach on the issue of school desegregation.

President Lincoln versus Chief Justice Taney

In most of the cases involving school desegregation, resistance to court orders came from governors, mayors, and school boards. What happens, though, when judges must decipher the constitutionality of actions taken by the president himself? Who will ensure that a court judgment against the commander in chief is enforced?

Given high visibility, the president generally will yield to court opinion, especially when public opinion is united and strong. It is for this reason, in part, that court and public opinion generally overlap (Barnum 1985; Comiskey 1994; Marshall 1989; Norpoth and Segal 1994). Public support raises the political costs associated with disregarding court opinion. When Richard Nixon announced that he intended to fire the special prosecutor investigating Watergate and disobey a court order directing him to turn over subpoenaed tapes, there "evoked a public reaction which his chief aide later described as a 'fire-storm'" (Siegel 1997). And not accidentally, within a matter of days Nixon promised to comply with the Court's ruling.

Focusing strictly on the costs of disregarding court rulings, however, is to miss the larger point. Indeed, there are costs associated with disputing any political act—court rulings are no exception. The essential point is that when challenged by the president, the courts have few powers of their own to compel executive adherence. Recall President Jackson's famous rebuttal to a Supreme Court that denied the states power to regulate Indian territory: "John Marshall has made his decision, now let him enforce it" (Roche and Levy 1964, 10–12). He obviously could not, and regulations proceeded.

President Lincoln's celebrated standoff against the Supreme Court illustrates the point most dramatically. During the Civil War, Lincoln took drastic steps to preserve the Union. He created an army, blockaded southern harbors, and appropriated funds, all without congressional approval. He also unilaterally ordered the arrest and trial of southern sympathizers and suspended the writ of habeas corpus.

The arrest and imprisonment of John Merryman on May 25, 1861, sparked a well-known showdown between Lincoln and the judiciary. Merryman challenged the constitutionality of his arrest, insisting that the Union army had violated his due process rights. That summer, Chief Justice Taney ordered General George Cadwalader to appear in court with Merryman. Neither the general nor the prisoner, however, ever showed up. Instead, an aide to the general informed Taney that the president had authorized Merryman's arrest, and therefore the Court had no jurisdiction on the matter.

It was clear, however, that the Supreme Court *did* have jurisdiction—the unilateral suspension of habeas corpus represented a fundamental constitutional breach. Lincoln, nonetheless, would have none of it, and Chief Justice Taney's efforts to contact both Merryman and General Cadwalader proved futile. In the end, Taney had to capitulate, lacking any means to enforce whatever decision he might want to render. "My duty was too plain to be mistaken," he later conceded. "I have exercised all the power which the Constitution and laws confer upon me, but that power has been resisted by a force too strong for me to overcome."[11]

Lincoln's actions must be understood within their context. Presidents have always garnered more power to strike out on their own during times of war than during times of peace. It is also true that presidents rarely outwardly and openly defy court orders. Historically, interactions between presidents and judges have been marked by efforts at conciliation. Lincoln's example, nonetheless, shaped the expectations and behaviors of future courts and presidents. A basic lesson was conveyed: "the courts are powerless to interfere with or control the actions of the President if he refuses to be bound by the judgment of the Court. The courts simply do not have the physical power to enforce their judgments" (Cash 1965, 116). When ruling on separation-of-powers issues, the courts must confront the possibility that a president may either ignore their decisions or simply refuse to actively enforce them. And without any way of compelling the president, save possibly appealing to a public that may defeat him or his party at the next election, the integrity of the courts may suffer.

Further Evidence: Court Doctrine

The "new institutionalism" argues quite convincingly that the legal principles used to resolve cases involving government actions emerge from larger institutional concerns about the judiciary's station within a system of separated powers (Clayton and Gillman 1999; Shapiro 1964). The canons of law are not handed down from on high. Rather, judges shape them in ways that promote their own institutional interests. In this sense, rather than providing an explanation for why judges are more or less likely to overturn presidential actions, jurisprudence serves as evidence to evaluate a prior institutional argument about judicial dependence on the executive branch of government, and the impact this has on judicial constraints on presidential power.

The Political Questions Doctrine

Historically, judges have made extraordinary efforts to avoid adjudicating separation-of-powers issues, especially where presidential actions are involved (Corwin 1957, 16). Rather than issue judgment, judges frequently claim that a case is not sufficiently "ripe" for consideration, or that "administrative avenues have not yet been exhausted," or that the issue is "moot" because of subsequent redress, or that parties "lack standing." When judges can find an escape hatch, they often take it.

The "political questions doctrine"—first articulated in *Marbury v. Madison* (1803)—is probably the most important legal basis upon which judges avoid cases involving presidential actions.[12] At the same time that John Marshall unleashed the awesome power of judicial review, the chief justice also supplied future judges with this ready escape clause from separation-of-powers cases.

> The province of the court is, solely, to decide on the rights of individuals, not to inquire how the executive, or executive officers, perform duties in which they have a discretion. Questions in their nature political, or which are, by the constitution and laws, submitted to the executive, can never be made in this court.[13]

"Never" was probably too strong. But Marshall's admission of the limitations of judicial power is profound. At the same time the Court asserted its power to review legislative enactments of Congress, it made sure that judges had a principled rationale for dismissing select cases involving executive powers.

The political questions doctrine claims that there are "political subjects" that concern the executive branch exclusively. If a case raises questions that either exceed the courts' competence, or if a judicial decision would express "lack of respect due coordinate branches of government," or if deciding the case might elicit the "potentiality of embarrassment," judges may reserve judgment.[14] To decide whether or not the political questions doctrine applies, judges distinguish "ministerial" actions (which are subject to judicial scrutiny) from "discretionary" actions (which are not).

These categories remain ambiguous, and judges retain considerable leeway when "deciding whether to decide" cases involving executive actions (Nagel 1989; Perry 1991). If public opinion generally matches judges' preferences, and judges believe that the executive branch will quickly and efficiently enforce their rulings, they may deem a unilateral directive "ministerial" and render judgment. On the other hand, if judges fear the embarrassment of issuing an opinion that the executive branch may not enforce, they can label an executive act "discretionary," invoke the political questions doctrine, and withdraw from the dispute entirely.

Statutory Interpretation

Clearly, judges cannot dismiss every case involving executive authority. When political avenues have been exhausted, and public attention is high, judges may consider challenges to presidential actions. What kind of reasoning, then, allows them to address these issues without either antagonizing the president or compromising the integrity of their institution? The answer lies in a jurisprudence that rests upon the notion of the "will of Congress."

Presidents usually justify their policy directives on the basis of powers vested in the Constitution and others found in statutes enacted by past and present congresses. When considering challenges to these actions, however, judges almost always restrict their evaluations to the latter criteria. "When constitutional issues are intermixed with statutory ones, courts ordinarily examine the statutory issues first, in hopes of avoiding a decision based on the Constitution" (Bruff 1982, 1). Statutory interpretation lies at the heart of judicial decision making in cases involving presidential power.

When interpreting the statutory basis for presidential directives, judges try to ascertain the intentions and policy interests of Congress. As long as the president can demonstrate that his actions comply with the expressed or implied will of Congress, then the courts will deem his actions constitutional. As Chief Justice Harlan Stone declared in *Yakus v. United States* (1944), "the only concern of courts is to ascertain whether the will of Congress has been obeyed."[15]

Consider, by way of example, the court's reasoning in *Contractors Association of Eastern Pennsylvania v. Shultz* (1971).[16] In this case, a group of local construction contractors brought suit against the Philadelphia Plan, a Department of Labor program that implemented President Johnson's executive order on affirmative action. The Philadelphia Plan required bidders on any federal or federally assisted construction contracts for projects in the five counties surrounding Philadelphia to submit an affirmative action program that included specific objectives for hiring minority workers. The plaintiffs argued that Johnson's order violated Titles VI and VII of the Civil Rights Act of 1964, as well as the National Labor Relations Act "by interfering with the exclusive union referral system to which the contractors have in collective bargaining agreements bound themselves" (43). Because the original order did not conform to the clear intent of Congress, the plaintiffs argued, the courts must overturn the plan that implements it.

A federal appeals court, however, disagreed. The panel of judges insisted that the plan was sufficiently narrow in scope (by targeting a single industry with a clear history of discrimination) to render the Civil Rights Act and National Labor Relations Act inapplicable. Instead, the court argued, the fact that Congress willingly appropriated funds for the Philadelphia Plan implied support for Johnson's original order. According to the Court, "When the Congress authorizes an appropriation for a program of federal assistance, and authorizes the Executive branch to implement the program by arranging for assistance to specific projects, in the absence of specific statutory regulations it must be deemed to have granted to the President a general authority to act for the protection of federal interests."

In this particular case, the courts sided with the president because Congress endorsed his actions. Often, though, courts find the justification they need to uphold a presidential directive not by examining what Congress has done, but what it has failed to do. If Congress has passed over opportunities to respond to the president, the courts assume that its members must have approved of the president's actions. Had they objected, the courts reason, they themselves would have overturned the president's actions long ago.

The "doctrine of acquiescence" dates back to *United States v. Midwest Oil Company* (1915).[17] In this case, the Court confronted an executive order that withdrew public lands from private parties, absent any specific authorization from Congress. It was clear that neither constitutional nor delegated powers justified the president's actions. Nonetheless, because Congress had known of similar orders in the past, and had chosen not to act, the court surmised that its continued silence implied consent. Absent a record of formal congressional opposition, courts tend to defer to the president (Cooper 1986).

Decades later, the doctrine of acquiescence remained a vital component of jurisprudence on separation-of-powers cases. In December 1978, President Carter unilaterally terminated the 1954 Mutual Defense Treaty with Taiwan, which for two decades had set a foundation for U.S.-Taiwanese relations. Senator Barry Goldwater (R-AZ) challenged what he perceived to be a patent abuse of executive authority.

The Supreme Court, however, would have none of it (*Goldwater v. Carter* 1979).[18] In his concurring opinion, Justice Lewis Powell noted, "Congress has taken no official action. . . . It cannot be said that either the Senate or the House has rejected the President's claim. If the Congress chooses not to confront the President, it is not our task to do so" (998). The irony could not be plainer. The Court would act provided Congress already had—exactly when judicial interference was unnecessary. But the Court refused to constrain the president in the absence of congressional action—precisely when judicial interference was needed most.

In *Youngstown v. Sawyer* (1952), perhaps the most important Supreme Court case involving presidential power during the twentieth century, Justice Robert Jackson established criteria for reviewing the statutory authority of executive actions.[19] When Congress has definitively prohibited certain acts, the Court ruled, the president's powers are at their weakest. When the president acts in the absence of statutory authority, he enters a "zone of twilight" where his actions are subject to judicial scrutiny. Finally, when the president follows the expressed or implied authorization of Congress, his authority is greatest.

For all intents and purposes, the Court has collapsed these last two categories. Because the absence of congressional action implies consent, the Court upholds the president in both these instances, and the "zone of twilight" becomes a nonoperative concept. The Court ruled against Truman in *Youngstown* only because Congress had considered, and voted down, an amendment to the Taft-Hartley Act that specifically addressed the president's power to intervene in labor disputes. Had Congress not considered the amendment, or had the amendment been broadly construed, then the Court may well have upheld Truman's actions.

Since *Youngstown*, the burden of proof required to establish congressional consent has dropped even further. "Recent cases indicate that in the zone of twilight the courts are increasingly insisting on more than a simple assertion of congressional will, looking instead for very specific and explicit legislation before they will rule against the president" (Silverstein 1997, 39). Rather than formally delegating certain powers to the president, now the mere absence of disapproval—and "specific" and "explicit" disapproval at that—satisfies the Court's requirement that the president's actions accord with the will of Congress.[20]

Where can judges hope to discover this purported will of Congress? As we have already seen, Congress occasionally takes subsequent actions that appear to endorse or refute a particular presidential directive. More often, though, in order to discern legislative intent, judges employ one of two strategies. Some focus on the "plain meaning of the text," confining their inquiry to the actual language of an enacted law. By studying the law, line by line, judges then determine whether the president complied with the wishes of Congress. Other judges, by contrast, believe that the meaning of a statute can only be understood by reference to the environment in which it was enacted; discerning its meaning, therefore, requires sorting through the debates and speeches and proposed amendments leading up to its enactment.[21]

In the end, however, neither approach is fail-safe. Laws are notoriously vague, filled with compromises, clauses and subclauses, conditions and qualifications. With the exception of particularly gross violations of a statute, it is almost never "plain" that the president has somehow breached the meaning of a text. Legislative histories, meanwhile, shed little additional light on the matter. Speeches delivered on floors, evidentiary documents, committee recommendations and reports, roll-call votes on proposed amendments, presidential signing statements, and the iterative drafts of multiple bills in two chambers all constitute the history of any particular law. Taken together, however, they rarely reveal a coherent "will" that binds together every member of Congress. At best, by wading through these materials, judges may determine whether Congress ever anticipated, and expressed an overwhelming preference with regard to, the precise presidential directive brought before the court. Given the rarity of such occurrences, compounded with the ambiguity of the laws themselves, judges usually can find any number of references needed to rule in ways that suit their institutional interests (Melnick 1993, 251–53). It is hard to imagine very many scenarios in which judges, owing to their discoveries in the language or history of a law, would be forced to issue a ruling against the president that they fear might not be enforced.

This brings us full circle. The courts have invented a notion of the will of Congress that requires the legislature to take definitive and positive steps before they will rule against the president. Anything less and they will support the president, for the absence of legislative action implies tacit consent. The flaw in this line of reasoning, however, is that congressional gridlock, rather than implying concurrence, may only signify an inability to act at all. "There is simply no good reason to assume that congressional silence does, in fact, imply consent" (Fleishman and Aufses, 1976). By assuming that it does, however, the courts retain a principled reason for ruling in favor of the president and thereby avoid an interbranch confrontation that they will likely lose.

Court Rulings

A small body of empirical work within political science examines the political conditions under which judges overturn the president (Ducat and Dudley 1989; Genovese 1980; King and Meernik 1999; Yates and Whitford 1998). For the most part, these scholars inventory district or Supreme Court cases involving exercises of presidential power. They find that judges are less likely to overturn presidents who appointed them to the bench, presidents who enjoy strong public approval ratings, and policies that involve foreign affairs—all findings that are quite consistent with those reported below.

The existing literature addresses two theoretical issues. First, it tests aspects of discretionary and rule-making models of judicial decision making and their relations to well-known theories of presidential power (see, especially, Ducat and Dudley 1989). Second, it examines whether judges appear more deferential to the president in some policy arenas than others. While these are interesting and important issues in their own right, they provide little insight into larger questions about how the institutional design of our system of separated powers defines the relationship between judges and presidents. No one, as far as I know, has systematically examined whether concerns about enforcement inform judges' rulings on cases involving presidential policy making.

Given the wide discretion judges have to dismiss cases involving presidential power, and a series of legal principles that broadly interpret statutory authority, there is good reason to expect presidents to fare well in the courts. Most of the time, challenges to presidential policy directives should not even go to trial. But among those that do, usually judges should support the president.

To test this supposition, I identified every challenge to an executive order heard in a federal court between 1942 and 1998. Challenges that were dismissed on the grounds of ripeness, mootness, justiciability, or the political question doctrine, all of which constituted de facto rulings in favor of the president, do not enter the database. By restricting the analysis to only those cases that actually go to trial, observed findings represent conservative estimates of judges' willingness to support the president. To the extent that any selection bias is introduced, it leads to an underestimation of presidential success in the judiciary.

I included cases at the district, appellate, and Supreme Court levels, relying upon the 1994 *Shepard's Code of Federal Regulations Citations* (and its subsequent supplements) to identify court decisions that mentioned executive orders. For some orders, such as Johnson's first affirmative action plan, literally hundreds of cases required examination; for others, only a handful.

To constitute a challenge, a case must raise questions about either the constitutionality or the statutory authority of an executive order issued by the president. The following kinds of cases, therefore, are excluded from the database: cases that challenge the constitutionality of an executive order issued by a mayor or governor (see, for example, *White v. Massachusetts Council of Construction Employers* [1983][22] or *Smith v. Avino* [1996][23]); cases in which an individual or firm are brought to court for violating an executive order issued by the president, but the only issue in dispute concerns the facts of the matter (see *Sierra Club v. Hodel* [1976][24] or *Fagundez v. Oakland Raiders Professional Football Club* [1974][25]); cases in which an individual or firm sued a government agency for not complying with an executive order (see *Itek Corporation v. First National Bank of Boston* [1983][26] or *EDF, Inc. v. Andrus* [1980][27]); and cases in which a private party or federal agency claimed exemption from a particular executive order (see *Chan v. Reno* [1997][28] or *Blanchette v. United States Environmental Protection Agency* [1977][29]).

Appendix 4 lists all eighty-three cases that challenged executive orders in the modern era. Some of the cases are well known, such as *Korematsu v. U.S.* (1944), which affirmed President Roosevelt's decision to intern American citizens of Japanese descent during World War II, or *Youngstown v. Sawyer* (1952), which overturned Truman's seizure of the steel mills during the Korean War. Other cases, meanwhile, are relatively obscure. *DeRieux v. The Five Smiths* (1974), *United States v. Pro Football Inc.* (1975), and *Oakland Raiders v. Office of Emergency Preparedness* (1974), for example, all concerned Nixon orders that temporarily fixed wages and prices; *Unidyne Corp. v. Iran* (1981), *Security Pacific National Bank v. Government of Iran* (1981), *Chase T. Main International v. Khuzestan Water* (1981), and *Power and American International Group v. Iran* (1981) centered on the constitutionality of Carter and Reagan orders that froze Iranian accounts in American banks.

These eighty-three cases challenged all sorts of executive orders, equally distributed between foreign and domestic policy.[30] Foreign orders primarily concern immigration issues, the appropriation of foreign accounts in domestic banks, the loyalty review guidelines established for federal employees, and the classification of national security information. Domestic orders concern the appropriation of private lands for national parks, patent infringements, the desegregation of public schools, and affirmative action guidelines. Figure 6.1 summarizes the kinds of executive orders disputed in the various court cases.

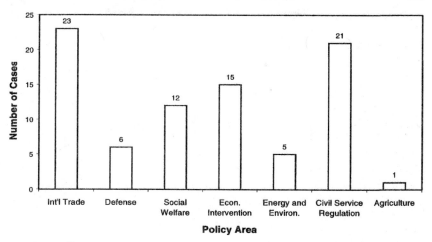

6.1 Court Challenges by Policy Area, 1942–1998. Eighty-three total federal court cases challenging executive orders.

District courts disposed of nineteen of the cases (or 24 percent) in the database, appellate courts fifty (60 percent),[31] and the Supreme Court thirteen (16 percent).[32] These data contrast markedly from the universe of cases brought before the federal courts, where approximately 75 percent of cases are resolved at the district level, 25 percent at the appellate level, and just 0.10 percent by the Supreme Court.[33]

While eighty-three separate court cases are included in this database, only forty-five separate executive orders (or sets of orders on the same subject) were actually challenged.[34] As Figure 6.2 shows, thirty executive orders were challenged just once, seven orders were challenged in two separate court cases, four were challenged three times, two four times, and three five or more times. As one might expect, Johnson's affirmative action order received the greatest amount of attention in the federal courts, the subject of fully eight separate federal court challenges between 1971 and 1984.

Individuals, interest groups, corporations, and political parties all challenged executive orders in these cases. In 15 percent of the cases, challenges constituted aspects of a defense against prosecution by a federal agency charged with enforcing an executive order. In *United States v. Pro Football Inc.* (1974), for example, the federal government alleged that the Redskins professional football team violated Executive Order 11723 (which established a ninety-day freeze on rents, wages, and salaries) by increasing the prices of their tickets. The Redskins did not dispute the facts of the case, but instead argued that the

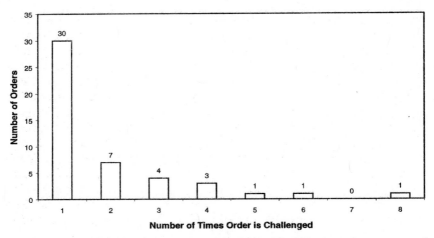

6.2 Frequency of Order Challenges, 1942–1998. 45 separate orders or sets of orders on the same subject challenged. 4,041 executive orders issued between 1942 and 1998 were never challenged in the courts.

executive order represented an "unconstitutional taking without just compensation."

In the remaining 85 percent of cases, executive branch officials represented the defendants. In 77 percent of such cases (or 66 percent of cases overall), presidents defended an executive order that they themselves had issued. Occasionally, however, presidents defended an executive order issued by a prior administration. In *Sale v. Haitian Centers Council* (1993), for example, the Haitian Centers Council challenged a Bush order that allowed the Coast Guard to return emigrants rescued at sea immediately to their native country. During the 1992 presidential election, candidate Bill Clinton announced his opposition to the Bush administration's policy. Concurrently, the United States Court of Appeals for the Second Circuit ruled that Bush's order violated the 1980 Refugee Act, but allowed the order to stand while the president's administration filed an appeal with the Supreme Court. As it worked out, a month after assuming office Clinton reversed his earlier stance and informed the Supreme Court that he now supported Bush's order. The Supreme Court promptly reversed the appellate decision and upheld the order.

Ultimately, when challenged in the courts, how did presidents fare? Quite well. Fully 83 percent of the time, the courts affirmed the president's executive order. Broken out by final level of disposition, presidents won 69 percent of the cases at the Supreme Court, 86 percent in appellate courts, and 85 percent in district courts.[35] Overall, the president lost only fourteen of eighty-three court challenges. By way of comparison, federal administrative agencies historically have won 73 percent of cases brought before the Supreme Court, and 58 percent before appellate courts (Humphries and Songer 1999; Sheehan 1990).

The remarkable won/lost record presidents have secured is not due to a handful of especially propitious years. As Figure 6.3 shows, modern presidents have fought and won challenges at about the same rate throughout the post–World War II period.[36] Only two presidents obtained a perfect record—Roosevelt and Johnson. For most presidents, the success rates fluctuated between 60 and 90 percent. While Reagan and Nixon participated in the largest number of cases involving executive orders, only Kennedy failed to defend any at all. The courts, it seems, have consistently sided with the president during most of the modern era.

While some of the more celebrated cases in the dataset (e.g., *Youngstown v. Sawyer* [1952] and *Cole v. Young* [1956]) certainly represent major defeats for the president, in the final analysis these cases are remarkable principally because they are so exceptional. In the vast majority of challenges to executive orders, the courts ruled in favor of the president, not only endorsing presidents' past actions, but occasionally providing rationales for future presidents to further expand their base of power.

Consider, for example, the growth of affirmative action programs established by executive order during the 1970s and 1980s. With each court victory, presidents found the justification they needed to expand the strength and scope of existing programs. Once the courts upheld the principle of affirmative action (in *Contractors Association of Eastern Pennsylvania v. Shultz* [1971]), presidents then established firm hiring quotas for federal agencies, stringent employment regulations for private companies competing for federal contracts, and punishments for individuals, agencies, and firms that violated them. While lower-court judges usually tailored their decisions on affirmative action policies to a narrow set of facts, appellate judges and Supreme Court justices occasionally expanded the scope and basis for their judgments. With each subsequent victory, presidents discovered new ways of justifying stronger and stronger affirmative action policies.

Not all court defeats, meanwhile, constituted major setbacks for the president. Take, for example, *Hampton v. Mow Sun Wong* (1976), which challenged the constitutionality of Executive Order 10577. This 1954 order delegated to the Federal Civil Service Commission (FCSC) the authority to set federal civil service eligibility guidelines. At the time, only United States citizens and permanent residents that owed their

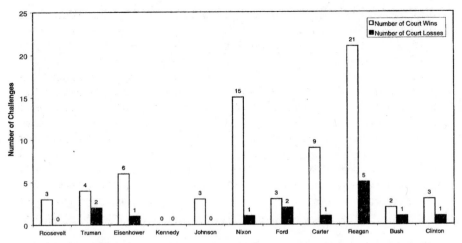

6.3 Challenge Outcomes by Administration Defending Order, 1942–1998. The 83 challenges are represented here by the administration that participated in oral arguments before the court of final disposition.

allegiance to the United States qualified to take the competitive civil service exam. With the discretion afforded them under Executive Order 10577, the FCSC in 1976 decided that residents of American Samoa qualified, while residents of Western Samoa did not.

After being denied the opportunity to take the civil service exam, Mow Sun Wong, who was a resident of Western Samoa, filed a class-action lawsuit against the FCSC. Wong argued that the commission's decision to bar resident aliens from competing for or holding federal civil service positions violated the due process clause of the Fifth Amendment. Further, Wong argued, the executive order that provided a basis for the commission's actions represented an overly broad delegation of power from the president to an administrative agency.

The Supreme Court agreed. "While overriding national interests may justify a citizenship requirement in the federal service even though an identical requirement may not be enforced by a State, the federal power over aliens is not so plenary that any agent of the Federal Government may arbitrarily subject all resident aliens to different substantive rules from those applied to citizens." The Court's objection, however, hinged upon the fact that neither Congress nor the president actually issued the restriction barring noncitizens from civil service employment. The Court implied that, had the decision come directly from one of these sources, then the plenary power interests of the government would outweigh the liberty interests of noncitizens.

In response to the Court's decision, President Ford immediately recast the civil service regulation as an executive order. When challenged once again (*Vergara et al. v. Hampton* [1978]), the policy survived judicial scrutiny. The Court ruled that the *Mow* precedent no longer applied because *Mow* did not preclude the direct exercise of authority by the president. In this instance presidential power "draws support from both the federal and political character of the power over immigration and naturalization." Claiming that the liberty and due process interests of noncitizens do not trump the president's power to regulate immigration, the Court upheld the executive order. The courts upheld the order once again when Mow himself challenged its constitutionality a second time in 1980 (*Mow Sun Wong v. Campbell*).

Explaining Variance

Given the courts' dependence on executive enforcement, we should expect judges generally to support the president. The data confirm as much. Ultimately, though, we need a theory that explains variance, predicting when judges will rule in favor of the president *and* when they will overturn him. Because judges always rely upon the executive branch for enforcement, however, it remains unclear when they might find against the president.

The variable costs to the president of ignoring a court ruling animate an otherwise static theory of judicial deference. Clearly, when presidents refuse to enforce a court order, they risk condemnation by Congress, interest groups, and the public. Each can hurt the president in different ways: killing aspects of his legislative agenda; manipulating media attention; or tossing him out of office at the next election.

When Congress, interest groups, or the public at large are mobilized against the president, the expected costs to the president of refusing to enforce a court order can be quite high. Judges, therefore, can proceed with relative confidence that other political actors will induce executive compliance. But when Congress and the president tend to agree with one another, when interest groups are not particularly concerned about the outcome of a case, or when the public holds the president in high regard, the political costs to the president of ignoring a court ruling (or simply overlooking its more objectionable aspects) are lower. Judges, in these instances, will almost always uphold the president.

To test this claim, I constructed three variables, each of which iden-

tifies a different source of presidential opposition: divided government, whether or not interest groups filed amicus briefs encouraging
the court to overturn an executive order,[37] and the president's job approval rating the week before a court case is decided.[38] The greater the
amount of opposition from either Congress, interest groups, or the
public at the time the judiciary considers a case, the more likely that
judges will rule against the president.[39]

The argument here is not that Congress, interest groups, or the
public inform the content of court rulings. Rather, their mobilized opposition is a precondition for judges to rule against the president.
During periods of divided government, or high interest group opposition, or low approval ratings, judges may well find in favor of the
president. But when the reverse conditions hold, judges should almost always uphold the president. Congressional, interest group, and
public opposition to the president frees up judges to rule on cases as
they see fit—which may very well involve assessments of the case's
legal merits or judges' own policy preferences (more on this below).

The data support this conjecture. Table 6.1 shows the percentage of
cases that presidents lose given different levels of political opposition.
Absent any opposition—for instance, during periods of unified government, when no amicus briefs were filed against the president, and
the president's approval ratings were above the lowest tenth percentile in the sample distribution—the president enjoyed a perfect success rate. When one source of opposition applied, the president lost
20 percent of the cases; when two applied, the president lost fully 31
percent of the cases. (To none of the eighty-three cases did all three
conditions apply.)[40]

Table 6.2 examines the direct impact of each source of political opposition on the likelihood that presidents win court challenges against
them. Simple logit models were calculated with robust standard errors to correct for heteroskedasticity. The dependent variable is coded
1 if the president won the case and zero otherwise. Table 6.3 provides
descriptive statistics for all variables included in the analyses.

The overall fit of the model is quite good. We can reject a constant-
only model at $p = .01$. Furthermore, all three political opposition
variables have the expected sign and are statistically significant.
Holding all other covariates at their means, during periods of divided
government presidents are 19 percent less likely to win a court challenge; when interest groups have mobilized against the president on a
particular issue, the president is 22 percent less likely to withstand a
challenge by the judiciary; and a shift from one standard deviation
below the mean of public approval ratings to one standard deviation
above translates into a 13 percent increase in the probability that

TABLE 6.1
President Success-Rates by Level of Political Opposition

	Level of Political Opposition Against the President		
	Low (1)	Medium (2)	High (3)
President Loses Case	0.0%	19.2%	30.8%
President Wins Case	100.0	80.8	61.2
Total	100.0%	100.0%	100.0%
(N)	18	52	13

Level of opposition is coded low during periods of unified government, when no opposing briefs are filed on a case, and the president's approval rating is above the tenth percentile in the sample distribution; medium when one of the previous conditions held; high when two held. In the eighty-three cases surveyed, there were no instances when all three conditions held. Pearson chi square (2) = 5.65, p = .06.

the president wins his case. A Wald test rejects the null hypothesis that $\beta_1 = \beta_2 = \beta_3 = 0$ at $p = .02$.

One might think that Supreme Court justices pay attention to the larger political environment, while appellate and district judges focuses on issues of fact and legal precedent. If so, dropping from the analysis the thirteen cases resolved by the Supreme Court should attenuate the estimated impacts of political opposition variables on court rulings. In fact, though, just the opposite occurs. During periods of unified government, presidents won every single case resolved at the district and appellate levels. The estimated impacts of presidential approval ratings and interest group opposition also retain their signs and significance.

Model 2A controls for the final level of disposition at which a case is decided. In this second model, the magnitude and significance of all three measures of political opposition increase. Meanwhile, presidents are significantly less likely to win cases decided by the Supreme Court. Our institutional theory lends one explanation for this finding. Because of these cases' high visibility, presidents have a much more difficult time escaping the scrutiny of politicians, interest groups, and the public at large. The costs of refusing to enforce a Supreme Court ruling exceed those of cases decided at the appellate or district level. Consequently, the issue of enforcement is less acute, and justices can feel free to overturn the president.

While all Supreme Court cases are relatively prominent, other cases resolved at the district or appellate levels nonetheless may attract

TABLE 6.2
When Presidents Win Court Challenges

	Presidential Success in Courts				
	Model 1 (1)	Model 2A (2)	Model 2B (3)	Model 3A (4)	Model 3B (5)
Political Opposition					
Divided Government	−1.41**	−2.55***	−2.02***	−2.55***	−2.24***
	(0.74)	(0.82)	(0.79)	(0.99)	(0.96)
Interest Groups	−1.25**	−1.50**	−1.41**	−1.31*	−1.24*
Oppose	(0.73)	(0.74)	(0.74)	(0.82)	(0.82)
Public Approval	4.15*	5.11**	4.41**	5.71**	4.69*
	(2.58)	(2.45)	(2.44)	(3.23)	(2.86)
Saliency of Case					
Supreme Court	—	−2.00**	—	−2.51**	—
		(1.03)		(1.50)	
Appellate Court	—	0.23	—	−0.13	—
		(0.83)		(1.25)	
New York Times	—	—	−1.21**	—	−1.32**
Coverage			(0.70)		(0.72)
Controls					
Last Year of Pres. Term	—	—	—	−2.43***	−2.33***
				(0.89)	(0.73)
War	—	—	—	0.22	0.06
				(0.95)	(0.92)
Foreign Policy	—	—	—	0.85	0.88
				(1.04)	(0.88)
Constant	0.89	1.70	1.67	2.29*	2.35**
	(1.36)	(1.41)	(1.31)	(1.65)	(1.42)
(N)	83 cases	83 cases	83 cases	83 cases	83 cases
Pseudo R^2	.10	.18	.14	.34	.30
Log Likelihood	−33.82	−30.98	−32.53	−24.91	−26.28
Wald Test	.02	.01	.01	.04	.07

Logit models estimated. The dependent variable is scored one if the president wins the challenge and zero otherwise. Robust standard errors reported in parentheses. * significant at .10 level, one-tailed tests conducted; ** significant at .05 level; *** significant at .01 level. Wald test reports the joint significance of the political opposition variables on a two-tailed test.

widespread attention. As another measure of issue saliency, therefore, I identified whether the *New York Times* covered each court case prior to the final decision being rendered. Model 3 contains the relevant indicator variable.[41] Because media coverage obviously increases the higher a case proceeds in the court system, this model omits the Supreme Court and appellate court indicators.

TABLE 6.3
Summary Statistics

	Mean (1)	Standard Deviation (2)	Min (3)	Max (4)	(N) (5)
Analysis of Case Outcomes					
President Wins Case	0.83	0.38	0	1	83
Divided Government	0.71	0.46	0	1	83
Interest Groups Oppose	0.12	0.33	0	1	83
President's Approval Ratings	0.50	0.13	0.25	0.74	83
Supreme Court	0.16	0.37	0	1	83
Appellate Court	0.60	0.49	0	1	83
District Court	0.24	0.43	0	1	83
New York Times Coverage	0.27	0.44	0	1	83
Last Year of President's Term	0.23	0.42	0	1	83
Foreign	0.36	0.48	0	1	83
War	0.28	0.45	0	1	83
Ideological Alignment of Deciding Court and President	0.48	0.50	0	1	83
Contemporary Citation of Authority	0.17	0.38	0	1	83
Analysis of Rulings Made by Individual Judges					
Judge Rules in Favor of President	0.75	0.43	0	1	277
Divided Government	0.60	0.49	0	1	277
Interest Groups Oppose	0.13	0.34	0	1	277
President's Approval Ratings	0.50	0.14	0.25	0.74	277
Supreme Court	0.37	0.48	0	1	277
Appellate Court	0.56	0.50	0	1	277
District Court	0.07	0.26	0	1	277
New York Times Coverage	0.44	0.50	0	1	277
Last Year of President's Term	0.23	0.42	0	1	277
Foreign	0.38	0.49	0	1	277
War	0.30	0.46	0	1	277
Ideological Alignment of Deciding Judge and President	0.54	0.50	0	1	277
Contemporary Citation of Authority	0.15	0.36	0	1	277
Annual Counts of Court Challenges, 1942–1998					
Number of Cases	1.46	1.92	0	12	57

TABLE 6.3
(continued)

	Mean (1)	Standard Deviation (2)	Min (3)	Max (4)	(N) (5)
Divided Government	0.60	0.49	0	1	57
President's Approval Ratings	0.56	0.13	0.26	0.78	57
Ideological Alignment of Supreme Court and President	0.63	0.48	0	1	57
Last Year of President's Term	0.25	0.43	0	1	57
War	0.33	0.48	0	1	57
Total executive orders Issued Previous Year	78.36	57.20	36	382	57

When the *New York Times* writes at least one article on a court case prior to the announcement of its final ruling, the chances that the president wins drop from 85 to 61 percent. Heightened public awareness of federal court cases involving challenges to executive orders rarely benefits the president. Presidents cannot easily ignore rulings that attract widespread public scrutiny. Knowing this *ex ante*, it appears that judges are more willing to overturn them.

One might expect judges to grant more discretionary authority to the president when he sets foreign policy or acts during a national crisis. The last two models, therefore, control for whether the challenged executive order involved foreign policy matters and whether the case was decided when the nation was at war. In addition, these models also control for whether or not the judiciary decided a case during the last year of a presidential term.

Little changes. The estimated impacts of the political opposition and saliency variables remain significant. Interestingly, when presidents defend an order during the last year of their term, judges are much more likely to rule against them. The reason may trace back once again to the issue of enforcement. Given some positive probability that a new president from a different party will be charged with enforcing the court's order, judges may feel emboldened to rule against the current president during the waning days of his administration. Indicator variables for war and foreign policy, meanwhile, have negligible impacts on outcomes.

There are a variety of competing explanations of judicial behavior. The attitudinal model of judicial decision making suggests that judges will support presidents who hold similar policy preferences, and

TABLE 6.4
Introducing Aspects of the Attitudinal and Legal Models

	Presidential Success in Courts			
	Model 1A (1)	Model 1B (2)	Model 2A (3)	Model 2B (4)
Political Opposition				
Divided Government	−3.28***	−2.97***	−3.61***	−3.33***
	(1.19)	(1.09)	(1.40)	(1.29)
Interest Groups Oppose	−1.69**	−1.64**	−1.39**	−1.51**
	(0.83)	(0.87)	(0.78)	(0.85)
Public Approval	7.65**	7.43**	8.59**	7.67***
	(3.52)	(3.20)	(3.91)	(3.21)
Saliency of Case				
Supreme Court	−2.49***	—	−3.69**	—
	(1.03)		(2.18)	
Appellate Court	0.46	—	−0.36	—
	(0.87)		(1.68)	
New York Times Coverage	—	−2.47***	—	−2.51***
		(0.85)		(0.78)
Attitudinal Model				
Partisan Alignment of	1.67**	2.09***	1.98***	1.93***
President and Court	(0.73)	(0.72)	(0.84)	(0.75)
"Legal" Model				
Contemporary Citation	1.87*	1.77*	1.22	1.71**
of Authority to Act	(1.23)	(1.24)	(1.15)	(0.95)
Controls				
Last Year of Pres. Term	—	—	−2.53**	−2.16***
			(1.08)	(0.80)
War	—	—	−0.15	−0.20
			(1.16)	(1.04)
Foreign Policy	—	—	0.32	0.61
			(0.98)	(0.88)
Constant	0.23	0.40	1.63	1.37
	(1.68)	(1.57)	(2.25)	(1.70)
(N)	83 cases	83 cases	83 cases	83 cases
Pseudo R^2	.28	.26	.42	.39
Log Likelihood	−27.16	−27.79	−21.98	−22.96
Wald Test	.01	.01	.01	.01

Logit models estimated. The dependent variable is scored one if the president wins the challenge and zero otherwise. Robust standard errors reported in parentheses. * significant at .10 level, one-tailed tests conducted; ** significant at .05 level; *** significant at .01 level. Wald test reports the joint significance of the political opposition variables on a two-tailed test.

overturn those who do not.[42] The models in Table 6.4, therefore, include controls for the partisan alignment of the court deciding the case and the president defending the executive order.[43]

According to legal models of judicial decision making, judges rule according to the dictates of law and the relevant facts in the case. Unfortunately, it is generally impossible to identify a clear, exogenous measure of such legal considerations. One source, however, is promising. When issuing executive orders, presidents routinely cite a formal basis of legal authority—usually some mix of laws and/or enumerated powers in the Constitution. While the choice is endogenous, all presidents want to proceed on the firmest ground possible. To the extent that there is sufficient variance in the sources of authority that presidents cite, and that judges scrutinize the statutory and constitutional bases of authority upon which presidents issue executive orders, we may have some grounds for evaluating the merits of the legal model.

When they can reliably identify delegated powers in a contemporary statute, presidents have strong legal standing with which to issue an executive order; when mining antiquated legislation for discretionary authority, or waving their hands about broader constitutional powers, the legal basis for an executive order is probably more suspect. The models in Table 6.4, therefore, include an indicator variable that is coded one when the president defends an executive order that cites legislation that was enacted while he was in office, and zero otherwise.[44]

In each of the models, divided government, interest group opposition, and public approval ratings have statistically significant impacts on the probability that the president wins the court case. Wald tests consistently reject the null hypothesis that the political opposition variables are jointly indistinguishable from zero. And as before, presidents are less likely to win court cases that attract considerable public attention.

The findings also support the predictions of the attitudinal and legal models. When the president defending an executive order comes from the same political party as a majority of the judges deciding the case, his chances of winning improve substantially. Similarly, presidents are significantly more likely to win court cases challenging executive orders that cite as legal authority recently enacted statutes. The impacts are consistently significant regardless of which measure of saliency we use and whether or not additional controls are introduced.[45]

The models in Tables 6.2 and 6.4 predict case outcomes, not the rulings of individual judges. At the district level, the two are synonymous. At the appellate court and Supreme Court levels, however, presidents typically stand before three and nine judges, respectively.[46] The models, therefore, may disregard considerable variation in judges' voting behaviors. In Table 6.5, therefore, the unit of analysis changes from 83 court rulings to 277 votes.[47] Standard errors have been adjusted to correct for clustering on each court case.[48] Again, Table 6.3 provides relevant summary statistics.

As before, political opposition and the case's saliency consistently improve the probability that judges will rule against the president. The greater the amount of political opposition to the president, and the higher profile the case, the more likely that judges overturn the challenged executive order.

The registered effects of some of the other variables, however, change slightly. Judges now appear more willing to support the president when the executive order concerns foreign policy. Further, the party alignment of the president and judge no longer increases the probability that the judge will rule in favor of the president; nor does the citation of statutory authority.

It is possible that the attitudinal and legal variables are simply too crude to detect effects. When substituting for the partisan alignment of judge and president an indicator variable for whether the deciding judge was appointed by the president defending the executive order—suggesting a tighter fit between the political preferences of the two actors, while possibly capturing some measure of deference on the part of the judge to the president who appointed her—the recovered point-estimates become positive and highly significant. Finer measures of legal considerations may also generate significant effects.

Recall, though, the nature of our original argument. When political opposition is mobilized against the president, and the issue of enforceability is essentially moot, judges may consider the statutory authority of the president's actions and their own political ideologies. But when Congress, interest groups, and the public at large generally support the president, legal and attitudinal considerations should have negligible effects on court rulings. While the main effects of attitudinal and legal variables are not significant, interaction terms may be.

Table 6.6 reports the effect of partisan alignment and the statutory basis for an executive order separately, depending upon the presence of political opposition against the president (as defined in Table 6.1).[49] Given some opposition to the president, both variables have a positive and statistically significant impact on the likelihood that the judge will uphold the president's actions. Absent political opposition, however, neither has much of an impact on the chances that the judge will

TABLE 6.5

How Individual Judges Vote on Challenges to Presidential Actions

	Presidential Success with Judges					
	Model 1A (1)	Model 1B (2)	Model 2A (3)	Model 2B (4)	Model 3A (5)	Model 3B (6)
Political Opposition						
Divided Government	-0.94***	-0.78**	-0.91**	-0.80**	-0.78**	-0.71*
	(0.40)	(0.39)	(0.42)	(0.44)	(0.45)	(0.50)
Interest Groups Oppose	-1.13***	-0.90**	-1.12***	-0.87**	-0.91**	-0.66*
	(0.47)	(0.50)	(0.49)	(0.51)	(0.54)	(0.49)
Public Approval Rating	2.87**	2.13*	2.84**	2.32*	2.01*	1.64
	(1.38)	(1.46)	(1.49)	(1.65)	(1.43)	(1.57)
Saliency of Case						
Supreme Court	-1.58**	—	-1.55**	—	-1.76**	—
	(0.71)		(0.70)		(0.77)	
Appellate Court	-0.17	—	-0.09	—	-0.44	—
	(0.72)		(0.70)		(0.77)	
New York Times Coverage	—	-1.08***	—	-1.12***	—	-0.98***
		(0.40)		(0.39)		(0.36)
Attitudinal Model						
Partisan Alignment of President and Judge	—	—	0.38	0.34	0.30	0.24
			(0.34)	(0.33)	(0.33)	(0.34)

	(1)	(2)	(3)	(4)	(5)	(6)
"Legal" Model						
Contemporary Citation of Authority to Act	—	—	0.64 (0.65)	0.65 (0.74)	0.44 (0.70)	0.51 (0.81)
Controls						
Last Year of Pres. Term	—	—	—	—	-0.91** (0.47)	-0.97** (0.43)
War	—	—	—	—	-0.21 (0.42)	-0.24 (0.43)
Foreign Policy	—	—	—	—	0.87** (0.45)	0.77** (0.45)
Constant	1.24* (0.93)	1.25* (0.82)	0.90 (0.99)	0.94 (0.88)	1.54* (0.98)	1.27* (0.86)
(N)	277 votes	277 votes	277 votes	277 votes	277 votes	277 votes
Pseudo R^2	.10	.07	.11	.09	.16	.13
Log Likelihood	-139.23	-142.82	-137.52	-141.25	-130.02	-133.66
Wald Test	.01	.03	.01	.05	.13	.27

Logit models estimated. The dependent variable is scored one if the judge supports the president and zero otherwise. Robust standard errors adjusted for clustering on the court case are reported in parentheses. * significant at .10 level, one-tailed tests conducted; ** significant at .05 level; *** significant at .01 level. Wald test reports the joint significance of the political opposition variables on a two-tailed test.

TABLE 6.6
The Conditional Effects of Attitudinal and Legal Considerations

	Presidential Success with Judges			
	Model 1A (1)	Model 1B (2)	Model 2A (3)	Model 2B (4)
Attitudinal Model				
Partisan Alignment (given political opposition)	0.74** (0.36)	0.68** (0.36)	0.66** (0.36)	0.55* (0.38)
Partisan Alignment (given no political opposition)	−0.98 (0.79)	−0.54 (0.77)	−1.01* (0.78)	−0.61 (0.80)
"Legal" Model				
Contemporary Citation (given political opposition)	1.58** (0.87)	1.82** (0.95)	1.64** (0.87)	1.88** (0.93)
Contemporary Citation (given no political opposition)	0.22 (1.13)	−0.63 (0.89)	−0.71 (1.13)	−1.53* (0.99)
Political Opposition				
Divided Government	−1.81*** (0.51)	−1.67*** (0.50)	−1.76*** (0.62)	−1.66*** (0.60)
Interest Groups Oppose	−1.30*** (0.53)	−0.97** (0.54)	−1.08** (0.58)	−0.77* (0.53)
Public Approval	5.33*** (1.96)	4.67*** (1.94)	4.72*** (1.88)	4.11*** (1.76)
Saliency of Case				
Supreme Court	−1.62** (0.70)	—	−1.77** (0.77)	—
Appellate Court	0.07 (0.72)	—	−0.22 (0.80)	—
New York Times Coverage	—	−1.32*** (0.39)	—	−1.19*** (0.38)
Controls				
Last Year of Pres. Term	—	—	−0.84** (0.50)	−0.88** (0.47)
War	—	—	−0.01 (0.46)	−0.08 (0.47)
Foreign Policy	—	—	1.13** (0.50)	1.13** (0.48)

TABLE 6.6
(*continued*)

| | Presidential Success with Judges | | | |
	Model 1A (1)	Model 1B (2)	Model 2A (3)	Model 2B (4)
Constant	0.22	0.42	0.61	0.60
	(1.06)	(1.02)	(1.03)	(0.94)
(N)	277 votes	277 votes	277 votes	277 votes
Pseudo R^2	.13	.11	.19	.17
Log Likelihood	−133.86	−137.28	−125.47	−128.39
Wald Test	.01	.01	.01	.01

Logit models estimated. The dependent variable is scored one if the judge supports the president and zero otherwise. Robust standard errors adjusted for clustering on the court case are reported in parentheses. * significant at .10 level, one-tailed tests conducted; ** significant at .05 level; *** significant at .01 level. Wald test reports the joint significance of the political opposition variables on a two-tailed test.

vote in favor of the president. When Congress, interest groups, and the public support the president, judges do not appear to consult their partisanship or the statutory authority upon which presidents base their actions. Within the domain of federal court cases involving presidential power, the effects of attitudinal and legal considerations are conditional upon the presence of some opposition against the president.

When Court Challenges Are Waged

Our theory has implications not only for how judges rule on cases involving presidential policy making, but also for when parties bring suit against the president. Presumably, individuals, corporations, and interest groups will go after the president when they stand the greatest chance of winning. And if politics define the president's odds in the judiciary, we should witness more challenges to executive orders when the president faces substantial opposition, and fewer when he enjoys widespread support.

Table 6.7 examines the impact of divided government and the president's public approval ratings on the number of cases challenging executive orders that are decided each year between 1942 and 1998.[50] Because we are working with event count data, I estimate Poisson models with robust standard errors. Table 6.3 summarizes the relevant descriptive statistics.

TABLE 6.7
Predicting the Annual Number of Court Challenges to Executive Orders,
1942–1998

	Annual Number of Court Challenges		
	Model 1A (1)	Model 1B (2)	Model 1C (3)
Political Opposition			
Divided Government	0.64**	0.66**	0.60**
	(0.28)	(0.27)	(0.30)
Public Approval	−2.84***	−2.82***	−2.85***
	(0.80)	(1.01)	(0.96)
Controls			
Support for President in S.C.	—	0.09	0.09
		(0.40)	(0.39)
War	—	0.02	0.12
		(0.34)	(0.35)
Last Year of Pres. Term	—	−0.16	−0.13
		(0.32)	(0.30)
Trend	—	—	0.02*
			(0.01)
Total executive orders Issued Prev. Year	—	—	0.003
			(0.003)
Constant	1.47***	1.42**	0.74
	(0.41)	(0.67)	(0.84)
(N)	57 years	57 years	57 years
Pseudo R^2	.08	.08	.09
Log Likelihood	−94.96	−94.71	−93.37
Wald Test	.01	.01	.01

Poisson models estimated. The dependent variable consists of the annual number of court challenges to executive orders decided at the final court of disposition. Robust standard errors are reported in parentheses. * significant at .10 level, one-tailed tests conducted; ** significant at .05 level; *** significant at .01 level. Wald test reports the joint significance of the two political opposition variables on a two-tailed test.

As the regression results clearly indicate, parties challenge executive orders more frequently during periods of divided government and less frequently when the president's approval ratings are relatively high. The effects, both individually and jointly, are highly statistically significant. During periods of divided government, the president faces, on average, one more court challenge each year. A shift from one standard deviation below the mean of public approval ratings to one standard deviation above correlates with roughly one fewer court challenge waged against the president.

When control variables are introduced for the partisan alignment of the Supreme Court and the president, periods of war, and the last year of the president's term, the impacts of the political opposition variables remain firm (see column 2). Nor does anything change when adding a trend term—meant to capture the rising litigiousness of the post–World War II era—and controlling for the number of executive orders issued during the previous year (see column 3). Just as judges look to sources of political opposition when deciding cases involving presidential policy making, so, too, do individuals and groups when deciding whether to challenge the president in the first place.

After the Rulings: The Logic of Anticipated Response

After every case that overturned an executive order, the president faithfully implemented the court's ruling. Just hours after the Supreme Court decided *Youngstown v. Sawyer*, Truman directed his secretary of commerce to relinquish control over the steel companies; after *Chamber of Commerce v. Reich*, Clinton willingly conceded that the federal government could not ban companies from permanently replacing striking workers. While a handful of historical examples of presidents standing up and outwardly defying the judiciary do exist—which, in addition to those already mentioned, might include Franklin Roosevelt's court packing scheme and President Bush's current hassling with district and appellate judges aiming to curtail his discretion to conduct a war on terrorism—they are few and far between.

Two conclusions are possible. First, observed behaviors by the president and the courts are in equilibrium. Judges never rule against the president when there is a high probability that the president will defy them; and presidents provide the necessary enforcement when they confront significant political opposition. Showdowns rarely occur between the president and judiciary because each effectively anticipates how the other will respond, and adjusts its actions accordingly.

On the other hand, the fact that presidents consistently implement court rulings against them may suggest that the issue of enforcement is essentially moot. Judges, by this account, can safely assume that presidents will faithfully and fully implement every aspect of their rulings. Why shouldn't they? Presidents have willingly abided by the vast majority of rulings that the judiciary has handed down against them.

Unfortunately, it is impossible to distinguish between these two possibilities. The logic of anticipated response keeps us from being able to infer from observed behaviors the prior strategic considerations that judges and presidents employ. Evidence of presidential compliance with judicial decisions, in and of itself, neither confirms nor refutes an underlying institutional argument about judicial dependence upon executive enforcement.

Discussion

In the unilateral politics model, the judiciary applies a strict decision rule to adjudicate challenges to unilateral directives. As long as the president does not exceed his discretionary authority, the judiciary upholds his actions. But any time that the president oversteps the assigned limits of his unilateral powers, the judiciary dutifully overturns him. Judges have no leeway on the matter.

The unilateral politics model does not explain how these limits are defined. Rather, the model takes the discretionary parameter (*d*) as given. Clearly, though, any number of factors help define the kinds of laws presidents legally can set on their own: powers enumerated in the Constitution, powers delegated to him by Congress, the ambiguity of certain statutes he is charged with enforcing. The difficulty is that neither the Constitution nor the corpus of delegated powers dictates unambiguously and authoritatively what the president legally can do, and what he cannot. When deciding the constitutionality or statutory authority of presidential actions, judges cannot methodically apply a clear and fixed set of standards. They must sort through legislative histories, interpret the meaning of the president's "executive power," create legal principles to guide their judgments. On many cases, given just a set of facts and standards for review, it is quite difficult to predict how judges ought to come out.

This chapter suggests that judges exploit the fact that the president's constitutional powers are ambiguous in order to serve their own interests, foremost among them being the preservation of their institution's reputation. Without any independent mechanism to enforce their rulings, judges proceed cautiously when issuing rulings generally. Judges consistently monitor the political winds, careful not to step too far out of line with public sentiment, or else risk a popular insurgence they have little means of quelling on their own. But the enforcement problem is full-blown when confronting a unilateral action taken by the president, for here judges must pass sentence on the very individual charged with enforcing their rulings. Should the president decide to ignore the judiciary's order entirely, or enforce only selections of it, then the reputation of the judiciary suffers, and the weight of judicial opinion subsequently diminishes.

Of course, lacking a window into their internal thought processes, we cannot know for sure whether judges seriously consider the possibility that presidents will ignore rulings against them and the impact this may have on the judiciary's reputation. All we observe are judges' actions—the legal doctrine they have erected to adjudicate separation-of-powers cases and the decisions they have rendered. We can only infer the basis on which such actions were made.

The jurisprudence and legal record, however, are remarkably consistent with an institutional explanation of judicial decision making based upon executive enforcement. Judges have created a whole line of principled rationales, foremost among them being the political questions doctrine, for refusing to hear challenges to the president. For the remaining cases, the judiciary has generally supported the president. Despite the fact that the Constitution says nothing about the president's power to issue executive orders, modern courts uphold the president in over 80 percent of the cases brought before them. Judges overturn the president only when Congress, interest groups, and/or the public opposes him, or when a case is particularly salient. The reason, I suggest, has much to with concerns about enforcement. Mobilized political opposition and heightened public scrutiny have the same effect: they increase the costs of defying a court order, and thereby increase the probability of executive compliance.

One feature of these findings deserves special attention: there exists a certain asymmetry working in favor of the judiciary. Should the president ignore a highly salient issue and get away with it, the judiciary's prestige suffers significantly more than when the president refuses to enforce a relatively obscure court ruling. The political costs to the president of ignoring salient issues, however, are probably higher than the costs of disobeying court rulings that do not attract significant public attention. Thus, where the costs are highest (both to the president and courts), the likelihood of executive compliance is greatest; and where the costs are reduced, the president is more likely to disobey the judiciary, but the damage of doing so to the judiciary's reputation is somewhat smaller.

Beyond these reputational effects, the data presented here support the notion that policy preferences and legal considerations influence judicial decision making. Judges appointed by Republican presidents generally support executive orders defended by Republican presidents, and likewise for Democrats. In addition, the source of authority that presidents cite when issuing an executive order appears to have some bearing on the rulings that judges deliver.

Judicial decision making on cases involving presidential power, however, is not just a mix of legal, attitudinal, and institutional considerations. There exists a logic that structures the conditional influences of different models of judicial decision making. Specifically, policy preferences and legal doctrine come into play only when the possibility of executive defiance is low. Not once in the modern era have the courts overturned a president who enjoys broad-based support from Congress, interest groups, and the public. Surely, though, there have been occasions when judges, owing to ideological precommitments or legal philosophies, would have liked to.

The institutional theory laid out here is far from complete. For one, the possibility that the executive will not enforce its rulings does not represent the only threat to the judiciary's reputation—should judges always find in favor of the president, their image as an impartial and independent arbiter of justice may also erode. In addition, greater attention needs to be paid to the substantive differences between overturning a presidential directive—such as an executive order, proclamation, or executive agreement—and overturning a rule or policy initiative set by an administrative agency or by Congress. Judicial deference may be the norm for all classes of cases, but for very different reasons.

Nonetheless, two points established here provide a useful starting point for future work on the subject. First, any theory of executive-judicial relations must explain why presidents fare so well in the judiciary. Rather than reviewing every order that the president issues and striking down those that breach the boundaries of executive authority, as the unilateral politics model depicts, in reality judges never review most executive orders, and of the few that they do, the vast majority are upheld. Second, the source of judicial deference cannot be found in the ideologies of individual judges or the case law that they write. Principles of law do not emerge from behind some Rawlsian veil of ignorance. Judges design them within particular political contexts in order to serve specific institutional needs. This is a matter of politics, not legal philosophy. And in politics, for reasons built into the design of a system of separated powers, judges almost always have cause to favor the president. When they do not, usually it is because other political actors oppose the president, and stand to defend a court order against him.

7

Conclusion

For forty years, scholars have advanced basically two views on presidential power. The first traces back to Richard Neustadt and focuses on the personal qualities of individual presidents. Power is measured by each president's skill, reputation, prestige, and unique ability to deploy these resources to persuade congressional representatives and bureaucrats to do things that he cannot accomplish on his own. Neustadt spawned an entire literature devoted to presidential leadership styles and personality types. And though the personal presidency literature's influence is waning, Neustadt's original formulation of presidential power remains conventional wisdom—presidents are powerful to the extent that they can drive their legislative agendas through Congress, bargain with bureaucrats, and breed loyalty within their administrations.

Recently, the new economics of organizations and positive political theory have taken a renewed interest in the formal powers of the presidency, especially the veto. These literatures formally demonstrate that with the power to veto legislation presidents can exact important policy concessions from Congress. It is only within the legislative process that presidents supposedly gain influence. As such, these literatures spotlight Congress, while presidents reside at the peripheries of lawmaking. Scholars gauge presidential power by the ability of each president to affect (if only indirectly) affairs transpiring in other parts of the federal government.

Because the presidency field has focused on the persuasive powers of the presidency, and the new institutions literatures consistently cast the president as little more than a veto player, scholars have lost sight of one of the most important ways in which presidents influence public policy in the modern era: that is, by setting policy on their own, by acting unilaterally. Indeed, a strong argument can be made that direct presidential actions constitute the distinguishing mark of the modern presidency. Using executive orders, proclamations, and other kinds of directives, presidents have helped define federal policies on civil rights, the environment, health care, and social welfare; and using executive agreements and national security directives, presidents since FDR have fastened their command over foreign policy.

At first glance, powers of unilateral action appear to grant presidents endless influence over public affairs. If they decide that national security interests require sending American troops to Africa or Central America or Eastern Europe, presidents need only issue the order; should the terms of domestic legislation or treaties face considerable opposition within Congress, the president can simply repackage the policies as executive orders or executive agreements; and should some economic or military crisis arise, the president can direct the nation's response, while judges retreat into their chambers and the 535 members of Congress deliberate on committees, subcommittees, and the floors of two chambers.

But there is a difference between celebrating presidential powers and thinking critically about the conditions under which presidents actually exercise them. Certainly, presidents have issued many highly controversial, and often times quite significant unilateral directives. Bush's oversight of the war on terrorism and Clinton's activities in health care, tobacco, federal lands, and civil rights make this abundantly clear. But presidents cannot do whatever they want, whenever they choose. There exist very real limits to these unilateral powers, as became abundantly clear when, in spring 1993, Clinton swore to overturn the ban on gays in the military and then quickly backtracked when Congress and the military establishment voiced fierce opposition. As one constitutional law scholar put it, the president "is not the Pied Piper, and the other branches of government and the American public are not the children of Hamelin" (Adler 1998, 38). Presidents cannot lead and expect everyone to automatically follow. Institutional constraints lie at the heart of a theory of direct presidential action for they determine what presidents can actually accomplish. The freedom the president has, at any moment, to unilaterally set public policy depends critically upon how the other branches of government will respond.

While its principal subject is the president, this book really is about Congress and the judiciary, and their respective abilities (and incentives) to reverse the president's actions. Indeed, it is impossible to articulate a theory of presidential power without having a theory of Congress and the judiciary. In this sense, the divisions between presidency, congressional, and judicial scholars appear entirely artificial. The influence each institution has over public policy depends on the checks that others place upon it. When Congress is weak and the judiciary lenient, presidents' powers of unilateral action flourish; when Congress is unified and strong and the judiciary takes a restricted view of presidential power, presidents can accomplish relatively little. A theory of direct presidential action, at base, must be a theory of political institutions.

The first half of this book is built around a formal representation of the institutional context in which presidents exercise their unilateral powers. The unilateral politics model specifies the precise conditions under which a president unilaterally changes public policy, given his preferences, a status-quo policy, a certain amount of discretion to act on his own, and the preferences of congressional representatives. The model demonstrates that under two circumstances presidents will bypass the legislative process in order to set policy on their own. First, when Congress is gridlocked on an issue (that is, a majority in Congress prefers some alternative to the status quo, but not the supermajority required to enact actual legislation) the president may circumvent the legislative process by issuing a unilateral directive. And second, when Congress is poised to enact new legislation that the president opposes, the president may unilaterally set a more moderate version of the bill in order to derail congressional support for more sweeping changes. In both of these scenarios, the president must take care not to shift public policy too far and provoke either Congress or the judiciary to overturn him. Still, the model shows that within certain limits presidents wield significant influence over final policy outcomes.

The unilateral politics model turns on its head the conventional account of presidential power. Strong presidents, it is generally supposed, distinguish themselves with a long record of legislative successes. The hallmark of weak presidents, meanwhile, is an inability to convince Congress to enact legislative proposals. Executive influence appears to hinge upon the capacity of each president, using whatever means are at his disposal, formal or informal, to convince congressional representatives to act on his behalf; and should they decide to ignore him, the president loses.

Direct presidential actions fashion an entirely different scenario. When presidents act unilaterally, they do not depend upon the active support or cooperation of Congress. Congressional and judicial neglect, in fact, signals presidential success. A unilateral directive retains the weight of law until and unless another institution overturns it.

The unilateral politics model clearly specifies the conditions under which presidents will act unilaterally, and how dramatically they can change public policy when they do. Still, though, there remain important aspects of politics that the unilateral politics model altogether omits. In the model, members of Congress do not confront any of the problems endemic to collective decision-making bodies. The legislative process, in fact, appears quite seamless. The judiciary, meanwhile, mechanically applies a strict decision rule when hearing challenges to presidential directives. Judges, presumably, have no interests with respect to policy outcomes. Their sole intent is to prevent presidents from traversing the appropriate boundaries of their authority.

The model, by its very nature, greatly simplifies the policy-making process. And the afforded gains in rigor and clarity may warrant such simplification. But by ignoring aspects of politics that may affect how Congress and the judiciary respond to the president, the model may misconstrue the politics of direct presidential action. The second half of this book, therefore, steps back and explores the broader institutional capacities of Congress and the judiciary to limit presidential power, delineating when the model overstates executive influence, and when it underestimates it.

Congress rarely can mount an effective and timely response to the president. In order to protect the efficacy of his orders, the president need only block bills, something easily done with the backing of a key committee member or a majority on the floor of one chamber. Historically, then, when Congress has succeeded in enacting legislation that responds to a unilateral directive, usually it is by way of support, either expanding the scope of the directive or simply codifying it in law.

The budget process, however, presents Congress with unique opportunities of influence. Congress can refuse to fund particularly controversial projects that the president creates on his own, or simply restrict how the funding is spent. Presidents must rally support within Congress if a unilaterally created agency or commission stands any chance of surviving in the long term. When his actions require appropriations, the president must engage Congress and persuade its members to support him—the strategy of blocking legislative attempts to overturn his directives no longer applies. Consequently, the influence of unilateral powers diminishes.

The courts, meanwhile, are something of a wild card in the politics of direct presidential action. Appointed for life and unfettered by the transaction costs and collective action problems that cripple the legislative process, judges ought to fare quite well when confronting the president. Indeed, some of the most important decisions the courts have rendered on separation-of-powers cases during the past fifty years have limited presidential power: *Cole v. Young, Youngstown v. Sawyer*. When contemplating a unilateral action, the president probably should fear the judiciary more than Congress.

Still, judicial deference to executive power remains the norm. Judges overturn only the most egregious of executive actions. While presidents have lost some court challenges over the past fifty years, they have won the vast majority. Federal judges ruled in favor of the president (or the party defending an order he issued) in fully 83 percent of the court challenges that went to trial between 1942 and 1998. The reason, in part, traces back to the design of our system of separated powers. The founders constructed a judiciary that can render judgment, but has no independent means to enforce it. For a ruling to have meaning, the executive branch must implement it. This is an important reason why judges stay carefully attuned to politics generally, but it has special relevance in cases involving unilateral directives. When interpreting the constitutionality or statutory authority of an executive order, judges find themselves in the awkward position of having to pass sentence on the very individual who is charged with enforcing their decision. Should the president decide to disobey the decision, or simply refuse to put the full weight of the executive branch behind it, he calls into question the integrity of the institution that delivered it.

How have judges responded? Generally, in one of two ways. Using a host of rationales, foremost among them being the political questions doctrine, judges have ready means to opt out of many challenges. When they can find a principled reason for dismissing a challenge to the president, judges often apply it. In the remaining cases, judges base their decisions on a theory of statutory interpretation that stacks the deck in favor of the president. As long as the president can show that his actions comply with either the expressed or implied will of Congress, judges will uphold his actions. Only when Congress explicitly forbids the presidents from taking certain actions, and public attention is high, will judges overturn the chief executive.

Macrotrends in Unilateral Policy Making

Since George Washington issued the Neutrality Proclamation in 1793, presidents have relied upon their unilateral powers to effect important policy changes. In the nineteenth century, Jefferson followed up with the Louisiana Purchase and Lincoln with the Emancipation Proclamation. In the early twentieth century, Theodore Roosevelt established the national parks system and Wilson issued more than 1,700 executive orders to guide the nation through World War I.

For the past fifty years, however, the trajectory of unilateral policy making has noticeably increased. While it was relatively rare, and for the most part inconsequential, during the eighteenth and nineteenth centuries, unilateral policy making has become an integral feature of the modern presidency. Presidents issue more unilateral directives today than ever before, steadily expanding their influence over all kinds of public policies, foreign and domestic. While there remain important fluctuations from year to year, and from administration to administration, the time-series of significant executive orders and executive agreements unmistakably rises.

In part, this is due to the overwhelming demands placed upon modern presidents. The public holds presidents responsible for all kinds of activities that previously either did not concern the federal government or rested solely within the domain of Congress. Presidents now develop policies on medical practices, racial discrimination, social welfare, labor and management relations, international trade, and education—areas that few presidents, prior to FDR, ever addressed. Indeed, it is difficult to think of a single area of governance that modern presidents can safely ignore. Modern presidents, in this sense, do more simply because the public expects them to.

In addition, presidential powers have expanded over the past half-century because the checks placed on them by Congress have subsided. As political parties have weakened, subcommittees have proliferated, and ideological divisions within Congress have heightened, Congress's ability to legislate has waned. So much so, in fact, that gridlock, while not constant, has become "a basic fact of U.S. lawmaking" (Krehbiel 1998, 4). This development has important implications for presidential power. As Congress weakens, the check it places on presidential power relaxes, and new opportunities arise for the president to strike out on his own. An expansion of presidential power then signals a shift in the overall division of powers—tipping the balance in favor of the president, and against Congress.

Two additional factors probably contributed to the overall increase in unilateral policy making during the latter half of the twentieth century. First, the time-series takes off in the late 1930s, just after the Supreme Court issued a series of rulings—*United States v. Curtiss-Wright* (1936); *United States v. Belmont* (1937); and *United States v. Pink* (1942)—that collectively fortified the president's legal authority to issue executive orders and executive agreements. With the official sanctioning of the Court, modern presidents proceeded with a greater measure of confidence when issuing executive orders and other unilateral directives. Second, many of these orders either created new administrative agencies or directed existing agencies to perform new functions. In this sense, the general trajectory of the significant executive order time-series maps the steady growth of the administrative state. Modern presidents did more simply because more needed to be done. Compared to their predecessors, modern presidents oversee more agencies that employ more employees that perform more tasks. As a consequence, it is little wonder that modern presidents rely upon the unilateral powers with greater frequency.

These trends, however, need not continue forever. There is nothing in the logic of the unilateral politics model that requires presidential power to increase monotonically over time. Quite the contrary, should a new consensus about policy matters emerge in Congress and legislative productivity displace gridlock, opportunities for presidents to act unilaterally may decline. Similarly, should executive actions attract heightened public scrutiny, judges may feel emboldened to overturn presidents with greater frequency.

The fact that presidents issue more unilateral directives now than ever before simply makes the subject matter particularly salient; a theory of unilateral action is unlikely to attract much attention in an era when presidents almost never set policies on their own. But a theory of unilateral action, like all theories, must be dynamic, capable of explaining when presidents will act unilaterally with increasing and decreasing frequency, from year to year, administration to administration, and epoch to epoch. This book, I hope, has taken some steps in that direction.

How Scholarly Research Ought to Proceed

This is the first book-length attempt to construct and systematically test a theory of direct presidential action. While scholars have developed numerous models of the legislative process and found novel ways of testing them, no one has carefully examined the conditions under which presidents can set public policy on their own. In this sense, this book breaks new ground. In doing so, however, it necessarily leaves a number of important questions about lawmaking and presidential power unanswered.

Constraints on Presidential Power. Surely, it seems, the public, interest groups, and bureaucratic agencies play important roles in the politics of direct presidential action. Congress is attentive to the concerns of its public constituents, and in this sense the public and interest groups find voice in the unilateral politics model. Still, presidents may refuse to issue executive orders that neither Congress nor the judiciary will overturn, fearing instead that certain interest groups will target them (and their supporters in Congress) at the next election. Similarly, bureaucratic agencies have considerable autonomy, and may effectively dissuade presidents from issuing orders that are not self-executing (Carpenter 2001). As a first cut, reducing the policy-making process to the three main constitutional branches of government makes good sense. Future work on unilateral powers, however, might consider how the public, interest groups, and administrative agencies affect presidents' decisions about whether to issue policy changes as executive orders, whether to propose legislation to Congress, or whether to do nothing at all.

Measurement Issues. When testing these propositions, scholars should develop finer measures of congressional and presidential preferences than either the partisanship of individual members or the highly aggregated, liberal/conservative NOMINATE scores. This, obviously, is a tall order—though one that a number of scholars are currently working on (see, for example, Clinton and Meirowitz 2001). Developing a set of scores that allow for cardinal and intertemporal comparisons, and identifying differences across policy domains, is anything but straightforward. Still, as data become available that reflect political actors' preferences within specific policy arenas, our empirical tests may better specify how the preferences of congressional members (and judges) impact the discretion presidents enjoy to unilaterally issue different kinds of public policy.

In addition, to properly test the unilateral politics model, and most other theories of lawmaking, we need some kind of measure of the status quo. All of the tests included in this book are necessarily probabilistic—an expansion of the gridlock interval, on average, corresponds to an increase in unilateral activity. To assess whether congressional gridlock will lead to the unilateral imposition of a particular public policy, however, we need to locate the status quo on the same dimension as that defined for congressional and presidential preferences. To date, such technologies remain outstanding.

Judicial Rulings. This book suggests that judges are fundamentally concerned about maintaining the integrity of their institution; and because they depend upon the executive branch to enforce their opinions, this usually involves ruling in favor of the president on cases involving presidential power. The extant political science literature on the judiciary, however, tends to cast judges in an entirely different light. Judges, like presidents and legislators, appear to have strong preferences with respect to policy outcomes. While they gesture toward a set of fixed principles of law, and claim to respect precedent, in reality judges behave much like other political actors—they have public policy interests and do what they can to impose them on others. To the extent that controversy on the matter persists among political scientists, it concerns whether Supreme Court justices act strategically, anticipating the responses of the presidents or Congress, or whether they simply write their sincere policy preferences into their rulings.

The findings presented in chapter 6 suggest a clear ordering of institutional explanations based on executive compliance and arguments about judges' policy preferences. Specifically, attitudinal considerations come into play only after the issue of enforcement is lifted. When they fear that presidents might ignore their rulings, judges rarely overturn executive orders; but when executive compliance is assured, judges freely turn to their ideologies to determine how they ought to rule.

Given that these findings depend upon a relatively small case base—83, to be exact—additional work clearly is warranted. An obvious place to begin is to extend the sorts of statistical models presented in this book to other kinds of unilateral directives: executive agreements, proclamations, administrative rulings, and memoranda. In addition, careful attention needs to be devoted to judicial decision making on cases involving the constitutionality of laws. Need judges worry about overturning federal laws that presidents actively support? And do presidents exert any influence over judicial decisions that state or county governments are charged with enforcing? These remain open questions. Answers, though, are essential if we want to better understand the institutional bases of executive-judicial relations.

Some of the most important topics involving unilateral politics have yet to be plumbed. This book, though, lays a foundation and sets an agenda for future work on the subject. It highlights an aspect of presidential power that scholars have ignored for far too long; it critically examines the conditions under which presidents can use this power to influence public policy; and it provides an important set of empirical findings about presidential activism, as well as the capacities of Congress and the judiciary to contain it. Through it all, the book presents a very different view of executive influence in the modern era—one that focuses less on bargaining and negotiating, and more on the institutional capacity of presidents to strike out on their own, set new policy, and place upon the legislative and judicial branches of government the onus of coordinating a response.

Revisiting September 11, 2001

During the weeks prior to the terrorist attacks of September 11, 2001, Bush enjoyed few friends within Congress. As David Broder noted on September 2, "It is good that President Bush had a long vacation at his Texas ranch, because this autumn is going to be sheer hell for him."[1] A waning economy, a disgruntled Democratic majority within the Senate, and a tax break over which the public was largely ambivalent left Bush with little political capital. Had he hoped to unilaterally impose aspects of his policy agenda, Bush would have to carefully monitor goings-on in Congress and the courts.

September 11 changed everything.

Congress reconvened two days after terrorists had flown planes into the World Trade Center, the Pentagon, and the hills outside of Pittsburgh. Members immediately pledged their allegiance to the president, vowing to support whatever measures Bush and his administration deemed proper to wage its war on terrorism. Senator Hillary Clinton's (D-NY) comments were typical, "I know that the most important thing now—having been at the other end of Pennsylvania Avenue for eight years—is for us to be united, united behind our president and our government, sending a very clear message that this is something that transcends any political consideration or partisanship."[2] Shortly thereafter, both chambers passed the USA Patriot Act, unanimously backing the use of force against the terrorists. The courts, throughout, were not to be heard from.

During that fall and winter the politics of direct presidential action were temporarily suspended. It mattered little whether preferences within Congress were cohesive or divided; whether governing majorities supported or opposed the president; whether Supreme Court justices shared the president's political preferences. All of the institutional constraints that play such vital roles in the unilateral politics model were temporarily lifted and the president could do whatever he liked to define and respond to the crisis, assured that no one would get in his way.

With time, though, institutional constraints invariably have reasserted themselves. As the nation has adjusted, and the sense of urgency has subsided, those constraints that define the boundaries of presidential power have become prominent once again. During the fall of 2001, dissension within Congress emerged over a proposed economic stimulus package and bailout of the airline industries; come March 2002, Democrats on the Senate Judiciary Committee had rejected the nomination of Judge Charles Pickering to the United States Court of Appeals for the Fifth Circuit; in May, memos by FBI personnel that had warned of a possible terrorist attack using commercial airlines came to light, and Democrats in Congress called for hearings to explore what the president knew, and did not know, in the months and weeks leading up to September 11; and as the campaign against terrorism continued into the summer of 2002, members cautiously began to question the military's long-term objectives in the Middle East. In a speech before the National Press Club just eight months after the terrorist attack, Senate Majority Leader Thomas A. Daschle (D-SD) declared that there was and continues to be an extraordinary degree of unity between Congress and this administration regarding the war on terror, both at home and abroad, and we're all agreed that much more needs to be done. But when we have concerns, Democrats will make them known, and when we have questions, those questions will be asked. . . . Despite what some in the administration have suggested, silence in the face of security lapses is not patriotism. If anything, it is the opposite. And the consequences of such silence can be devastating.[3]

Members of Congress, and especially the Democratic leadership, appeared determined to be silent no more.

At roughly the same time, the courts began to object—if ever so cautiously—to aspects of the war on terrorism. On August 2, U.S. District Court Judge Gladys Kessler ordered the Justice Department to release the names of roughly 1,200 detainees suspected of terrorism. "Secret arrests are a 'concept odious to a democratic society,' and profoundly antithetical to the bedrock values that characterize a free and open one such as ours."[4] That national security concerns occasionally trump civil liberties, Kessler ruled, did not justify the Justice Department's concealment of the detainees' identities.

While arguably a rather impotent affront to presidential power, Kessler's ruling marked the judiciary's first serious foray into the national debate over the war on terrorism. It reasserted the judiciary's role in establishing boundaries on executive authority and protecting basic civil liberties. True, the order met strong resistance from the Bush administration, prompting Kessler to issue a stay while the government prepared its appeal—actions fully consistent with the theory of judicial deference outlined in chapter 6. Still, a basic message was sent: the president hereafter would have to consider the judiciary as it conducted its war on terrorism.

Later that month, a federal appeals court dealt its first blow to the administration. A three-judge panel in the U.S. Circuit Court of Appeals for the Sixth Circuit in Cincinnati ruled that the press and public cannot be barred from immigration hearings for individuals rounded up after September 11 (*Detroit Free Press v. John Ashcroft*).[5] Commenting upon a Justice Department order that closed hearings deemed to be of "special interest" to the terrorism investigation, Senior Judge Damon J. Keith wrote in the majority opinion that "the executive branch seeks to uproot people's lives, outside the public eye and behind a closed door." "Democracies die behind closed doors. When the government begins closing doors, it selectively controls information rightfully belonging to the people. Selective information is misinformation."[6] As of this writing, the administration—which claims that civilian courts have no authority over the detentions—has not decided whether to appeal the case. Regardless of its decision or the eventual outcome, the judiciary officially had returned as a check on presidential power.

Ultimately, though, it was Iraq that finally voided the blank check that September 11th conferred upon the Bush administration. During the late summer of 2002, members of the administration—most notably Vice-President Dick Cheney and Secretary of Defense Donald Rumsfeld—began to cast aspersions at Saddam Hussein, decrying the dictator's development of chemical and biological weapons and support for terrorism worldwide. In an August 26 speech before the Veterans of Foreign Wars' National Convention, Cheney detailed the threats to national security posed by the Hussein regime, insisting that "wars are never won on the defensive. We must take the battle to the enemy. We must take every step necessary to make sure our country is secure, and we will prevail. . . . The risks of inaction are far greater than the risk of action."[7] Many, however, were not persuaded. The possibility of a major military offensive against Iraq met widespread opposition among Democrats generally, key members of the Republican Party leadership, and certain corners of the military. Bush Senior's national security adviser, Brent Scowcroft, and ex–Secretary of State James Baker both publicly expressed caution about a possible military strike against Iraq. Above all, Secretary of State Colin Powell stood out for his reluctance to openly endorse the administration's Middle East plans.

That fall, Bush finally conceded that Congress, the public, and the international community had a legitimate stake in the Administration's decision about whether to exercise force abroad. "I believe it's really important for the United States Congress to have an open dialogue about how to deal with [Saddam Hussein]," Bush announced at a September 4 press conference after briefing congressional leaders on Iraq. "This is the debate the American people must hear, must understand. And the world must understand as well that its credibility is at stake."[8] The conversation about whether, and when, to preemptively strike Iraq widened considerably in the proceeding weeks, as Bush tried to justify his position to international allies and domestic parties In a highly partisan vote just before the mid-term elections, Congress would later authorize the use of force against Iraq; shortly thereafter, the United Nations' Security Council unanimously voted in favor of a resolution demanding that Iraq disclose and, if need be, destroy all of its weapons of mass destruction. Still, though, doubts lingered, and Bush remained subject to levels of scrutiny not seen during the weeks and months immediately following September 11. The constraints on presidential power displayed prominently in this book had returned to the fore, and Bush's free pass, at last, had expired.

So it is with national crises. The sinking of the Lusitania, the bombing of Pearl Harbor, and the capture of the Mayaguez all interrupted the conventional politics of unilateral action, temporarily lifting legislative and judicial checks on executive power. These instances also are the exceptions that prove the rule: powers of unilateral action are fundamentally defined by the institutional constraints that Congress and the courts place upon presidents. In the weeks and months following all of these crises, first Congress, and later the courts, reclaimed a measure of influence over public policy making and challenged the president once again. Thereafter, when contemplating a policy change, presidents had to ask not one question, but two: What do I want? *and* what can I get away with?

Appendix 1 _____

Coding of Executive Orders

VIRTUALLY all executive orders easily fell into one of the following thirteen categories. King and Ragsdale (1988), who coded executive orders issued between 1949 and 1984, developed these categories. I simply extended the time-series back to 1920 and up to 1996, making minor modifications as needed.

1. Foreign Trade
- Orders that define terms of trade with individual nations
- Trade tariffs, sanctions, or embargoes
- Trade committees, boards, and organizations: for example, President's Export Council
- Changes to Generalized System of Preferences
- Orders that concern the Panama Canal Zone
- Orders that create foreign relations committees, boards, and organizations: for example, the President's commission on the Holocaust and the Board of Foreign Service
- Selecting and defining powers of ambassadors/consulars
- Financial relations with foreign countries over such matters as loans, stocks, bonds
- Immigration quotas; passport disbursements

2. Foreign Aid
- Orders that refer to "foreign assistance" or provide aid to individual countries or areas
- Administration of aid (often military), development programs, information agencies
- Designating countries as "economically less developed"
- Financial relations with international banks

3. Defense
- Defense departments, committees, boards, agencies: for example, NASA, Foreign Intelligence Board, Department of Transportation
- Defense and emergency programs: for example, development of naval nuclear propulsion, the Foreign Intelligence Board, the Sinai Support Mission, EURATOM
- Disclosure of Classified Information
- Restoring domestic order, city riots

- Orders concerning military personnel, military pay, the draft, Military Reserve Forces (note: orders concerning veterans are coded as 11).
- Orders affecting materials, weapons, bases and military reservations, lands transferred to the military
- Orders that expressly note "threats to national security and/or foreign policy"
- Actions taken in times of war such as designating combat zones and providing health care for military personnel

4. Social Welfare
- All orders relating to education
- Orders directed at the federal judiciary: civil courts; designation of district judges; justice councils, committees such as Federal Legal Council
- Orders that establish policy and organizations concerning women (Advisory Committee for Women) or minorities (equal employment)
- Orders concerning Indian reservations
- Federal programs on drug policy, health care, the disabled, welfare, food stamps
- Private business matters: employee safety, retirement, insurance, minority businesses
- Federal and private sector collaboration projects: for instance, technology sharing and research

5. Government
- Government interventions into the economy: resolution of labor disputes, inflation controls, changes in the deficit or budget
- Allotment of funds to governments of American territories
- Boards, councils, and agencies that are set up for brief periods of time to perform multiple functions that cannot be categorized by a single code
- Orders that continue or revoke more than one federal advisory committee

6. Natural Resources/Energy/Public Lands
- Orders concerning the environment: for example, pollution, recycling, power/energy efficiency, nuclear power, and ride-sharing programs
- Protection of certain areas: for example, wetlands, animal preserves
- Public lands (national parks, lighthouses, and homesteads) designated for resurvey, classification—this constituted the largest category between 1920 and 1945
- Land transfers from military to Department of Interior

7. Agriculture
- Orders that establish committees, organizations to advise the president on agriculture-related matters

- Federal agriculture programs: growth, harvest and trade of certain products

8. Seals, Symbols; Awards, Medals; Recognition of noted deceased
- Establish seals, symbols, and/or flags for national organizations: for example, seal for U.S. Court of Military Appeals
- Official observances for noted deceased
- Medals/awards for distinguished individuals
- Creation and dictation of qualifications of award

9. Intergovernmental Powers/Presidential Delegations of Power
- Orders that reorganize powers of government councils and committees
- Orders that create a committee and dictate its membership, functions, and active period

10. Arts and Humanities
- Orders that affect historic sites and monuments; deals almost exclusively with the Advisory Council on Arts and Humanities
- Some public land orders fall under this category

11. Federal and Civil Service Employment
- Deals primarily with the employment status (retirement, raises, promotions, holidays, firings) of certain groups, firms, individuals
- Orders concerning military veterans and court-martials
- Orders that create federal inspection organizations: for example, the Council on Integrity and Efficiency

12. Taxes
- Orders that direct inspections of firms' and individuals' income tax returns
- Internal Revenue Districts

13. Alien Property Custodian—"Trading with the Enemy Act"
- Orders concerning property seized from foreign citizens during wars by the Alien Property Custodian—most of these orders relate to the sale and trade of confiscated property.

Appendix 2 _____

Proofs of Propositions in the Unilateral Politics Model

Proof of Propositions 1A and 1B

The proof is by backwards induction, and builds upon definitions 1–4 that are proved in Krehbiel 1996. Here we derive $p^*(q, d)$, given the equilibrium strategies employed by the median legislator, the filibuster-pivot, the veto-pivot, and the judiciary. All equilibrium strategies calculated below apply for $p > v > m$; for $p < v < m$, the proof is symmetric and therefore details are omitted. The optimal bill $p^*(q, d)$ depends upon the location of the status quo and the amount of discretion afforded the president. I consider each location of q and possible values of d:

For $q < 2f - m$, the median legislator is unconstrained by subsequent optimizing players and therefore, absent presidential action in the first period, maximizes her utility by proposing her ideal point, $c(q) = m$. If the president cannot set $p(q, d) > m$ without being overturned by the judiciary, then he will not act at all and $p^*(q, d) = \emptyset$. For $\mid v - q \mid > d \geq \mid m - q \mid$, however, the president's optimal strategy is to set $p^*(q, d) = q + d$ (the upper bound of the judiciary's no-overturn set), which the median legislator will not try to change and the judiciary will uphold. Finally, for $d \geq \mid v - q \mid$, the president will set $p^*(q, d) = v$, again which the median legislator will not try to change and the judiciary will uphold. If the president were to set $p(q, d) > v$, the median legislator would be able to introduce a $c(p) < v$, which is an element of both the veto-pivot's no-override set and the filibuster-pivot's no-filibuster set, and which will then become law; the order $p^*(q, d) = v$ then, is the best the president can do.

For $2f - m \leq q < f$, the median legislator is constrained by the filibuster-pivot, and therefore, should the president not act in the second stage of the game, she will introduce $c(q) = 2f - q$, which will become law. Therefore, the president will only set a new policy if $p(q, d) > 2f - q$, which is entirely dependent upon the size of d. For $d < \mid 2f - q \mid$, the president is better off not acting at all and therefore $p^*(q, d) = \emptyset$. For $\mid v - q \mid > d \geq \mid 2f - q \mid$, the president's optimal strategy is to set $p^*(q, d) = q + d$ (the upper bound of the judiciary's no-overturn set), which the median legislator will not try to change and the judiciary will uphold. Finally, for $d \geq |v - q|$, the president will set $p^*(q, d) = v$, applying the same logic as above.

For $f \leq q < v$ and $q < m$, the median legislator can do no better than not to act; therefore, if the president does not introduce $p(q, d) \neq q$, q will remain law. Two scenarios present themselves. For $d < |v - q|$, the president's optimal strategy is to set $p^*(q, d) = q + d$ (the upper bound of the court's no-overturn set), which the median legislator will not try to change and the judiciary will uphold. And again, for $d \geq |v - q|$, the president can do no better than to set $p^*(q, d) = v$.

For $f \leq q < v$ and $q \geq m$, again the median legislator's optimal strategy is not to act, but now d points away from p. If the president does not act at all, then $c(p) = \varnothing$, and q will remain law. Should the president set a policy such that $v > p(q, d) > q$, then the median legislator will not introduce any $c(p)$, but the judiciary will overturn the president's order and policy will revert back to q. Should the president set a policy such that $2q - v > p(q, d) > v$, the median legislator will act strategically, and rather than introducing $c(p) = 2v - p(q, d)$, she will not act at all; the judiciary will overturn the president's order and policy will revert back to q, making the median legislator better off than if she introduced $c(p)$ in the previous period. Should the president set a policy such that $p(q, d) > 2q - v > v$, the median legislator will introduce $c(p) = 2v - p(q, d)$, which will become law. Finally, should the president set $p(q, d) < q$, such that $|p(q, d) - q| < d$ and $p(q, d) > f$, the median legislator will not introduce any $c(p)$ and the judiciary will uphold the president's actions. None of these instances, though, enhance the president's utility relative to $p(q, d) = \varnothing$. Thus, $p^*(q, d) = \varnothing$ is utility-maximizing and q remains law.

For $v \leq q < 2v - m$, the median legislator is constrained by the veto-pivot and therefore, absent presidential action in the first period, $c(p) = 2v - q$. For $d < |q - v|$, the president maximizes his utility by setting $p^*(q, d) = q - d$, the lower bound of the judiciary's no-override set; the median legislator will then propose $c^*(p) = 2v - p(q, d)$, which will become law, but which is greater than $2v - q$. For $d \geq |q - v|$, the president will set $p^*(q, d) = v$, which the median legislator will not try to change and the judiciary will uphold.

For $q > 2v - m$, the median legislator is no longer constrained by the veto-pivot and therefore, absent presidential action in the first period, $c(q) = m$. The president, then, will try to shift q all the way to v, or as far into interval IV as possible, in order to constrain the median legislator's proposal (which must be an element of both the filibuster-pivot's no-filibuster set and the veto-pivot's no-veto set) in the subsequent period. For $d \geq |q - v|$, the president will set $p^*(q, d) = v$, which the median legislator will not try to change and the judiciary will uphold; for $d < |q - v|$, the president maximizes his utility by setting $p^*(q, d) = q - d$, the lower bound of the judiciary's no-overturn set; the median legislator will then propose $c^*(p) = 2v - p(q, d)$, which will become law.

Proof of Propositions 2A and 2B

The discretionary parameter (d) now is assumed to point away from m. Nonetheless, much the same logic used in the previous proof applies here. All equilibrium strategies calculated below apply for $p > v > m$; for $p < v < m$, the proof is symmetric and therefore details are omitted. And again, the optimal bill $p^*(q, d)$ depends upon the location of the status quo and the amount of discretion afforded the president.

For $q < 2f - m$, the median voter is unconstrained by subsequent optimizing players and therefore, absent presidential action in the first period, maximizes her utility by proposing her ideal point, $c(q) = m$. The president can never set $p(q, d) > m$ without being overturned by the judiciary, in which case policy reverts back to q. Thus, $p^*(q, d) = \varnothing$ is the president's optimal strategy.

For $2f - m \leq q < f$, the median legislator is constrained by the filibuster-pivot, and therefore, should the president not act in the first stage of the game, she will introduce $c(q) = 2f - q$, which will become law. Again, the president can never set $p(q, d) > 2f - q$ without triggering a reversal by the judiciary. The president maximizes his utility, however, by setting $p^*(q, d) = q - d$ (the lower bound of the judiciary's no-overturn set), giving the median legislator the leverage needed to propose $c^*(p) = 2[p(q, d)] - f = m$, where $c^*(p) > c(q)$; and because $c^*(p)$ is an element of both the veto-pivot's no-veto set and the filibuster-pivot's no-filibuster set, $c^*(p)$ will become law.

For $f \leq q < v$ and $q < m$, the median legislator can do no better than not to act; therefore, if the president does not act at all, q will remain law. For $d \geq 2(|q - f|)$, the president will set $p^*(q, d) = q - d$; the median legislator then will set $c^*(p) = 2f - p(q, d)$, such that $c^*(p) > q$, which becomes law. For $d < 2(|q - f|)$, $p^*(q, d) = \varnothing$, and therefore q remains law.

For $f \leq q < v$ and $q > m$, we have the same scenario as for $f \leq q < v$ and $q < m$ in the previous proof. Two scenarios, again, require consideration. For $d < |v - q|$, the president's optimal strategy is to set $p^*(q, d) = q + d$ (the upper bound of the judiciary's no-overturn set), which the median legislator will not try to change and the judiciary will uphold. And again, for $d \geq |v - q|$, the president will set $p^*(q, d) = v$.

For $v \leq q$, the president cannot set any $p(q, d)$ that either further constrains or eliminates the median legislator's ability to set $c(q)$ any closer to her ideal point; note that even if the president set $p(q, d)$ to the left of q, in the hopes of triggering a reversal by the judiciary so that final policy reverts back to q, the median legislator remains no less constrained, for subsequent players will remain strategic, and knowing that the reversion point is q, and not $p(q, d)$, will behave no differently than if the president had not acted at all. Therefore, $p^*(q, d) = \emptyset$ is weakly utility-maximizing and $c^*(q) = 2v - q$ (for $v \leq < 2v - m$) or m (for $2v - m \leq q$) becomes law.

Appendix 3 _____

Identifying Congressional Challenges
to Executive Orders

VIA three sweeps of primary sources, I assembled a list of bills introduced to Congress between 1945 and 1998 that sought to amend,
overturn, or codify in law an executive order.

The first sweep relied upon electronic sources. Using *Washington
Alert* and *Thomas: Legislative Information on the Internet*, both online
legislative clearinghouses, I identified seventy-seven bills introduced
between 1973 and 1998 that attempted to amend, extend, overturn, or
codify in law a particular executive order. *Washington Alert*'s database
goes back to 1990, and *Thomas*' to 1973. These sites also include detailed legislative histories and descriptive information on every bill
introduced to Congress.

The second sweep covered 1945 to 1998, and involved various
source materials. The appendix of every *Congressional Record* contains
a list of executive orders introduced to the floor of the House or Senate. I determined whether Congress introduced any legislation in
conjunction with the mentioned executive order. If the information
collected was in any way incomplete, or if I could not identify a congressional action on the matter, I then searched through the *Congressional Quarterly Almanac* for that year, and the years immediately pre-
ceding and following the citation in the *Congressional Record*. Again, if
any information was missing, or if I still had not identified a bill introduced to Congress, I repeated this procedure using the *Commerce
Clearinghouse Legislative Histories*. If after searching through all three
sources I still had not discovered any legislative activity, I then concluded that Congress did not introduce a bill. The conclusion is reasonable, for frequently congressional members introduce an executive
order into the *Congressional Record* simply to express their endorsement or opposition to the president's action. This second sweep un-
covered fifty-four relevant bills.

The third and final sweep relied upon the *Congressional Information
Service* (CIS), a computer database that contains information on congressional hearings and selected bills introduced to Congress between
1789 and the present. I searched this database for all bills passed between 1945 and 1998 that contained the words "executive order" in

their legislative histories or descriptions. This sweep identified just eight bills.

Because the first sweep is more comprehensive than either the second or third, the data collected for the post-1973 years is most complete. Consequently, we cannot make intertemporal comparisons of congressional activism. We can, nonetheless, gauge the threat Congress poses to presidents who are deciding whether or not to act unilaterally. And to the extent that any bias is present, these data probably overestimate legislative success. A bill that eventually became a law has a much greater chance of being in this database than a bill that died in committee. Of those bills that the three sweeps missed, the vast majority surely did not proceed very far through the legislative circuit.

Frequently, members will introduce more than one version of a bill, presenting a basic dilemma. Should we include all versions (including duplicates), and risk overestimating congressional activism? Or should we limit ourselves to only one version, and risk underestimating Congress's attempts to modify executive orders? I settled on a compromise. When members introduced multiple, but identical, bills, I entered into the database the one that proceeded furthest along the legislative route. When members introduced qualitatively different versions of a bill, however, I included them all.

Federal Court Challenges to Executive Orders

Date	Case Name	E.O. Challenged	Case Number	Decision
1 43/06/21	Hirabayashi v. U.S.	9066	320 U.S. 81	For President
2 43/07/14	U.S. v. Von Clemm	8405	136 F. 2d 968	For President
3 44/12/18	Korematsu v. U.S.	9066	323 U.S. 214	For President
4 46/07/29	Wilcox v. Emmons	9066	67 F. Supp. 339	For President
5 50/03/22	International Workers Order v. McGrath	9835	182 F. 2d 368	For President
6 50/04/17	Washington v. McGrath	9835	182 F. 2d 375	For President
7 51/04/30	Bailey v. Richardson	9835	341 U.S. 918	For President
8 51/04/30	Joint Anti-Fascist Refugee Committee v. McGrath	9835	341 U.S. 123	Against
9 52/06/02	Youngstown Sheet & Tube Co. v. Sawyer	10340	343 U.S. 579	Against
10 53/05/25	Perko et al. v. United States	10092	204 F. 2d 446	For President
11 55/07/14	National Lawyers Guild v. Brownwell	9835, 10450	225 F. 2d 552	For President
12 56/06/11	Cole v. Young	10450	351 U.S. 536	Against
13 57/05/09	Lithuanian Workers v. Brownwell	9835, 10450	247 F. 2d 64[1]	For President
14 58/04/28	Jackson v. Kuhn	10730	254 F. 2d 555	For President
15 58/05/19	Moreno Rios v. U.S.	10653	256 F. 2d 68	For President
16 58/08/15	Eastern States Petroleum v. Seaton	10761	165 F. Supp. 363	For President
17 65/05/03	Zemel v. Rusk	11037	381 U.S. 1	For President
18 66/11/23	McBride v. Roland	10173	369 F. 2d 65	For President
19 67/03/23	Rose v. McNamara	10713	375 F. 2d 924	For President
20 69/07/25	Kahn v. Secretary of HEW	10450	302 F. Supp. 178	For President
21 70/12/21	Williamson v. Alldridge	10713	320 F. Supp. 840	For President
22 71/03/31	United Federation of Postal Clerks v. Blount	11491	325 F. Supp. 879	For President

(*continued*)

Date	Case Name	E.O. Challenged	Case Number	Decision
23 71/04/22	Contractors Assoc. of E. Penn. v. Shultz	11246	442 F. 2d 159	For President
24 71/09/23	Ogletree v. McNamara	11246	449 F. 2d 93	For President
25 71/10/07	Calif. Teachers Assoc. v. Newport Mesa USD	11615	333 F. Supp. 436	For President
26 71/11/03	Gordon v. Blount	10450	336 F. Supp. 1271	For President
27 71/11/30	U.S. v. Intone Corporation	11615	334 F. Supp. 905	For President
28 72/07/14	Jennings v. Connally	11627	347 F. Supp. 409	Against
29 72/11/24	United Black Fund v. Hampton	10927	352 F. Supp. 898	For President
30 73/04/18	Ray Baille Trash Hauling v. Kleppe (SBA)	11625	477 F. 2d 696	For President
31 73/09/01	Western States Meat Packers Assoc. v. Dunlop	11723	482 F. 2d 1401	For President
32 73/12/20	League of Voluntary Hospitals v. Local 1199	11695	490 F. 2d 1398	For President
33 74/01/02	Oakland Raiders v. Office of Emergency Preparedness	11615	380 F. Supp. 187	For President
34 74/01/11	Jolly v. U.S.	11491	488 F. 2d 35	For President
35 74/06/20	DeRieux v. The Five Smiths (Atlanta Falcons)	11615	499 F. 2d 1321	For President
36 75/04/15	U.S. v. Pro Football Inc.	11723	514 F. 2d 1396	For President
37 76/06/01	Hampton v. Mow Sun Wong	10577	426 U.S. 88	Against
38 76/08/19	Aviation Consumer Action Project v. CAB	11920	418 F. Supp. 634	For President
39 76/09/22	National Treasury Employees Union v. Fasser	11491	428 F. Supp. 295	Against
40 76/11/24	Kaplan v. Corcoran	10096	545 F. 2d 1073	For President
41 77/02/16	Ramos v. U.S. Civil Service Commission	11935	430 F. Supp. 422	For President

(continued)

Date	Case Name	E.O. Challenged	Case Number	Decision
42 78/07/25	Daughtrey v. Carter	11967	584 F. 2d 1050	For President
43 78/08/24	Vergara v. Hampton	11935	581 F. 2d 1281	For President
44 78/10/05	Jalil v. Campbell	11935	590 F. 2d 1120	For President
45 79/06/22	AFL-CIO v. Kahn	12092	618 F. 2d 784	For President
46 79/06/27	United Steal Workers v. Weber	11246	443 U.S. 193	For President
47 79/07/20	Uniroyal v. Marshall	11246	482 F. Supp. 364	For President
48 80/09/02	Mow Sun Wong v. Campbell	11935	626 F. 2d 739	For President
49 80/10/22	Nat'l. Bank of Commerce of San Antonio v. Marshall	11246, 11375	628 F.2d 474	For President
50 81/01/09	Liberty Mutual Insurance Co. v. Friedman	11246	639 F. 2d 164	Against
51 81/02/02	Levy v. Urbach	11157	651 F. 2d 1278	Against
52 81/03/06	U.S. v. Mississippi Power and Light Co.	11246	638 F. 2d 899	For President
53 81/03/30	Unidyne Corp. v. Iran	12294	512 F. Supp. 705	For President
54 81/04/30	Security Pacific National Bank v. Gov't. of Iran	12294, 12285	513 F. Supp. 864	For President
55 81/05/22	Chase T. Main Int'l. v. Khuzestan Water and Power	12276–12285	651 F. 2d 800	For President
56 81/06/05	American International Group v. Iran	12294	657 F. 2d 430	For President
57 81/06/29	Haig v. Agee	11295	453 U.S. 280	For President
58 81/07/02	Dames & Moore v. Regan	12170	453 U.S. 654	For President
59 81/07/10	Marschalk v. Iran National Airlines	12276–12285	657 F. 2d 3	For President
60 81/07/15	Electronic Data Systems v. Social Security Org. of Iran	12294	651 F. 2d 1007	For President
61 81/09/03	National Treasury Employees Union v. Regan	12171	108 L.R.R.M. 2948	For President
62 83/02/09	Behring International v. Imperial Iranian Air	12294	699 F. 2d 657	For President

(*continued*)

Date	Case Name	E.O. Challenged	Case Number	Decision
63 83/07/15	NAACP v. Devine	12404	727 F. 2d 1247[2]	Against
64 84/01/23	New Orleans Public Service v. U.S.	11246	723 F. 2d 422	Against
65 84/07/12	Florsheim Shoe Co. v. U.S.	12204	744 F. 2d 787	For President
66 84/07/17	United Presbyterian Church v. Reagan	12333	738 F. 2d 1375	For President
67 84/09/21	Ozonoff v. Berzak	10422	744 F. 2d 224	Against
68 85/07/02	Cornelius v. NAACP	12404, 12353	473 U.S. 788	For President
69 86/04/08	Hinton v. Devine	10422	633 F. Supp. 1023	Against
70 86/07/17	Heinemann v. U.S.	10096	796 F. 2d 451	For President
71 86/09/11	U.S. v. Hescorp Heavy Equip. Sales Corp.	12205, 12211	801 F. 2d 70	For President
72 87/01/09	Haitian Refugee Center v. Gracey	12324	809 F. 2d 794	For President
73 87/03/27	National Assoc. of Air Traffic Specialists v. Dole	12564	1987 WL 348512	For President
74 88/09/22	Belk v. U.S.	12276–12285	858 F. 2d 706	For President
75 88/10/13	Chang v. U.S.	12543, 12544	859 F. 2d 893	For President
76 89/01/05	Conservation Law Foundation v. Clark	11644	864 F. 2d 954	For President
77 89/03/24	American Federation of Gov. Employees v. Reagan	12559	870 F. 2d 723	For President
78 92/02/04	Haitian Refugee Center v. Baker	12324	953 F. 2nd 1498	For President
79 92/07/29	Haitian Centers Council v. McNary	12807	969 F. 2d 1350[3]	Against
80 93/02/26	U.S. v. Arch Trading Co.	12722, 12724	987 F. 2d 1087	For President
81 93/06/21	Sale v. Haitian Centers Council	12807	509 U.S. 155	For President
82 96/02/02	Chamber of Commerce v. Reich	12954	74 F. 3d 1322	Against
83 97/02/14	U.S. v. Harold Nicholson	12949	955 F. Supp. 588	For President

1. Judgment subsequently vacated, 355 U.S. 23 (1957)
2. Judgment subsequently reversed, 473 U.S. 788 (1985)
3. Judgment subsequently reversed, 509 U.S. 155 (1993)

Notes

Preface

1. Neustadt defines presidential power as a "personal capacity to influence the conduct of the men who make up government," a formulation that accounts for both the construction and implementation of public policy (1991 [1960], 4).

2. See, for example, *Congressional Information Services Index 1986*; Office of the Federal Register, 1990. *Codification of Presidential Proclamations and Executive Orders: April 13, 1945–January 20, 1989*. Washington, D.C.: Government Printing Office.

3. The only exceptions are Mayer 2001 and Mayer and Price 2002, both of which code the significance of a random sample of executive orders.

Chapter 1
Presidential Power in the Modern Era

1. See Howell and Pevehouse 2002 for an analysis of the presidential use of force.

2. William Safire, "Voices of Negativism," *New York Times*, 5 Dec. 2001, p. A35.

3. William Safire, "Seizing Dictatorial Power," *New York Times*, 15 Nov. 2001, A31; Anthony Lewis, "Wake Up, America," *New York Times*, 30 Nov. 2001, A27; Stephen Gillers, "No Lawyer to Call," *New York Times*, 3 Dec. 2001, A19.

4. The Terrorism Tribunal Act would have formally authorized Bush's actions. The bill was referred to the House Judiciary and Armed Services committees in December 2001. As of this writing, it has yet to emerge for a floor vote.

5. *Coalition of Clergy v. George Walker Bush* (2002) U.S. Dist. LEXIS 2748.

6. Final regulations have the force of law once they are printed in the *Federal Register*.

7. Quotes in "Clinton's Lands Designation Refuels Efforts to Narrow Monuments Law," *CQ Weekly*, 15 Jan. 2000, p. 86. In 1999, the House passed H.R. 1487, which would have restricted the president's authority to designate national parks, but the bill died in the Senate.

8. The coding scheme builds on the one developed by King and Ragsdale (1988). King and Ragsdale coded all orders between 1947 and 1986. To code orders passed between 1920 and 1947 and after 1983, I relied upon *The Federal Register*, 1983–1998 editions, and the *CIS Index to Presidential Executive Orders and Proclamations*. Almost every order easily fell within one of the following categories: foreign trade; foreign aid; defense; social welfare; government in-

tervention into the domestic economy; public lands/energy conservation; agriculture; seals, symbols, and awards; presidential delegations of power; arts and humanities; civil service; taxes; and orders that relate to the "Trading with the Enemy Act." See Appendix 1 for the coding rules.

9. This book treats the executive, legislative, and judicial branches as constitutional entities. It does not differentiate the president from the White House staff from members of the Executive Office of the President from civil servants in the executive branch, generally. As a consequence, the book attributes unilateral policy changes to the president alone. Of course, directives regularly rise from below, at the behest of cabinet members, undersecretaries, or agency heads. While the president has considerable discretion over whether or not to sign off on these directives, he does not always have complete control over their content. Future work should examine how administrative agencies can leverage their informational advantages to shape executive orders, memoranda, proclamations, and other administrative directives to suite their individual interests.

10. The percentages do not sum to 100 only because some directives fit into multiple categories. U.S. House of Representatives, *Presidential Directives and Records Accountability Act: Hearing Before a Subcommittee on the Committee on Government Operations*. 100th Congress, 2d Session (Washington, D.C.: U.S. Government Printing Office, 1988), p. 83.

11. The full text of N.S.C. 68 is available at http://www.Fas.org/irp/offdoes/nsc-hst/nsc-68.htm.

12. 6 U.S. (2 Cranch) 170, 179 (1804).

13. See, for example, *Gelston v. Hoyt* (3 Wheat) 246 (1818); *Blake v. United States*, 103 U.S. 227 (1881); *Ex parte Merryman*, 17 Fed. Cas. 144 (1861).

14. 299 U.S. 304 (1936).

15. 301 U.S. 324 (1937).

16. 315 U.S. 203 (1942).

17. Susan Page, "When a law is unlikely, often an order will do," *USA Today*, 11 Aug. 1997, 7A.

Chapter 2
A Formal Representation of Unilateral Action

1. These certainly are not the first, or only, efforts to apply game theory to studies of the presidency. See, for example, Matthews 1989; Sullivan 1990.

2. Given the form of the game, providing an option to the president to propose legislation to Congress would not lend any additional influence over the final public policy that is enacted. To generate equilibrium outcomes that support such influence, at a minimum, additional restrictions would have to be placed on the range of legislative alternatives to the president's proposal that Congress could consider.

3. For other examples of formal models that represent Congress as a unicameral body, see Baron and Ferejohn 1989, Diermeier 1995, and Krehbiel 1998. To the extent that a bicameral Congress makes the legislative process more cumbersome, modeling both chambers would effectively increase the

number of status-quo policies that the president can unilaterally change without being overturned by Congress.

4. Clearly, Congress has at its disposal other mechanisms by which to respond to the president. Especially with regard to reorganization efforts, Congress has used the legislative veto to constrain the president's exercise of his unilateral powers; similarly, the appropriations process has been an effective means by which to limit the president's capacity to make law. In chapter 5, we consider these avenues in greater detail.

5. Because the judiciary constrains the president, but not Congress, it makes no difference to the equilibrium strategies calculated below whether the court moves right after the president or at the end of the legislative process. Because of the sheer length of time it generally takes for cases to reach, and then be adjudicated in, federal courts, I positioned the judiciary at the end of the unilateral politics model.

6. Mayer 2001 provides a thorough historical overview of the president's use of executive orders to effect changes in these three policy domains.

7. The latter half of the inequality rules out scenarios where the president, without being overturned by the judiciary, sets $p(q, d)$ on the opposite side of m than q, and where $| m - p(q, d) | > | m - q |$.

8. The issue of whether the judiciary should interpret the intent of the current or enacting Congress was raised in *Bob Jones University v. United States*, 103 S.Ct. 2017 (1983). In this case, the Court upheld a 1971 Internal Revenue Service (IRS) ruling that denied tax exemption to educational institutions that discriminated against blacks. The statutory basis on which the IRS acted, however, came from two sections of the 1894 Internal Revenue Code, which was then updated in 1917. Neither the original law nor its update denied exemptions to institutions that discriminated on the basis of race; what is more, Congress never subsequently revisited the issue. The Court majority, nonetheless, argued that the original statute reserved exemptions "for organizations which further the public welfare as defined by *present-day* observers" (Rose-Ackerman 1990, 24; italics in original). The dissent, lead by Justice William Rehnquist, argued that the relevant intent was not that of the current Congress, which clearly disapproved of racial discrimination, but that of the enacting Congress, which likely would have permitted such discrimination. "I agree with the Court that Congress has the power to further this policy by denying . . . [tax-exempt] status to organizations that practice racial discrimination. But as of yet Congress has failed to do so. Whatever the reasons for the failure, this Court should not legislate for Congress."

9. This definition of the "gridlock interval" depends upon this particular array of preferences. For extreme locations of p, as depicted here, the gridlock interval is bounded by the filibuster-pivot's ideal point (f) and the veto-override player's ideal point (v). There really are, however, two filibuster-pivots, one at the fortieth Senator ($f1$), the other at the sixtieth ($f2$). If $f2 < p < v$, then the gridlock interval is bounded by $f1$ and p. And for even more moderate presidents, where $m < p < f2$, then the gridlock interval is bounded by $f1$ and $f2$.

10. For $p < m$, the exact same logic applies.

11. Policy outcomes are a function of both the location of status-quo policies and the amount of discretion associated with them. To graph these equilibrium outcomes within a two-dimensional space, therefore, I've simply fixed d for all q to be the distance between m and f, with the one restriction being that for $m - |v - m| \leq q \leq m + |v - m|$, $d = |m - q|$. Thus, the d associated with extreme status-quo policies will be larger than that associated with more moderate policies.

12. The fact that the size of the shaded region on the left is smaller than that on the right is an artifact of this particular array of preferences and the restriction that for $m - |v - m| \leq q \leq m + |v - m|$, $d = |m - q|$.

13. If d were relatively small, the president would not be able to give the median legislator the leverage she requires to enact a superior $c(p)$, and thus the president will do nothing, and deadlock will persist.

14. If f does not act as a constraint, then there is no reason to shift q further away from m; the median legislator will set $c(p)$ at m regardless.

15. Given this decision rule, the order of the game *does* affect the equilibrium strategies employed by all players. Assume that the judiciary acts strategically, that it moves immediately after the president, and that it has the same ideal point as the median legislator. Here, all of the advantages afforded to the president by preempting Congress disappear entirely, while the range of status-quo policies within the gridlock interval that he can unilaterally shift remains intact. By placing the judiciary at the end of the game, there are no policy gains to be achieved by acting strategically.

16. One might incorporate both a discretionary parameter (d) and judicial policy preferences. A revised judicial decision rule, then, might go as follows: the judiciary always overturns the president if he shifts policy outside of the bounds set by d; the judiciary, though, chooses whether or not to uphold values of $p(q, d)$ that are set within the bounds of d depending upon whether or not the $p(q, d)$ is closer to j than q.

Chapter 3
Bridge Building

1. Indeed, it had come before. In 1942, the National Association for the Advancement of Colored People (NAACP) and the Urban League threatened to march on Washington, as well. Congress then introduced civil rights legislation, but all proposals died either in committee or on the floor. Roosevelt responded just days before the scheduled march by creating the Federal Employment Practices Commission (FEPC). While it delayed civil protests, the FEPC did little of substance to solve the problems of race and racial discrimination in the defense industries. The Commission never established standards of discrimination and failed to allocate direct enforcement powers. By signaling the willingness of presidential administrations to respond to NAACP demands, however, Roosevelt's order set the stage for continued activism after World War II.

2. 304 U.S. 333.

3. For a summary of bills introduced to Congress, see the *Congressional*

Quarterly Almanac 1991, 314; *1992*, 361; *1993*, 396–97; *1994*, 402–3; *1995*, 7–8; and *1996*, 7–13.

4. For the sake of consistency, in all of these examples I have placed the president's ideal point to the right of the median legislator's. Clearly, this misrepresents Clinton. To interpret the substantive meaning of the deadlock politics figure as it relates to this case, therefore, simply reverse the identification of liberal and conservative in the underlying dimension.

5. *Chamber of Commerce of the United States v. Reich* (D.C. Cir. 1996). The appellate court overturned a district court ruling in favor of the president.

6. Interestingly, the substance of Clinton's defense was that the 1948 Procurement Act, and not the 1933 Fair Labor Standards Act, provided the president the discretion he needed to issue Executive Order 12954. The president was fully aware that his actions could not be justified by reference to the Fair Labor Standards Act alone. But rather than roll over and admit defeat, Clinton just selected another act passed by Congress and insisted that it gave him the statutory authority required to issue his executive order.

This suggests that rather than being tied to a single q, presidents can actually choose from many different status-quo policies when deciding to act unilaterally. In this instance, Clinton lost, not least because Congress and the Supreme Court had already spoken directly to the issue of the permanent replacement of striking workers: But to the extent that there is any ambiguity about the value of d different status-quo policies confer, presidents will surely have even more latitude to set new policy than the unilateral politics model suggests.

7. In all of these cases, the president is located to the right of the median legislator. Should the president move to the left, exactly the same logic applies throughout.

8. When d points in either direction of q, then an expansion of the gridlock interval always increases the probability that the president will act unilaterally, no matter how status-quo policies are distributed. If this prediction holds for unidirectional values of d as well, then, we can be confident that our prediction about the relationship between the size of the gridlock interval and presidential policy making is the right one.

9. For status-quo policies to the left of $2f_2 - m$, the probability that the president will act unilaterally is the same at times T1 and T2, for in both cases $c(q) = m$.

10. I purposefully set up this example so that f and v were equidistant from m. It is possible, though, that the distribution of senators' preferences are skewed, in which case one may be further away from the other; and post-1975, the filibuster-pivot moves from the two-thirds position to the three-fifths position, making it all the more likely that f will be closer to m than v. Given a unidirectional d, it should then be the case that the losses experienced between v_1 and v_2 from moving from T1 to T2 will not be entirely offset by the gains from moving from f_1 to f_2. These differences, though, are marginal, and on the whole should not affect our prediction of the overall impact of an expanding gridlock interval.

11. This suggests a related hypothesis, one that is easily calculated by per-

forming the same steps as above. Rather than letting the gridlock interval vary, we might shift the location of p. While the probability that the president will act unilaterally does not change among those values of p that lay outside of the gridlock interval, the probability increases markedly when p moves inside. Thus, we might expect that relatively moderate presidents will issue more executive orders than relatively extreme presidents, where moderate and extreme are defined by whether the presidents ideal point lies inside or outside of the gridlock interval. Unfortunately, there has been only one president (Eisenhower) in the last sixty years to fall within the gridlock interval, making it impossible to actually test this hypothesis.

12. The exact same logic applies when the Republicans control Congress.

13. Recall the distinction between the enacting and current Congress. It could be the case that d points in the direction of the m_{gop}, the median legislator of the Republican party, even though the Democrats are currently the majority party; in this case, the preferences of a prior Congress, rather than the current Congress, constrain what the president can accomplish. Should this scenario occur with much frequency, the job of calculating the effect of divided government is significantly more complex. If we assume, however, that the majority party remains constant—as it does for the vast majority of the modern era—the difficulties associated with differentiating between the current and enacting Congress are put to rest, and the subsequent calculations are greatly simplified.

Chapter 4
Theory Testing

1. By using this approach, we cannot identify which particular orders are significant during this time period. Predicted values only specify how many orders we can expect to make the cut. Nonetheless, by coding the orders mentioned in each source and rerunning the analysis, we can break out these findings by policy area, or any other criteria of interest.

2. These post–World War II figures are slightly lower than legislative outputs. Elsewhere I show that roughly 13 percent of all laws passed between 1945 and 1994 can be considered "non-trivial" (Howell et al. 2000). This definition was based upon each law's coverage in the *New York Times*, the *Washington Post*, and the annual almanacs assembled by *Congressional Quarterly*.

3. The significant executive order time-series levels off after 1985. This trend may be due to limitations in the generation of predicted values. Alternatively, some scholars have noted that presidents increasingly are substituting memoranda (which do not have strict reporting requirements) for executive orders (which do). If so, then the significant executive order time-series may overlook important developments in unilateral policy making. See Cooper 2002, 114–15.

4. These latter peaks are somewhat more difficult to see in the first panel, given the range of the y-axis. They become quite clear, though, if one drops the pre-1950 observations, thus allowing us to shrink the range of the y-axis.

5. When taking the larger of the House and Senate majorities, equivalent results are generated.

6. The LPPC score for either chamber in any given term is calculated as follows: Chamber LPPC = [(majority party size in percent) × (cohesion of majority party)] − [(minority party size in percent) × (cohesion of minority party)]. Typically, *Congressional Quarterly*'s party unity scores are utilized.

7. Alternatively, to test Hypothesis 1, one might calculate the length of the gridlock interval directly using NOMINATE or ADA scores (Groseclose, Levitt, and Snyder 1999; McCarty and Poole 1995; Poole 1998). This strategy has the advantage of providing the tightest possible link between theory and data. The trouble with this approach, however, concerns the number of assumptions that must be made to generate scores that allow for intertemporal and cardinal comparisons. Further, at least when applied to legislative outputs, the measure appears to lack face value. When estimating the length of the gridlock interval using DW-NOMINATE scores, I found that the 89th Congress (which was by far the most productive Congress in the post–World War II era) had one of the largest values, while congresses in the late 1950s and early 1970s (which were not exactly bustling with legislative activity) had the smallest. This is precisely why Keith Krehbiel, when testing the pivotal politics model, examined changes in the partisan makeup of Congress, and chose not to estimate the length of the gridlock interval directly (1998, 74, n. 28).

8. None of the findings reported below change significantly when estimating models that use annual counts of significant orders issued. In addition, findings are stable when taking the logistic transformation of the number of significant orders issued, an adjustment that decreases the influence of outliers in the time-series.

9. To formally assess the structural properties of the time-series, I applied a battery of Augmented Dickey-Fuller tests (Enders 1995, 256–58). I estimate the following model: $\Delta y_t = a_0 + \gamma y_{t-1} + a\tau + \beta_1 \Delta y_{t-1} + \epsilon_t$, where Δy_t is the first difference of the significant order time-series, y_{t-1} is the one period lag of the times-series, τ is a time trend, and Δy_{t-i} is the ith period lag of the first differenced time-series. γ, the variable of interest, is estimated to be −0.46 with a standard error of 0.12 for the Congress/court time-series. Using the critical values from a Dickey-Fuller test, we can reject the null that γ is zero, indicating that the significant order time-series does not contain a unit root, and hence is stationary.

10. Poissons, nonetheless, present one potential complication: they generally assume that observations within each time period are independent of one another. Given that presidents frequently issue executive orders that overturn prior orders, assuming independence may be problematic. The results reported below, nonetheless, are not sensitive to this choice of model estimation. Various versions of least squares regressions (ordinary least squares, generalized least squares) and negative binomials all generated almost identical results.

11. I suspect that the lack of dynamics in the significant executive order time series derives from the fact that observations are aggregated by Con-

gress. When examining the annual number of significant orders issued during the post-War era, a slight dampening dynamic process is observed, suggesting the need to estimate linear Poisson autoregressive models.

12. As an alternative to including fixed effects, one might simply control for each president's propensity for activism. Unfortunately, though, it is almost impossible to come up with such a measure without sampling on the dependent variable.

13. Models that exclude fixed effects for presidents position considerably poorer than those that do. F-tests of their joint significance reject the null at $p < .01$. In addition, observed impacts for regime variables differ noticeably when fixed effects are excluded.

14. When examining the creation of administrative agencies by executive order, departmental order, and reorganization plans, Lewis (2003) and Howell and Lewis (2002) also observe a negative relationship between the size of congressional majorities (as well as other direct measures of preference divergence) and levels of unilateral activity. Presidents appear especially likely to construct new administrative agencies on their own when Congress is least capable of legislating.

15. Holding all variables at their means, the models predict that presidents issue, on average, eighteen significant executive orders each Congress (regardless of which version of congressional weakness one employs).

16. For the sake of simplicity, in this and all subsequent tables, I have omitted the presidential indicator variables, most of which follow the same patterns as noted in Table 4.2.

17. In addition, we might want to control for the relative size of the federal government. The rise in executive orders may simply derive from the number of responsibilities cast upon the president, and have little to do with the particular institutional environment within which each president finds himself. Testing this proposition, however, is less than straightforward, if only because the executive branch in many ways has grown at the hand of presidents exercising their unilateral powers. Presidents have issued all sorts of unilateral directives to construct federal agencies: the Peace Corps, the now-defunct Loyalty Review Board, the Environmental Protection Agency, the Occupational Safety and Health Organization are but a few examples. Rather than being a cause of presidential policy making, then, the expansion of the federal government is actually an outcome. To control for it would mistakenly assign the direction of causality.

18. War receives values of one during the Korean War (1950–53), the Vietnam War (1965–75), and the Persian Gulf War (1990–91).

19. I suspect that the differences in estimated coefficients on *Administration Change* for the two series concern the source materials consulted and not the different time periods covered. In an effort to highlight differences between newly elected presidents and their predecessors, the *New York Times* regularly featured articles on executive orders that amended or overturned a prior administration's policies.

20. When estimating these models without the variables *War, Unemployment*, and *First-Term*, the coefficients on the majority party variables remain negative and statistically significant, the effects of *Divided Government* become

negative and statistically significant in both time-series, and the effect of a change in presidential administrations remains positive and significant only in the *New York Times* series.

21. *First-Term* had a spurious relationship with *Divided Government* and therefore was dropped from the analysis. When included, it had a positive and significant relationship with outcomes, but the *Divided Government* variable became positive and significant.

22. Models that use as the dependent variable the percentage of executive orders issued during the previous presidential term that the current president amends or overturns show strong positive effects for changes in presidential administration and first congressional term—presidents amend and overturn a much higher percentage of the previous administration's orders during the first two years of their term, and when the previous presidential administration is from the opposite party.

23. Howell et al. (2000) used these count data to test whether Congress enacts fewer important laws during periods of unified than divided government. They find that while *Divided Government* depressed the number of landmark laws enacted, it has no effect on the number of important and ordinary enactments, and has a positive effect on the number of trivial laws passed each Congress between 1945 and 1994. For the analyses conducted for this chapter, I updated the time-series through 1998.

Chapter 5
Congressional Constraints on Presidential Power

1. See Moe 1987 for a review of these models.

2. U.S. House of Representatives, *Presidential Directives and Records Accountability Act: Hearing Before a Subcommittee on the Committee on Government Operations*. 100th Congress, 2d Session (Washington, D.C.: U.S. Government Printing Office, 1988), 2, 29.

3. A variety of unilateral directives, for example memoranda, are still not subject to any reporting requirements. At the president's discretion, however, most are placed in the *Federal Register*, the *Weekly Compilation of Presidential Papers*, or *The Public Papers of the President*.

4. Members of Congress, in fact, passed the 1977 and 1979 amendments to the Case Act in order to address this very issue. Members feared that presidents would continue to issue the same unilateral directives they had before, and just insist that their orders fell outside of the definition of an "international agreement" and therefore were not subject to "public notice or legislative accountability." For further discussion of the Senate's deliberations on the matter, see the 1974 *Report of the Special Committee on National Emergencies and Delegated Emergency Powers, Executive Orders in Times of War and National Emergency*. 93d Congress, 2d Session (Committee Print).

5. The Resolution actually limits the engagement to sixty days, but allows presidents an additional thirty days when troops must either be protected or withdrawn.

6. The Bricker Amendments represented Congress's best attempt to negate the president's powers of unilateral action. Between 1953 and 1956, Senator

John Bricker of Ohio introduced six versions of the amendment, each of which declared that "a treaty shall become effective as internal law in the U.S. only through the enactment of appropriate legislation by the Congress." The constitutional amendment would thus have eliminated the president's authority to issue executive agreements. If a deal was to be made, Congress would have to be a party to it. Nonetheless, none of these amendments ever passed the Senate—though one version failed by just one vote. When Senator Bricker lost his 1958 reelection bid, congressional efforts to eliminate executive agreements were laid to rest.

7. Wawro (2000) examines the behaviors of "legislative entrepreneurs" who attend to the intra-institutional difficulties that impede legislative action. He says less, however, about those members of Congress who address broader balance-of-powers issues across the branches of government.

8. The one exception involves cases where the status-quo policy is located in intervals IV or V, but the president lacks the discretion to shift policy all the way back to v. In equilibrium, the president will set policy at $q - d$, and the median legislator will then introduce a new legislative proposal at $2v - (q - d) > m$.

9. These findings are consistent with those of other scholars. When Hugh Keenan reported to the U.S. Senate's 1974 hearing on the use of executive orders during wartime, he claimed that Congress had repealed only five executive orders in the first 200 years of the nation's history (Keenan 1974, 16–17).

10. Simple resolutions require the support of just a majority of the House or Senate; concurrent resolutions require the support of a majority of both chambers.

11. Members of Congress also use resolutions to express praise for particular orders issued by the president.

12. Under what conditions can Congress credibly threaten to punish the president along one dimension in order to keep him from acting along another? Consider two policies—unilateral directive x and policy initiative y. Four conditions must hold if Congress' threat to kill y is to persuade the president not to unilaterally issue x. First, the president must care more about y than x. Second, the president cannot be able to issue policy y on his own; that is, to become law, policy y must take the form of legislation. Third, there must exist enough votes in Congress in support of policy initiative y that it would otherwise pass. Clearly, threatening to kill a bill that stands no chance of being enacted is hardly a threat at all. And finally, there must exist a critical number of legislators with the following preference ordering: $[(\sim x, y), (\sim x, \sim y), (x, y), (x, \sim y)]$. That is, absent the president's unilateral directive x, these members would enact y. But because they so object to x, they would prefer that neither x nor y become law to a situation where the president issues x and Congress enacts y.

13. For a summary of the legal arguments for and against drug testing in the workplace, see Peter Susser 1985, "Issues Raised by Drugs in the Workplace," *Labor Law Journal* 36, no. 1, 42–54.

14. 57 USLW 4324.

15. 57 USLW 4338.

16. "Supply Management: Improving Marine Corps Procedures for Phasing out Equipment: Report to the Commanding General." Marine Corps Logistics Base, Albany, Georgia. (Washington, D.C.: General Accounting Office, 1986).

17. *Mitchell v. Laird*, 476 F. 2d 533, 538.

18. The only difference between executive and secretarial orders concerns the signatory; the president generally signs executive orders while agency heads usually sign secretarial orders.

19. In part, these differences are due to source bias. *Congress and the Nation* focuses explicitly on congressional affairs and only covers presidential acts when they receive some measure of attention within Congress. It is no surprise, then, that agencies created by legislation receive more coverage than do agencies established by executive or department orders.

20. *INS v. Chadha*, 462 U.S. 919.

21. Notable exceptions include the Foreign Claims Settlement Commission and the Government Patents Board.

22. See U.S. Equal Employment Opportunity Commission. *Legislative History of Titles VII and XI of Civil Rights Act*. (Washington, DC: U.S. Government Printing Office, 1968).

23. *Federal Register* 8, no. 106 (1943): 7183.

24. Congress once again introduced legislation (H.R. 2232 and the "Norton Bill") that would have made the FEPC a permanent agency. Despite the support of the Rules Committee Chairman Adolph Sabath, the bills were locked in committee.

25. Supplement to the Code of Federal Regulation of the United States of America (Washington, D.C.: Government Printing Office, 1945).

26. For a history of FEPC acts introduced to Congress, see *Congressional Quarterly Almanacs: 1947*, 651–52, 654–55, 681–82, and 766–67; *1948*, 230–32 and 444–46; *1949*, 455–56 and 854–55; *1950*, 375–83.

27. 59 Stat. 134. In addition to several civil rights commissions, future presidents used this statute to justify the funding of such commissions as the President's Commission on Registration and Voting Participation (1963), the President's Commission on the Patent System (1965), the National Advisory Commission on Food and Fiber (1965), and the National Advisory Commission on Health Manpower (1966).

Chapter 6
The Institutional Foundations of Judicial Deference

1. For examples of the attitudinal model, see Segal and Cover 1989; Segal and Spaeth 1993; and Segal, Epstein, Cameron and Spaeth 1995; for the strategic model, see Epstein and Knight 1998; Gelly and Spiller 1992; Kornhauser 1992; Schwartz 1992.

2. For this reason, federal judges expressed deep ambivalence about deciding cases pertaining to slavery and Native American lands in the nineteenth century, and reapportionment and integration in the twentieth (Burgess 1994; Roche 1955; Strum 1974, 36–96; Woolhandler and Collins 1995). On these particular matters, resistance from state governments was probable and execu-

tive backing uncertain. See, for example, *Texas v. White*, 7 Wall 700, 729 (1866); *Mississippi v. Johnson*, 4 Wall. 475 (1866); and *Georgia v. Stanton*, 6 Wall. 50 (1867).

3. *Virginia Coupon Cases*, 114 U.S. at 288.

4. 347 U.S. 483 (1954).

5. *Cooper v. Aaron*, 358 U.S. 1 (1957). Interestingly, the Court did not append the justices' opinions until several weeks after the actual judgment was rendered. This action is virtually unheard of, and reflects the deep ambivalence the justices felt about having to rule on an issue they knew they could not enforce.

6. Gary Orfield and John T. Yun, "Resegregation in American Schools," Civil Rights Project, Harvard University, 1999, Table 6. Paper available at *www.law.harvard.edu/civilrights/publications*.

7. 36 U.S. 19.

8. 402 U.S. 1.

9. *Milliken v. Bradley I*, 418 U.S. 717; *Milliken v. Bradley II*, 433 U.S. 267 (1977).

10. Orfield and Yun, "Resegregation."

11. 17 F. Cas. 144 (C.C. D. Md. 1861) at 153.

12. 5 U.S. (1 Cranch) 137.

13. Ibid. at 170.

14. *Baker v. Carr*, 369 U.S. 186 (1962); *Armstrong v. U.S*, 759 F.2d 1378 (1985).

15. 321 U.S. 414 at 425.

16. 442 F.2d 159.

17. 236 U.S. 456.

18. 343 U.S. 635.

19. 444 U.S. 997.

20. This practice pervades administrative law. In *Chevron U.S.A. Inc. v. Natural Resources Defense Council*, the Supreme Court declared that "to uphold an agency's construction of a statute that is silent or ambiguous with respect to the question at issue, a reviewing court need not conclude that the agency construction was the only one it permissibly could have adopted, or even the reading the court would have reached if the question initially had arisen in a judicial proceeding"; 467 U.S. 837 (1984). Where a statute is ambiguous, administrative agencies (and, by extension, presidents) enjoy "broad discretion" to interpret and implement the law as they see fit. Only when an agency (or president) contravenes "narrowly construed" and "unambiguous" aspects of a statute will the Court intervene.

21. For a discussion of the two approaches, see the concurring and dissenting opinions in *United States v. Thompson/Center Arms Co.*, 504 U.S. 505 (1992). For analyses of the use of legislative histories in statutory interpretation, see Carro and Brann 1982; Wald 1982, 1990.

22. 103 S. Ct. 1042.

23. 91 F.3d 105.

24. 544 F.2d 1036.

25. 498 F.2d 1394.

26. 704 F.2d 1.

27. 619 F.2d 1368.

28. 113 F.3d 1068.

29. 551 F.2d 906.

30. Given that presidents issue, on average, twice as many significant domestic executive orders as foreign orders, foreign orders actually have a higher probability of being challenged in the courts. See chapter 6.

31. While the Washington, D.C., circuit court heard the most cases in the database, all eleven circuits (plus the federal circuit) heard at least one. The president's chances of winning a case, however, did not depend upon the circuit in which it was heard.

32. The breakdown of votes at the appellate and Supreme Court levels were roughly comparable when ruling in favor of the president or when overturning him. Appellate-level decisions were almost always unanimously decided. Majority opinions at the Supreme Court level typically were signed by six or seven of the nine Justices.

33. These data come from the Administrative Office of the United States for the 1997 calendar year. While the figures vary somewhat from year to year, the vast majority of both civil and criminal cases never make it to the Supreme Court.

34. This represents roughly 9 percent of all "significant" executive orders issued between 1942 and 1998.

35. These figures reflect rulings at the final level of disposition. Cases decided at the Supreme, appellate, and district level each count as a single observation.

36. Between 1789 and 1956, state and federal courts overturned a grand total of sixteen executive orders (Schubert 1973, 361–65).

37. In two of these cases, members of Congress, rather than interest groups, actually filed the briefs. When parties on both sides of the issue filed briefs, this variable was coded zero. The variable was coded one only when all amicus briefs opposed the president's order, which occurred 12 percent of the time.

38. This variable catalogues the last Gallup poll that included a question about the public's approval of the president's performance before a court ruling was released. In most instances, this occurred about one week beforehand. At the Supreme Court level, justices often decide cases long before actually publishing their opinions. As a robustness check, I collected public support data after the first day that arguments were held on these cases. The impacts recovered from this measure virtually replicate those reported below.

39. There is good cause for including variables that measure the specific opposition of interest groups and the more diffuse opposition of Congress and the public. Interest groups selectively monitor the president's implementation of court rulings. Dynamics involving Congress, the public, and the president, however, operate at multiple levels. Members of Congress from the opposite party may care very little about a particular executive order issued by the president. Still, should the president ignore a court order against him during periods of divided government, the majority party in Congress may use the opportunity to decry perceived abuses of executive authority and undermine support for other aspects of his legislative agenda. Similarly, the

public generally pays very little attention to court proceedings involving executive orders. Its support, nonetheless, may bolster the president's political capital, and with it his freedom to implement only those aspects of a court ruling that he favors.

40. When examining individual votes, rather than court outcomes, judges find in favor of the president 88, 73, and 64 percent of the time during periods of low, medium, and high political opposition, respectively.

41. Substituting a variable that counts the actual number of articles on each court case generates virtually identical point estimates. Among the 21 cases that are mentioned at least once in the *New York Times*, the mean number of mentions is 4.6 with a standard deviation of 5.0. As one might expect, the most frequently mentioned case in the database is *Youngstown v. Sawyer*, about which 23 stories were written.

42. As previously mentioned, strategic models of judicial decision making also assume that judges are primarily interested in asserting their policy preferences. Attitudinal and strategic models, however, differ over whether court rulings represent judges' sincere policy preferences, or whether judges shape their decisions to conform to a host of exogenous constraints.

43. This is simply an indicator variable that is coded one if the president defending the executive order is from the same party as the district court judge (or majority of judges at the appellate and Supreme Court levels) deciding the case.

44. Among the court cases in this database, 17 percent of the time presidents defended an executive order that cited as its basis for legal authority a legislative enactment that they themselves signed; 47 percent of the cases involved an executive order that cited a statute that was enacted prior to the defending president's administration; in 26 percent of the cases, the president defended an order that cited only broad constitutional powers.

45. Models that do not control for the political opposition variables or the level of final disposition do not generate statistically significant impacts for either the alignment of court/president policy preferences or the contemporary citation of authority to act.

46. A panel of nine judges ruled on one appellate case in the database.

47. *Bailey v. Richardson*, 341 U.S. 918, was decided per curiam, affirming the appellate court decision by an equally divided Court; Justice Tom Clark withdrew from the decision. The Supreme Court, however, did not release how the remaining eight justices voted. For this analysis, therefore, I used the three appellate-level votes that were published on this case. Also, in four cases in this database, one judge abstained; and in one Supreme Court case, two judges abstained. These five observations have been dropped from the analysis.

48. The models presented below estimate basic logistic regressions that take account of clustering on each case. Such models adjust for correlation among votes, but do not make any assumptions about the form of the correlation. Other kinds of statistical models that correct for correlated data, such as marginal models (or population-averaged models) and conditional models (or cluster-specific models), generate virtually identical results.

49. Because presidents never lost a case during periods of unified government, when interest groups did not file amicus briefs against him, and his public approval ratings were above the lowest tenth percentile, we cannot calculate interactive effects when the dependent variable involves court rulings rather than the decisions of individual judges.

50. We also might count the number of cases that are decided each year at the lowest court of disposition. While this measure does not account for the willingness of an individual or corporation to appeal an unfavorable lower court decision, it arguably does a better job of identifying the precise moment when a party decides to bring suit against the president. Fortunately, the results do not hinge upon any particular decision rule. When estimating models that use as the dependent variable the number of cases decided at the lowest court of disposition, virtually identical results as those presented in Table 6.7 are observed. The only substantive difference is that the impact for the number of executive orders issued the previous year becomes positive and highly statistically significant.

Chapter 7
Conclusion

1. David Broder, "Now Comes the Hard Part," *Washington Post*, 3 Sept. 2001, B7.

2. Alison Mitchell and Katharine Seelye, "Horror Knows No Party As Lawmakers Huddle," *New York Times*, 12 Sept. 2001, A20.

3. Senator Thomas A. Daschle (D-SD), speech before the National Press Club, 22 May 2002.

4. *Center for National Security Studies v. United States Department of Justice.* Civil action 01-2500, August 2, 2002. Full text of case is available at http://www.dcd.uscourts.gov/01-2500.pdf.

5. 2002 FED App. 0291P, August 26, 2002.

6. Full text of opinion is available at http://pacer.ca6.uscourts.gov/cgi-bin/getopn.pl?OPINION=02a0291p.06.

7. Full text of the speech is available at http://www.whitehouse.gov/news/releases/2002/08/20020826.html.

8. Full text of the remarks is available at http://www.whitehouse.gov/news/releases/2002/09/20020904-1.html.

Bibliography

Abraham, Henry. 1996. *The Judiciary: The Supreme Court in the Governmental Process.* New York: New York University Press.

Adler, David. 1998. "Court, Constitution, and Foreign Affairs." In David Adler and Larry George (eds.), *The Constitution and the Conduct of American Foreign Policy.* Lawrence, KS: University of Kansas Press.

Arnold, Peri. 1998. *Making the Managerial Presidency: Comprehensive Reorganization Planning, 1905–1996.* Lawrence, KS: University Press of Kansas.

Banks, Jeffrey. 1991. *Signaling Games in Political Science.* Reading, UK: Harwood Academic Publishers.

Barber, James David. 1972. *The Presidential Character: Predicting Performance in the White House.* Englewood Cliffs, NJ: Prentice Hall.

Barnum, David. 1985. "The Supreme Court and Public Opinion: Judicial Decision Making in the Post-New Deal Period." *Journal of Politics* 47: 652–66.

Baron, David. 1996. "A Dynamic Theory of Collective Goods Programs." *American Political Science Review* 90(2): 316–30.

———. 1991. "Majoritarian Incentives, Pork Barrel Programs, and Procedural Control." *American Journal of Political Science* 35: 57–90.

———. 1989. "A Noncooperative Theory of Legislative Coalitions." *American Journal of Political Science* 33: 1048–84.

Baron, David, and John Ferejohn. 1989. "Bargaining in Legislatures." *American Political Science Review* 83(4): 1181–1206.

Bickel, Alexander. 1962. *The Least Dangerous Branch: The Supreme Court and the Bar of Politics.* Indianapolis, IN: Bobbs-Merrill.

Bond, Jon and Richard Fleisher. 2000. *Polarized Politics: Congress and the President in a Partisan Era.* Washington, D.C.: Congressional Quarterly Press.

———. 1990. *The President in the Legislative Arena.* Chicago: University of Chicago Press.

Bowles, Nigel. 1999. "Studying the Presidency." *Annual Review of Political Science* 2: 1–23.

Box-Steffensmeier, Janet M., and Renee M. Smith. 1996. "The Dynamics of Aggregate Partisanship." *American Political Science Review* 90(3): 567–580.

Brady, David. 1988. *Critical Elections and Congressional Policy Making.* Stanford, CA: Stanford University Press.

Brady, David, and Craig Volden. 1998. *Revolving Gridlock.* Boulder, CO: Westview Press.

Brandt, Patrick T., and John T. Williams. 2001. "A Linear Poisson Autoregressive Model: The Poisson AR(p) Model." *Political Analysis* 9(2): 164–84.

Brandt, Patrick T., John T. Williams, Benjamin O. Fordham, and Brian Pollins. 2000. "Dynamic Modeling for Persistent Event-Count Time Series." *American Journal of Political Science* 44(4): 823–43.

Brigham, John. 1987. *The Cult of the Court.* Philadelphia: Temple University Press.

Bruff, Harold. 1982. "Judicial Review and the President's Statutory Powers." *Virginia Law Review* 68(1): 1–61.

Burgess, Christine. 1994. "When May a President Refuse to Enforce the Law?" *Texas Law Review* February: 631–67.

Burke, John P. 1991. *The Institutional Presidency*. Baltimore, MD: Johns Hopkins University Press.

Cameron, Charles. 2000. *Veto Bargaining: Presidents and the Politics of Negative Power*. New York: Cambridge University Press.

Canes-Wrone, Brandice. Forthcoming. *Who Leads Whom? The Policy Effects of Presidents' Relationship with the Masses*. Book manuscript.

———. 2001. "A Theory of Presidents' Public Agenda Setting." *Journal of Theoretical Politics* 13(2): 183–208.

Canes-Wrone, Brandice, Michael C. Herron, and Kenneth W. Shotts. 2001. "Leadership and Pandering: A Theory of Executive Policymaking." *American Journal of Political Science* 45(3): 532–50.

Canes-Wrone, Brandice, William Howell, and David Lewis. 1999. "The Two-Presidencies in the Legislative and Executive Arenas." Paper presented at the Annual Meeting of the Midwest Political Science Association, Chicago, IL.

Carey, John, and Matthew Shugart. 1998. *Executive Decree Authority*. New York: Cambridge University Press.

Carpenter, Daniel. 2001. *The Forging of Bureaucratic Autonomy: Reputations, Networks, and Policy Innovations in Executive Agencies, 1862–1928*. Princeton, NJ: Princeton University Press.

Carro, Jorge, and Andrew Brann. 1982. "The U.S. Supreme Court and the Use of Legislative Histories: A Statistical Analysis." *Jurimetrics Journal* 22: 293–303.

Cash, Robert. 1965. "Presidential Legislation by Executive Order." *University of Colorado Law Review* 37: 116.

Cavanaugh, Ralph, and Austin Sarat. 1979. "Thinking about Courts: Toward and Beyond a Jurisprudence of Judicial Competence." *Law and Society Review* 14: 371–419.

Chemerinsky, Erwin. 1987. "A Paradox without Principle: A Comment on the Burger Court's Jurisprudence in Separation of Powers Cases." *Southern California Law Review* 60 (May): 1087–96.

———. 1983. "Controlling Inherent Presidential Power: Providing a Framework for Judicial Review." *Southern California Law Review* 56 (May): 863–913.

Choper, Jesse. 1980. *Judicial Review and the National Political Process*. Chicago, IL: University of Chicago Press.

Clayton, Cornell, and Howard Gillman. 1999. *Supreme Court Decision-Making: New Institutionalist Approaches*. Chicago: University of Chicago Press.

Clinton, Joshua and Adam Meirowitz. 2001. "Agenda Constrained Legislator Idea Points and the Spatial Voting Model." *Political Analysis* 9: 242–59.

Cohen, Jeffrey, and George Krause. 1997. "Presidential Epochs and the Issuance of Executive Orders, 1901–1994." Paper presented at the annual meeting of the Midwest Political Science Association, Chicago, IL.

Comiskey, Michael. 1994. "The Rehnquist Court and American Values." *Judicature* March–April: 261–67.

Conley, Patricia. 2001. *Presidential Mandates: How Elections Shape the National Agenda.* Chicago: University of Chicago Press.

Cooper, Joseph, David W. Brady, and Patricia A. Hurley. 1977. "The Electoral Basis of Party Voting: Patterns and Trends in the U.S. House of Representatives, 1887–1969." In Louis Maisel and Joseph Cooper, eds., *The Impact of the Electoral Process.* Beverly Hills, CA: Sage Publications.

Cooper, Phillip. 2002. *By Order of the President: The Use and Abuse of Executive Direct Action.* Lawrence, KS: University Press of Kansas.

———. 1997. "Power Tools for an Effective and Responsible Presidency." *Administration and Society* 29(5): 529–56.

———. 1986. "By Order of the President: Administration by Executive Order and Proclamation." *Administration and Society* 18: 233–62.

Corwin, Edward. 1957. *The President, Office and Powers, 1787–1948: History and Analysis of Practice and Opinion.* New York: New York University Press.

Cox, Gary, and Mathew McCubbins. 1999. "Agenda Power in the U.S. House of Representatives." Paper presented at Conference on the History of Congress, Stanford University, 15–16 January, Stanford, California.

———. 1993. *Legislative Leviathan: Party Government in the House.* Berkeley, CA: University of California Press.

Cronin, Thomas. 1989. *Inventing the American Presidency.* Lawrence, KS: University of Kansas Press.

Cronin, Thomas, and Michael Genovese. 1998. *The Paradoxes of the American Presidency.* New York: Oxford University Press.

Deering, Christopher, and Forrest Maltzman. 1998. "The Politics of Executive Orders: Legislative Constraints on Presidential Power." Unpublished manuscript. George Washington University.

Dickinson, Matthew. 2000. "Staffing the White House, 1937–1996: The Institutional Implications of Neustadt's Bargaining Paradigm." In Robert Shapiro, Martha Kumar, and Lawrence Jacobs (eds.), *Presidential Power.* New York: Columbia University Press.

Diermeier, Daniel. 1995. "Commitment, Deference, and Legislative Institutions." *American Political Science Review* 89(2): 344–55.

Dixit, Avinash. 1996. *The Making of Economic Policy: A Transaction-Cost Politics Perspective.* Cambridge, MA: MIT Press.

Ducat, Craig R., and Robert L. Dudley. 1989. "Federal district judges and presidential power." *Journal of Politics* 51(1): 98–118.

Eastland, Terry. 1992. *Energy in the Executive: The Case for the Strong Presidency.* New York: Free Press.

Edwards, George C., III. 1989. *At the Margins: Presidential Leadership of Congress.* New Haven, CT: Yale University Press.

———. 1986. "The Two Presidencies: A Reevaluation." *American Politics Quarterly* 14(3): 247–63.

Enders, Walter. 1995. *Applied Econometric Time Series.* New York: John Wiley & Sons.

Epstein, David, and Sharyn O'Halloran. 1999. *Delegating Powers.* Cambridge: Cambridge University Press.

Epstein, Lee, and Jack Knight. 1998. *The Choices Justices Make*. Washington, D.C.: Congressional Quarterly.

Epstein, Lee, and Jeffrey A. Segal. 2000. "Measuring Issue Salience." *American Journal of Political Science* 44(1): 66–83.

Eskridge, William. 1994. "Overriding Supreme Court Statutory Interpretation Decisions." *The Yale Law Journal* 101: 331–425.

———. 1991. "Reneging on History? Playing the Court/Congress/President Civil Rights Game." *California Law Review* 79: 613–84.

Eskridge, William, and John Ferejohn. 1992a. "Making the Deal Stick: Enforcing the Original Constitutional Structure of Lawmaking in the Modern Regulatory State." *Journal of Law, Economics and Organization* 8(1): 165–89.

———. 1992b. "The Article I, Section 7 Game." *Georgetown Law Journal*. 80: 523–63.

Eskridge, William, and Philip Frickey. 1988. *Statutes and the Creation of Public Policy*. Minneapolis, MN: West Publishing Company.

Fenno, Richard F. 1966. *The Power of the Purse: Appropriations Politics in Congress*. Boston: Little, Brown.

Ferejohn, John, and Charles Shipan. 1990. "Congressional Influence on Bureaucracy." *Journal of Law, Economics and Organization* 6: 1–20.

Ferejohn, John, and Barry Weingast. 1992. "Limitation of Statutes: Strategic Statutory Interpretation." *Georgetown Law Journal* 80(3): 565–82.

Fisher, Louis. 2000. *Congressional Abdication on War and Spending*. College Station, TX: Texas A&M University Press.

———. 1998. *The Politics of Shared Power: Congress and the Executive*. 4th Edition. College Station, TX: Texas A&M University Press.

———. 1975. *Presidential Spending Power*. Princeton, NJ: Princeton University Press.

Fleisher, Richard, and Jon R. Bond. 1988. "Are there Two Presidencies? Yes, But Only for Republicans." *Journal of Politics* 50(3): 747–67.

Fleishman, Joel, and Arthur Aufses. 1976. "Law and Orders: The Problem of Presidential Legislation." *Law and Contemporary Problems* 40(3): 1–46.

Franck, Thomas M., and Edward Weisband. 1979. *Foreign Policy by Congress*. New York: Oxford University Press.

Frye, Alton, 1975. *A Responsible Congress*. New York: McGraw-Hill.

Gelly, Rafael, and Pablo Spiller. 1992. "A Rational Choice Theory of Supreme Court Statutory Decisions with Applications to the State Farm and Grove City Cases." *Journal of Law, Economics and Organization* 6: 263–300.

Genovese, Michael. 1980. *The Supreme Court, The Constitution, and Presidential Power*. Lanham, MD: University Press of America.

George, Alexander. 1974. *Presidential Personality and Performance*. Boulder, CO: Westview Press.

Gilligan, Thomas and Keith Krehbiel. 1990. "Organization of Informative Committees by a Rational Legislature." *American Journal of Political Science* 34: 531–64.

———. 1987. "Collective Decision-Making and Standing Committees: An Informational Rationale for Restrictive Amendment Procedures." *Journal of Law, Economics and Organization* 3: 287–335.

Goldsmith, William. 1974. *The Growth of Presidential Power*. New York: Chelsea House Publishers.

Gomez, Brad, and Steven Shull. 1995. "Presidential Decision Making: Explaining the Use of Executive Orders." Paper presented at the annual meeting of the Southern Political Science Association, 2–4 November, Tampa, Florida.

Greene, William. 1997. *Econometric Analysis, 3rd Edition*. Upper Saddle River, NJ: Prentice Hall.

Greenstein, Fred. 2000. *The Presidential Difference: Leadership Style from FDR to Clinton*. New York: Martin Kessler Books.

Groseclose, Tim, Steven Levitt, and James Snyder. 1999. "Comparing Interest Group Scores across Time and Chambers: Adjusted ADA Scores for the U.S. Congress." *American Political Science Review*. 93(1): 33–50.

Haight, David, and Larry Johnston. 1965. *The President: Roles and Powers*. Chicago: Rand McNally.

Hall, Kermit (ed.). 1992. *The Oxford Companion to the Supreme Court of the United States*. Oxford: Oxford University Press.

Hall, Richard. 1996. *Participation in Congress*. New Haven, CT: Yale University Press.

Hamilton, Alexander, James Madison, and John Jay. 1999 (1788). *The Federalist Papers*. New York, NY: Mentor.

Hargrove, Erwin C. 1974. *The Power of the Modern Presidency*. New York: Alfred A. Knopf.

———. 1966. *Presidential Leadership, Personality and Political Style*. New York: Macmillan.

Hart, John. 1995. *The Presidential Branch From Washington to Clinton*. Chatham, NJ: Chatham House Publishers, Inc.

Havemann, Judith. 1986. "Reagan Sets Drug Tests for Sensitive U.S. Jobs; $900 Million Proposal Sent to Congress." *Washington Post*, 16 September, A1.

Hebe, William. 1972. "Executive Orders and the Development of Presidential Power." *Villanova Law Review* 17: 688–712.

Hogg, Robert, and Elliot Tanis, 1993. *Probability and Statistical Inference*. New York: Macmillan Publishing Company.

Howell, William, Scott Adler, Charles Cameron, and Charles Riemann. 2000. "Divided Government and the Legislative Productivity of Congress, 1945–1994." *Legislative Studies Quarterly* 25: 285–312.

Howell, William, and David Lewis. 2002. "Agencies by Presidential Design." *Journal of Politics*. 64(4): 1095–1114.

Howell, William and Jon Pevehouse. 2002. "Presidents, Congress, and the Use of Force." Harvard University Typescript.

Humphries, Martha Anne, and Donald R. Songer. 1999. "Law and Politics in Judicial Oversight of Federal Administrative Agencies." *Journal of Politics* 6: 207–220.

Jones, Charles. 1994. *The Presidency in a Separated System*. Washington, D.C.: The Brookings Institution Press.

Katyal, Neal K., and Laurence H. Tribe. 2002. "Waging War, Deciding Guilt: Trying the Military Tribunals." *Yale Law Journal* 111(April): 1259–1310.

Kaufman, Herbert. 1976. *Are Government Organizations Immortal?* Washington, D.C.: The Brookings Institution Press.

Keenan, Hugh C. 1974. "Executive Orders: A Brief History of their Use and the President's Power to Issue Them" (revised 26 February 1974 by Grover S. Williams), in U.S. Senate, *Report of the Special Committee on National Emergencies and Delegated Emergency Powers, Executive Orders in Times of War and National Emergency.* 93rd Congress, 2nd Session (Committee Print).

Kernell, Samuel. 1986. *Going Public.* Washington, D.C.: Congressional Quarterly Press.

Key, V. O. 1964. *Politics, Parties and Pressure Groups.* New York: Crowell.

Kiefer, Francine. 1998. "Clinton Perfects the Art of Go-Alone Governing." *Christian Science Monitor* 24 July, 3.

King, Anthony. 1983. "A Mile and a Half is a Long Way." In Anthony King (ed.), *Both Ends of the Avenue.* Washington, D.C.: American Enterprise Institute, 246–73.

King, Gary. 1989. "A Seemingly Unrelated Poisson Regression Model." *Sociological Methods and Research* 17(3): 235–55.

King, Gary, and Lyn Ragsdale. 1988. *The Elusive Executive: Discovering Statistical Patterns in the Presidency.* Washington, D.C.: Congressional Quarterly Press.

King, Kimi Lynn, and James Meernik. 1999. "The Supreme Court and the Powers of the Executive: The Adjudication of Foreign Policy." *Political Research Quarterly* 52: 801–24.

Kirst, Michel. 1969. *Government Without Passing Laws: Congress' Nonstatutory Techniques for Appropriations.* Chapel Hill, NC: University of North Carolina Press.

Kluger, Richard. 1975. *Simple Justice: The History of Brown v. Board of Education and Black America's Struggle for Equality.* New York: Vintage Books.

Kornhauser, Lewis. 1992. "Modeling Collegial Courts II: Legal Doctrine." *Journal of Law, Economics and Organization* 8: 441–70.

Kramer, Gerald. 1986. "Political Science as Science." In *Political Science: The Science of Politics,* ed. Herbert Weisberg. New York: Agathon Press.

Krause, George, and David Cohen. 2000. "Opportunity, Constraints, and the Development of the Institutional Presidency: The Case of Executive Order Issuance, 1939–1996." *Journal of Politics* 62: 88–114.

———. 1997. "Presidential Use of Executive Orders, 1953–1994." *American Politics Quarterly* 25(October): 458–81.

Krehbiel, Keith. 1998. *Pivotal Politics: A Theory of U.S. Lawmaking.* Chicago: University of Chicago Press.

———. 1996. "Institutional and Partisan Sources of Gridlock: A Theory of Divided and Unified Government." *Journal of Theoretical Politics* 8: 7–40.

———. 1993. "Where's the Party?" *British Journal of Political Science* 23(April): 235–66.

———. 1992. *Information and Legislative Organization.* Ann Arbor, MI: University of Michigan Press.

Landy, Marc, and Sidney Milkis. 2000. *Presidential Greatness.* Lawrence, KS: University of Kansas Press.

Lewis, David E. 2003. *Presidents and the Politics of Agency Design*. Stanford, CA: Stanford University Press.

Light, Paul C. 1999. *The President's Agenda: Domestic Policy Choice from Kennedy to Clinton*. 3d ed. Baltimore: Johns Hopkins University Press.

Lindsay, James M., and Wayne P. Steger. 1993. "The 'Two Presidencies' in Future Research: Moving Beyond Roll-Call Analysis." *Congress & the Presidency* 20(2): 103–17.

Locke, John. 1988 [1689]. *Two Treatises of Government*. Cambridge: Cambridge University Press.

Marshall, Thomas. 1989. *Public Opinion and the Supreme Court*. Boston: Unwin Hyam.

Martin, Lisa. 1999. *Democratic Commitments: Legislatures and International Cooperation*. Princeton, NJ: Princeton University Press.

Matthews, Steven. 1989. "Veto Threats: Rhetoric in a Bargaining Game." *Quarterly Journal of Economics* 347–69.

Mayer, Kenneth. 2001. *With the Stroke of a Pen: Executive Orders and Presidential Power*. Princeton, NJ: Princeton University Press.

———. 1999. "Executive Orders and Presidential Power." *Journal of Politics* 61: 445–466.

———. 1996. "The Importance of Moving First: Executive Order and Presidential Initiative." Paper delivered at the 1996 annual meeting of the American Political Science Association, San Francisco, California, August 29–September 1, 1996.

Mayer, Kenneth, and Kevin Price. 2002. "Unilateral Presidential Powers: Significant Executive Orders, 1949–99." *Presidential Studies Quarterly* 32(2): 367–86.

Mayhew, David. 1991. *Divided We Govern*. New Haven, CT: Yale University Press.

———. 1974. *Congress: The Electoral Connection*. New Haven, CT: Yale University Press.

McCarty, Nolan. 1997. "Presidential Reputation and the Veto." *Economics and Politics* 9(1): 1–26.

McCarty, Nolan, and Keith Poole. 1995. "Veto Power and Legislation: An Empirical Analysis of Executive and Legislative Bargaining from 1961–1986." *Journal of Law, Economics and Organization* 11: 282–312.

McCubbins, Mathew, Roger Noll, and Barry Weingast. 1989. "Structure and Process, Politics and Policy: Administrative Arrangements and the Political Control of Agencies." *Virginia Law Review* 3: 243–77.

McDonald, Forrest. 1994. *The American Presidency: An Intellectual History*. Lawrence, KS: University of Kansas Press.

McKelvey, Richard. 1976. "Intransitivities in Multidimensional Voting Models and Some Implications for Agenda Control." *Journal of Economic Theory* 12: 471–82.

Melnick, Shep. 1993. *Between the Lines: Interpreting Welfare Rights*. Washington, D.C.: The Brookings Institution Press.

Mikva, Abner, and Eric Lane. 1997. *An Introduction to Statutory Interpretation and the Legislative Process*. New York: Aspen Law and Business.

Miller, Gary. 1993. "Formal Theory and the Presidency." In *Researching the Presidency: Vital Questions, New Approaches*, ed. George C. Edwards, John H. Kessel, and Bert A. Rockman. Pittsburgh, PA: University of Pittsburgh Press, 289–337.

Moe, Terry. 1999. "The Presidency and the Bureaucracy: The Presidential Advantage." In *The Presidency and the Political System*, 5th edition, ed. Michael Nelson. Washington, D.C: Congressional Quarterly Press.

———. 1993. "Presidents, Institutions, and Theory." In *Researching the Presidency: Vital Questions, New Approaches*, ed. George C. Edwards, John H. Kessel, and Bert A. Rockman. Pittsburgh, PA: University of Pittsburgh Press, 337–387.

———. 1989. "The Politics of Bureaucratic Structure." In *Can the Government Govern?* ed. John E. Chubb and Paul E. Peterson. Washington, D.C.: The Brookings Institution Press.

———. 1985. "The Politicized Presidency." In *The New Direction in American Politics*, ed. John E. Chubb and Paul E. Peterson. Washington, D.C.: The Brookings Institution Press.

Moe, Terry, and William Howell. 1999a. "The Presidential Power of Unilateral Action." *Journal of Law, Economics and Organization*. 15(1): 132–79.

———. 1999b. "Unilateral Action and Presidential Power: A Theory." *Presidential Studies Quarterly* 29(4): 850–72.

Moe, Terry, and Scott Wilson. 1994. "Presidents and the Politics of Structure." *Law and Contemporary Problems* 57: 1–44.

Moreno, Paul. 1996. "Racial Proportionalism and the Origins of Employment Discrimination Policy, 1933–1950." *Journal of Policy History* 8(4): 410–39.

Morgan, Ruth. 1970. *The President and Civil Rights*. New York: St. Martin's Press.

Morrison, David. 1986. "The Pentagon's Drug Wars." *The National Journal*. 18(36): 2104.

Morrow, William L. 1968. "Legislative Control of Administrative Discretion: The Case of Congress and Foreign Aid." *Journal of Politics* 30: 986.

Nagel, Robert F. 1989. "Political Law, Legalistic Politics: A Recent History of the Political Question Doctrine." *University of Chicago Law Review* 56: 643–69.

Nathan, James, and James Oliver. 1994. *Foreign Policy Making and the American Political System*. Baltimore, MD: Johns Hopkins University Press.

Nathan, Richard. 1983. *The Administrative Presidency*. New York: Wiley.

———. 1969. *Jobs and Civil Rights: The Role of the Federal Government in Promoting Equal Opportunity in Employment and Training*. Washington, DC: Government Printing Office.

Neighbors, William. 1964. "Presidential Legislation by Executive Order." *University of Colorado Law Review* 105(37): 105–18.

Neustadt, Richard E. 1991 [1960]. *Presidential Power and the Modern Presidents*. New York: Free Press.

Norpoth, Helmut, and Jeffrey Segal. 1994. "Popular Influence on Supreme Court Decisions." *American Political Science Review* 88: 711.

Page, Benjamin, and Robert Shapiro. 1992. *The Rational Public: Fifty Years of Trends in Americans' Policy Preferences*. Chicago: University of Chicago Press.

Paige, Joseph. 1977. *The Law Nobody Knows: Enlargement of the Constitution—Treaties and Executive Agreements*. New York: Vantage Press.

Pear, Robert. 1998. "The Presidential Pen is Still Mighty." *New York Times*, 28 June, K3.

Pepper, Donald. 1975. "The Two Presidencies Eight Years Later." In *Perspectives on the Presidency*, ed. Aaron Wildavsky, Boston: Little, Brown, and Co.

Perret, Geoffrey. 1999. *Eisenhower*. New York: Random House.

Perry, H. W. 1991. *Deciding to Decide: Agenda Setting in the United States Supreme Court*. Cambridge, MA: Harvard University Press.

Persson, Torsten, and Guido Tabellini. 1990. *Macroeconomic Policy, Credibility and Politics*. Reading, UK: Harwood Academic Publishers.

Peterson, Mark. 1990. *Legislating Together: The White House and Capitol Hill from Eisenhower to Reagan*. Cambridge, MA: Harvard University Press.

Pfiffner, James. 1989. *The Presidency in Transition*. New York: Center for the Study of the Presidency.

Poole, Keith. 1998. "Estimating a Basic Space from a Set of Issue Scales." *American Journal of Political Science* 42: 954–93.

Poole, Keith, and Howard Rosenthal. 1997. *Congress: A Political-Economic History of Roll Call Voting*. New York: Oxford University Press.

Powell, Colin. 1998. *President Truman and the Desegregation of the Armed Forces*. Washington, D.C.: National Legal Center for the Public Interest.

Reeves, Richard. 2001. *President Nixon: Alone in the White House*. New York: Simon and Schuster.

Relyea, Harold. 1988. "The Coming of Secret Law." *Government Information Quarterly* 5(2): 97–116.

Robinson, Greg. 2001. *By Order of the President*. Cambridge, MA: Harvard University Press.

Roche, John. 1955. "Judicial Self-Restraint." *American Political Science Review* 49(3): 762–72.

Roche, John, and Leonard Levy. 1964. *The Presidency*. New York: Harcourt, Brace and World.

Rodgers, William. 2001. "Executive Orders and Presidential Commands: Presidents Riding to the Rescue of the Environment." *Journal of Land, Resources, and Environmental Law* 21: 13–24.

Rose-Ackerman, Susan. 1990. "Comment on Ferejohn and Shipan's 'Congressional Influence on Bureaucracy.'" *Journal of Law, Economics and Organization* 6: 21–27.

Rosenberg, Gerald. 1991. *The Hollow Hope: Can the Courts Bring About Social Change?* Chicago: University of Chicago Press.

Ross, Sonya. 1999. "Searching for a Way to Make History Forget Impeachment." 20 December, posted on CNN.com.

Rossiter, Clinton. 1956. *The American Presidency*. New York: Harcourt, Brace and World.

Ruchames, Louis. 1953. *Race, Jobs and Politics: The Story of the FEPC*. New York: Columbia University Press.

Rudalevige, Andrew. 2002. *Managing the President's Program: Presidential Leadership and Legislative Policy Formation*. Princeton, NJ: Princeton University Press.

Sala, Brian, 1998. "In Search of the Administrative President: Presidential 'Decree' Powers and Policy Implementation in the United States." In *Executive Decree Authority*, ed. John Carey and Matthew Shugart. Cambridge: Cambridge University Press: 254–73.

Scharpf, Fritz. 1966. "Judicial Review and the Political Question: A Functional Analysis." *Yale Law Journal* (75): 517–38.

Schubert, Glendon. 1973. *The Presidency in the Courts*. New York: Da Capo Press.

Schwartz, E. P. 1992. "Policy, Precedent, and Power: A Positive Theory of Supreme Court Decision-Making." *Journal of Law, Economics, and Organization* 8: 219–52.

Segal, Jeffrey, and Albert Cover. 1989. "Ideological Values and the Votes of U.S. Supreme Court Justices." *American Political Science Review* 83: 557–65.

Segal, Jeffrey, and Harold Spaeth. 1993. *The Supreme Court and the Attitudinal Model*. New York: Cambridge University Press.

Segal, Jeffrey, Lee Epstein, Charles Cameron, and Harold Spaeth. 1995. "Ideological Values and the Votes of U.S. Supreme Court Justices Revisited." *Journal of Politics* 57: 812–22.

Shane, Peter, and Harold Bruff. 1988. *The Law of Presidential Power*. Durham, NC: Carolina Academic Press.

Shapiro, Martin. 1964. *Law and Politics in the Supreme Court: New Approaches to Political Jurisprudence*. New York: Free Press.

Sheehan, Reginald S. 1990. "Administrative Agencies and the Court: A Reexamination of the Impact of Agency Type on Decisional Outcomes." *Western Political Quarterly* 43: 875–85.

Shepsle, Kenneth. 1986. "Institutional Equilibrium and Equilibrium Institutions." In *Political Science: The Science of Politics*, ed. Herbert Weisberg. New York: Agathon Press.

Siegel, Jonathan. 1997. "Suing the President: Nonstatutory Review Revisited." *Columbia Law Review*. 97: 1612–1709.

Sigelman, Lee. 1979. "A Reassessment of the Two Presidencies Thesis." *Journal of Politics* 41(4): 1195–1205.

Silverstein, Gordon. 1997. *Imbalance of Powers: Constitutional Interpretation and the Making of American Foreign Policy*. New York: Oxford University Press.

———. 1992. "Judicial Enhancement of Executive Power." In *The President, The Congress and the Making of Foreign Policy*, ed. Paul E. Peterson. Norman, OK: University of Oklahoma Press.

Skowronek, Stephen. 1993. *The Politics Presidents Make: Leadership from John Adams to George Bush*. London: Belknap Press.

Spitzer, Robert. 1993. *President and Congress: Executive Hegemony at the Crossroads of American Government*. New York: McGraw-Hill.

Stimson, James. 1999. *Public Opinion in America: Moods, Cycles, and Swings*. Boulder, CO: Westview Press.

Strum, Phillipa. 1974. *The Supreme Court and "Political Questions": A Study in Judicial Evasion*. Tuscaloosa, AL: University of Alabama Press.

Sullivan, Terry. 1990. "Bargaining with the President: A Simple Game and New Evidence." *American Political Science Review* 84(4): 1167–95.

Susser, Peter. 1985. "Issues Raised by Drugs in the Workplace." *Labor Law Review* 36(1): 42–54.

Wald, Patricia. 1990. "The Sizzling Sleeper: The Use of Legislative History in Construing Statutes in the 1988–89 Term of the United States Supreme Court." *American University Law Review* 39: 277–88.

———. 1982. "Some Observations on the Use of Legislative History in the 1981 Supreme Court Term." *Iowa Law Review* 68: 195–201.

Wawro, Gregory. 2000. *Legislative Entrepreneurship in the U.S. House of Representatives.* Ann Arbor, MI: University of Michigan Press.

Wayne, Stephen. 1978. *The Legislative Presidency.* New York: Harper and Row.

Weiner, Tim. 1999. "Pentagon Misused Millions in Funds, House Panel Says." *New York Times,* 22 July, A1.

Weingast, Barry. 1995. "The Economic Role of Political Institutions: Market-Preserving Federalism and Economic Development." *Journal of Law, Economics and Organization* 111(1): 1–31.

Weingast, Barry, and William Marshall. 1988. "The Industrial Organization of Congress." *Journal of Political Economy* 96: 132–63.

Weiss, Nancy. 1997. *"We Want Jobs": A History of Affirmative Action.* New York: Garland Publishing.

Whitnah, Donald R. 1983. *Government Agencies.* Westport, CT: Greenwood.

Wigton, John. 1991. "Recent Presidential Experience with Executive Orders." *Presidential Studies Quarterly* 26: 473–84.

Wildavsky, Aaron. 1966. "The Two Presidencies." *Trans-Action* 4(December): 7–14.

Wilhoit, Francis. 1973. *The Politics of Massive Resistance.* New York: George Braziller.

Willoughby, W. F. 1913. "Allotment of Funds by Executive Officials: An Essential Feature of Any Correct Budget System." In the *Proceedings of the American Political Science Association, 9th Annual Meeting,* 28–31 December, 80.

Wilson, James Q. 1989. *Bureaucracy: What Government Agencies Do and Why They Do It.* New York: Basic Books.

Wilson, Woodrow. 1961 [1908]. *Constitutional Government in the United States.* New York: Columbia University Press.

Woolhandler, Ann, and Michael Collins. 1995. "State Standing." *Virginia Law Review* 81(March): 387–520.

Yates, Jeff, and Andrew Whitford. 1998. "Presidential Power and the United States Supreme Court." *Political Research Quarterly* 51: 539–50.

Zeidenstein, Harvey. 1981. "The Two Presidencies Thesis is Alive and Well and has been Living in the U.S. Senate Since 1973." *Presidential Studies Quarterly* 11(4): 511–25.

———. 1978. "The Reassertion of Congressional Power: New Curbs on the President." *Political Science Quarterly* 93: 393–409.

Index

Page locators in **boldface** indicate figures and tables.